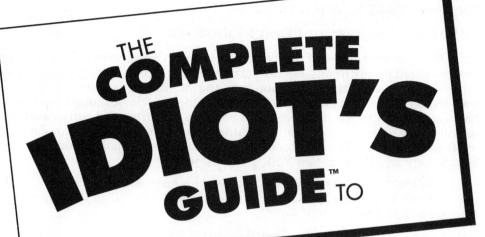

THE COMPLETE IDIOT'S GUIDE™ TO

Great Customer Service

by Ron Karr
and
Don Blohowiak

alpha
books

A Division of Macmillan General Reference
A Simon and Schuster Macmillan Company
1633 Broadway, New York NY 10019-6785

For Cindy, Janet P., and Dick Staron.

©1997 by Ron Karr and Don Blohowiak

Macmillan Publishing books may be purchased for business or sales promotional use. For information please write: Special Markets Department, Macmillan Publishing USA, 1633 Broadway, New York, NY 10019-6785.

International Standard Book Number: 0-02-861953-6 (pbk.)
Library of Congress Catalog Card Number: 97-073148

99 98 97   4 3 2

Interpretation of the printing code: the rightmost number of the first series of numbers is the year of the book's printing; the rightmost number of the second series of numbers is the number of the book's printing. For example, a printing code of 97-1 shows that the first printing occurred in 1997.

Printed in the United States of America

Brand Manager
Kathy Nebenhaus

Director of Editorial Services
Brian Phair

Executive Editor
Gary M. Krebs

Managing Editor
Bob Shuman

Senior Editor
Nancy Mikhail

Development Editor
Nancy D. Warner

Production Editors
John Carroll
Mark Enochs

Editorial Assistant
Maureen Horn

Illustrator
Judd Winick

Book Designer
Glenn Larsen

Cover Designer
Michael Freeland

Indexer
Joe Long

Production Team
Angela Calvert
Laure Robinson
Megan Wade

Contents at a Glance

Contents

Foreword

At first glance, the title of this book seems to suggest that great customer service is so simple, any "idiot" is up to the task. Yes, the principles are very simple, but providing great customer service—embracing those principles, applying them on a daily basis, instilling them in your corporate culture—is not an easy task.

The customers have spoken and they aren't happy. According to *Fortune* magazine, "customers were cranky in 1996...Overall, the corporations listed in this year's American consumer satisfaction index...were judged by consumers to be...*less* friendly than they were last year." Frankly, that is not surprising. In this low-touch, high-tech society, we seem to crave more human interaction. Instead, we get voicemail prompts and e-mail messages. But while the consumer environment has become more demanding, and certainly more volatile, customer service professionals are working harder than ever to please. As the Executive Director of the International Customer Service Association (ICSA), I am constantly impressed with the dedication of our members to providing the highest levels of customer service; their commitment to research and education; and in general, their desire to raise the level of customer service across the board.

So why the negative image? Simple. The customer service industry is largely based on consumer perceptions. Thanks to an increased media and consumer awareness of customer service, those perceptions have risen more quickly than most companies' budget-conscious customer service functions. Promises of "anything for the customer," have raised the bar to new heights, but downsizing-related budget cuts have left customer service teams fighting to catch up with heightened consumer expectations. It can be difficult to tangibly express the importance of customer satisfaction to senior management and shareholders with eyes fixed intently on the bottom line. Often, in response to tighter operating budgets, customer service functions feel the squeeze. What looks like an easy solution on the financial statement can lead to bigger problems in the future.

As you read this book, one theme becomes increasingly clear. Customer service is no longer a department, it is a culture cultivated throughout the organization. Perfect. Frame that phrase and hang it in your office, make copies, put them in everyone's inbox. Too often customer service is considered one branch of a company, one arm of a manufacturer, the counter person at a fast food restaurant. That's where the problem begins, with the mentality that customer service is simply a front line entity, an independent facade not directly connected with the rest of the group. The authors, Ron Karr and Don Blohowiak, note that "Every individual has a direct effect on the organization's ability to provide its customers with [great customer service]." In short, everyone is a customer service representative.

The *Complete Idiot's Guide to Great Customer Service* is an excellent reference tool for professionals at all levels from the front lines to the executive offices. Written with the understanding that the reader is the customer, it is very user-friendly, easy to follow, and divided into logical sections like "What Exactly Is Customer Service?" and "Build It and They Will Come: Creating a Customer Service Organization." There are several chapters devoted to the possibilities and pitfalls associated with emerging customer service technology, as well as excellent case studies and a list of helpful resources.

True, customer service can be a challenging profession, but also an extremely rewarding one. Regardless of where you are in terms of reaching your customer service goals, you can always find time to celebrate the positives. National Customer Service Week (annually the first full week of October) is designed to spotlight the numerous acts of great service that happen daily but never reach the headlines. If you would like ideas on how to celebrate and promote this event, please call ICSA at 800-360-ICSA(4272).

Great customer service can make the difference, and set your company apart from the pack. If you aren't already, become known for your great customer service. The benefits will carry your company to greater heights and healthier profits.

Brenda Anderson

Executive Director
International Customer Service Association

Introduction

To Serve and to Please—The Service Difference

Service. Service. Service! Open a newspaper, turn on a radio or a TV—you'll see and hear endless ads that boldly shout that you should spend your money at this place or that one because of the *customer service*. No matter how big or small your business, how simple or sophisticated your product or service, customer service has become the enduring ingredient in the elusive formula for success.

Each of us gives and receives service constantly. As consumers, we demand great service, and as service-providers we're obligated to give great service—because if we don't, people just won't do business with us. Today's business reality is that simple and that harsh. But don't despair!

The Service Difference

This book is about not only how to give your customers the kind of service that they expect, but the kind they'll remember and like so much that they return to spend even more money with you time and time again.

This book is about creating what we call *The Service Difference*. That's service so special that it genuinely pleases your customers and sets your organization apart from the pack. Most importantly, when you deliver The Service Difference, you create lasting, profitable customer loyalty that encourages customers to do business with you rather than a competitor. It's loyalty that even a slightly better mousetrap, or a slightly lower price, can't yank away.

The Thinking Behind This Book

We could write a very short book on customer service. It could say something like this: Good customer service is being nice to customers, and not being rude to them. Good customer service comes from treating people in the way they'd like to be treated.

Yes, that would be a short book. And one you really wouldn't need to buy. Because it wouldn't begin to describe what it really takes to give your customers truly great service today.

The Whole and the Parts

Competing in today's ruthlessly competitive business environment means that your company's customer service effort is part of a much more complex system. Great service isn't merely saying, "How may I help you?" "Thanks for your business," and "Have a nice day."

Sure, that would be a good start. And certainly many businesses we know would benefit immensely by just starting there. But that's not the stuff of customer service that will help you compete against world class competitors.

Competing in customer service requires you to understand what good service is and why it's so vitally important. Competing on the basis of service means making great customer service an essential—no, an *indispensable*—part of your daily operation.

Competing in service means:

➤ Possessing a deep understanding of your market

➤ Organizing and running your business in a special way

➤ Hiring people in a certain way

➤ Training them to behave in certain ways

➤ Operating to standards

➤ Using technology to its fullest

➤ And much more

In short, a book on creating and consistently delivering great customer service is a book about rethinking and redesigning your business, and managing it as though you were starting from scratch.

Practical Bias

Wherever we can, we list the action steps as simply as *insert tab A into slot B*. There's a whole lot of that throughout the book.

In the first few chapters we orient you to today's brave new world of service. The one that's driven by catering to customers, treating them as though they are valued, special, and the very reason your business exists. We try to explain in straightforward terms why great customer service is a business necessity, and why it's a much bigger job than just being nice to customers, picking up the phone by the second ring, or waiting for the customer to hang up the phone before you do.

What You'll Find in This Book

An old Spanish proverb holds that, "It is one thing to speak of bulls, it is another to be in the bullring." This book will enable you to bravely enter the ring, boldly face the snorting bulls of commerce, and happily prevail. Because we suspect you'd rather find out what works rather than be preached at, the book is short on *shoulds* and long on *how tos*.

We've divided the book into several major parts, each focusing on a particular aspect of delivering The Service Difference.

Part 1: What Exactly Is Customer Service?

Customer service, like art, is many different things to many people. But unlike art, The Service Difference can be precisely defined and consistently delivered. This section describes in detail what The Service Difference is, why it's so vitally important, and how you can make it an integral part of your organization's very heart and soul. We show you how to get past the lip-service of merely saying "service, service, service" to making The Service Difference an essential part not only of what your organization stands for, but of the way every employee in it *behaves* day in and day out. You'll learn how to operate your business in a way that consistently encourages customers to *want* to spend their money with you.

Part 2: Service Is Communication

The roots of great customer service, The Service Difference, are in one-to-one communication between your individual employees and your individual customers. Customer service is based on human-to-human interaction. In this section, we take a close look at the dynamics of effective communication. You'll find very specific information about how you can avoid communication break-downs. And how you can maximize understanding between you and your customer when you interact face to face, over the phone, in letters, through your instruction manuals, and even when your customer is very angry with your company *and* you're having an absolutely rotten day.

Part 3: So, How Am I Doing?

Your customers' needs, wants, and preferences change. All the time. The key to making The Service Difference really work for your organization is to continuously stay responsive and relevant to your customers. Customer satisfaction surveys are part of the answer, but there's much more to it. We cover it all in this section about gathering and using information from your customers. You'll learn how to keep your organization in-touch and on top.

Part 4: Build It and They Will Come: Creating a Customer Service Organization

Delivering The Service Difference requires you to do much more than simply issue memos, policies, and directives about giving good service. To truly deliver The Service Difference, your whole organization has to breathe, eat, and sleep service. This section shows you, in great detail, how to make that happen. It covers hiring, training, motivating, rewarding, and supporting your service staff. You'll even learn how to give great service to *internal customers* across the hall, as well as to customers far flung around the globe—separated from you by language, time, and a few oceans and continents.

Part 5: The Gizmos & Gadgets of Great Service

To be sure, great service is high-touch (human to human contact), yet we live in a highly technical age. The Service Difference is supported by sophisticated technology that enables you to serve customers in wonderful ways that you simply couldn't do without the electronics. Even if you can't program your VCR (and who can?!), you'll get a solid grounding on how you can put to work the whiz-bang, gee-whiz high-tech stuff that's revolutionizing customer service.

Appendix A: Resources

We've worked hard to make this book a complete guide to how you can create The Service Difference in your organization. And we know that putting these ideas into reality in your company is a big job. You might want to get some more help. In this section, you'll find listings for other consultants, trainers, technology vendors, call center outsourcing firms, and so on. We're in there, too, and would love to discuss with you how we might be of further assistance.

Extras

To make the learning experience as easy and as fun as possible, we've highlighted lots of tips and facts along the way. Look for the following elements in the book to guide you along.

Tales from the Real World

It's one thing for us to give you important principles, guidelines, checklists, charts, and lists of Dos and Don'ts. But there's nothing like a good example to drive home a point.

Voltaire, a French philosopher in the Age of Enlightenment, once asked, "Are there any so wise as to learn from the experience of others?" In *Tales from the Real World*, you'll find stories that illustrate The Service Difference in action.

Since we're pretty sure that you've experienced plenty of bad service as a customer yourself, we're going to highlight, as much as possible, people doing things right.

Quote, Unquote

The wisdom of the wise, and the experience of ages, may be preserved by quotation, English author Isaac D'Israeli observed. We've included some especially apt quotes for your enlightenment and entertainment.

Watch It!

Warnings, cautions, and "heads up" notes appear in the little box titled *Watch It!* You still might want to do something that we warn you against, but at least we can say, "We told you so!"

At Your Service

As you read the book, these little boxes will key in on important ideas and offer additional helpful tips.

Word to the Wise

We've tried to avoid *buzz words* and arcane jargon, but there may be some terms you're not familiar with. So *Word to the Wise* defines some less common terms we use in the text. You can find a Glossary for all those terms in the back of the book.

At Your Service

To help you help others (and in the process, help your employer and yourself), the authors of this book brought together more than four decades of experience of serving demanding customers in a wide variety of industries. Our collective experience includes far more than management consulting and speaking at conferences around the globe.

Sure, we've served big-name companies in industries as varied as heavy equipment rentals, disability and life insurance, healthcare, elevator manufacturing, hospitality, newspaper publishing, banking, pharmaceuticals, defense contractors, grocery stores, mining, telecommunications, chemical producers, government agencies, and on and on, all over North and South America, Europe, and beyond.

But just as importantly, we've been employees in firms from New York to California—in big companies, little companies, and not-for-profits. We learned about the world of service by painting houses and commercial buildings, working as a farmhand and a hospital security guard, cooking in a fast food restaurant, stocking shelves, tending bar, rescuing people, writing radio commercials, selling computer systems and information services, reporting news, marketing cable television services, advertising professional reference libraries, managing a satellite information system, conducting market research, teaching college, taking Scouts camping, helping the school board pass a needed tax hike, teaching literacy to immigrants and quality to prisoners (really!), reading for the blind, and donating blood.

In short, we've spent lots of time in the real world dealing with and working to please demanding customers. We've made it our life's work to help organizations of all sizes and types to be the best they can be. To truly provide the service difference.

Now *you* are our customer. We consider it a privilege and a joy to serve you. We hope you find this book an invaluable resource for giving your customers both their money's worth and a truly delightful experience. We know if you implement the ideas, strategies, and tactics in this book, you will gain The Service Difference and profitably stand out.

In fact, we can't wait to hear of your success. We invite you to submit your "tales from the real world," as well as any other comments or suggestions you may have. Please send them to either one of us; our contact information appears in the Resources appendix at the back of the book.

Acknowledgments

We're thankful to our clients who helped us see that The Service Difference really does make a meaningful difference in reaching and sustaining a high level of success.

We're grateful to Dick Staron of Macmillan, who championed this project, and his team who brought it to life, Howard Jones, John Carroll, and especially Nancy Warner.

We offer a very special thank you to Sandy Lang of Kaset International for her careful reading of the manuscript and her many thoughtful suggestions that improved the work.

And we deeply appreciate the many people who shared their insights and information with us so that we could bring them to you in this book. You'll find many of their names in the Quote, Unquote sections, in the credit lines beneath material we've reproduced for you, and in the Resources section. We must extend special thanks to Bill Bonstetter of TTI Performance Systems, and Judy Suiter and Randy Jay Widrick for their incredibly valuable work in the area of behavioral profiles.

To the others who quietly gave us a helping hand not wanting anything in return, *thank you* for your help; your selfless example teaches us much about great customer service.

There's a lot of really important, really cool information between these covers. Let's get to work!

Special Thanks from the Publisher to the Technical Reviewer

The Complete Idiot's Guide to Great Customer Service was reviewed by an expert who not only checked the technical accuracy of what you'll learn in this book, but also provided invaluable insight and suggestions.

Our special thanks are extended to Alexandra Lang, corporate communications manager for Kaset International. She is responsible for internal and external newsletters, public relations, and article writing for publications. Kaset International is a recognized leader in service quality training and consulting. Since 1973, Kaset has worked with leading public and private sector organizations to help them maintain a competitive advantage through customer loyalty. Kaset, a Times Mirror company, is based in Tampa, Florida.

Lang, who has been with Kaset for 17 years, has managed Kaset's quarterly customer publication, *in-touch*, since 1984. She has interviewed and written about customer-focused executives throughout North America, the Bahamas, and the United Kingdom.

Lang earned her BA from The College of Wooster in Wooster, Ohio, with a major in chemistry. She also attended the University of Southwest Florida in Pensacola and Tidewater Community College in Virginia Beach, VA. Her first love has always been writing, however.

Part 1
What Exactly Is Customer Service?

Economists tell us we live in a "service economy." So everyone is exposed to—and giving—lots of service. With all that experience with service, our customers have a pretty good idea of what good service is.

Their expectations for good service run awfully high, and get higher and higher every day.

Firms that provide outstanding *customer service (the kind you typically receive while wandering Disney World on a good day, or visiting your grandma's house, especially when grandpa's in a good mood) will prosper in our service economy.*

Those who only provide good *service might survive. Everyone else is doomed. And we're not exaggerating.*

The upcoming chapters describe The Service Difference. *The Service Difference is both the operating principles and the specific processes that combine to give your customers a warm feeling of satisfaction, maybe even* joy, *from interacting with your organization.*

Chapter 1

Customer Service: A Many Splendored Thing

In This Chapter

➤ Defining customer service

➤ Expanding the idea of who is a customer

➤ Understanding the difference between good service and *great* service

➤ Winning customers for life

➤ Generating a service reputation

News Item: Washington, D.C.—Lt. Gen. Joe N. Ballard, Chief of Engineers, announced the implementation of the plan released earlier this year to restructure the U.S. Army Corps of Engineers into eight divisions. "The new structure of the Corps will ensure continued customer service," said Gen. Ballard.

Wait a second. "Continued customer service"… at the Army Corps of Engineers? (*"Good day, ma'am. Please forgive the intrusion. See, we need to raise just a bit of dust, and we beg your pardon for that slightly inconvenient noise while we blast that darn dam and reroute the river. Appreciate your kindly understanding. Would you mind terribly if, on our way out, we plant a few petunias and pansies? It's our pleasure to serve. By the way, sure would appreciate your filling out this customer satisfaction survey. We really do want to be your earth modifiers of choice! Y'all have a nice day now, hear?"*)

What's going on here? Welcome to the New Age of Customer Service. *Everyone* has jumped on the customer service bandwagon. (By the way, Gen. Ballard's press release mentions that the new plan "optimizes support to military forces, minimizes district realignments, and maintains geographical balance." In other words… you know, better customer service.)

Customer Service. You know what that is, right?

Define It

Try this little experiment. Ask five people to define "customer service."

Don't be surprised if you get 20 different answers! Customer service could be…

➤ Receiving a quick, friendly greeting in a retail store.

➤ Getting the balance on your heating bill straightened-out.

➤ Having the repair technician show up at your business to fix your copier just an hour after you called for service.

➤ Ordering flowers for your Mom's birthday, on your computer, at 3 in the morning, for delivery later that day.

➤ Spending more than 24 seconds with your doctor, who's caring and not abrupt; and not having to wait 90 minutes surrounded by old, tattered, germ-covered magazines in the waiting room for the privilege.

➤ Calling a vendor to order materials and getting the price, delivery, and credit details worked out all in one call.

➤ Experiencing a no-hassle exchange for that goofy tie you received as a gift.

➤ Talking with someone who actually understands the problem you're having with your software—and getting an immediate answer that actually solves your problem right then and there.

➤ Calling a store and having a nice, helpful person tell you if they carry such-and-such an item, and whether they have it in stock.

➤ Encountering a helpful salesperson who takes the time to ask what features *you* think the product should have to meet your needs.

These are all examples of what people describe as *customer service*. And to be sure, customer service is all of these things and more.

But Don't Confine It

In some companies the term *customer service* has a very restrictive definition. To them, customer service is a *specific department* dedicated to one or a few tasks. Those tasks might include one or more of the following:

➤ Quoting prices to customers

➤ Entering customer orders into a computer

➤ Telling customers the status of their orders

➤ Explaining an invoice

➤ Dispatching a truck to pick up or deliver something

➤ Resolving billing questions

➤ Investigating or approving credit

➤ Collecting overdue bills

➤ Repairing malfunctioning products made by the company

> **Word to the Wise**
> Your organization's *constituencies* are all the people served by it. They could include the owners, stockholders, employees, customers, joint venture partners, members of the community, government officials, and even suppliers. Constituents are your company's very important people, no matter who or where they are.

While these are all customer service functions that may be best handled by a customer service department, we have a broader concept in mind. In this and the next few chapters, we're going to describe customer service as an objective for your company that is so vitally important to its success that it goes beyond the traditional customer service department. In fact, it even goes beyond the traditional idea of what constitutes a *customer*.

> **Tales from the Real World**
>
> Don once worked with a colleague responsible for hundreds of sales people who referred to their employer's customer service department as the "sales prevention department." The sales folks kept "trying to get the business" but ran into a brick wall erected by the customer service department. The customer service department dutifully enforced some terribly rigid (and probably unreasonable) company rules, making it difficult to please more customers and make more sales.
>
> Eventually, under intense competitive pressure, a major restructuring aligned the sales, credit, and customer service groups toward common purposes. They, along with technical support, all began working together to please more customers—and make more sales. The upshot: sales, customer satisfaction, and employee satisfaction all increased.

To us, customer service is everything your company does—and everything it doesn't do—to create *Personally Pleasing Memorable Interactions* (or PPMI) with the company's many different *constituencies*. We coined this catchy little mouthful to capture the essence of great service: Truly great service pleases a customer according to his or her *individual* preferences—so much so that the customer feels special and *remembers* the interaction with the company. And wants to come back for more again and again.

Human to Human

Customer service injects humanity into a business transaction. There are two vital components to every interaction you have with a customer:

1. The purchase or transaction
2. The relationship

Good customer service always builds the relationship and completes the transaction. As you will see, it also is the relationship that often builds more sales.

Every business interaction involves the twin dimensions of business: the transaction and the relationship.

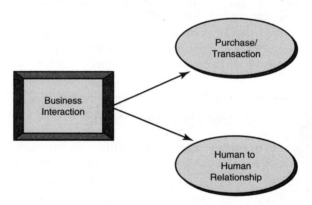

Copyright©1997 by Don Blohowiak

Customer: Far Beyond "Buyer"

When you think of customer service as encompassing all the activities that can create Personally Pleasing Memorable Interactions (PPMI) with many different very important people, you certainly include the work done by traditional, more narrowly-defined customer service departments. Yet, for those departments to be most effective in their dealings with customers, a broader idea of what customer service is needs to take hold in the organization.

Let's dissect the term customer service.

Customer, as the dictionary defines it, translates into buyer. And while buyers are mighty important, heck, let's say absolutely indispensable, to your company's success, how you

6

treat your buyers depends largely on how your company treats lots of other important people (like you and your fellow employees, for instance).

Tales from the Real World

Gordon Bethune, Chairman and CEO of Continental Airlines, knows what it takes to transform a company from the brink of bankruptcy to being an industry leader. In 1993, Continental came out of bankruptcy protection. Just three years later, Continental was named Airline of the Year by Air Transport World for being in the top three of all four Department of Transportation customer satisfaction measures—on time performance, baggage handling, fewest customer complaints, and fewest involuntary denied boardings. When you ask Bethune or any of his employees how they accomplished this feat, you hear the unanimous answer that both the employees and customers were treated as valued stakeholders in Continental's overall success.

When you think of your company's customers as including many more people beyond those who simply buy from your company, three interesting things result:

At Your Service
Thinking of customer service as giving good service merely to buyers is extremely limiting. An organization tends to give much better service to buyers when it serves well *all* the people who are important to it.

1. You make delivering great customer service the responsibility of many more people beyond those in the customer service department.

2. Your company tends to give better service to many more people.

3. Far more people begin to think of your company and talk about it as one that really cares and provides really great service. And that should encourage more people to buy from you.

Service: Far Beyond "May I Help You?"

You don't need to read this or any other book to know that good service starts with politeness and a helpful attitude. You should also understand that politeness and a helpful attitude do not equal good service.

Everyone who comes in contact with your company wants to be treated nicely, fairly, and promptly. But truly good service is more than that.

Good service is:

➤ Getting help, getting a problem solved—competently with no hassle, no run-around, and no delay

➤ Dealing with people who know their stuff

➤ Dealing with people who are authorized to provide information, right a wrong, or make things happen for a customer without passing the buck or begging permission

➤ Being treated in the way that the customer wants, which usually means with respect, a quick response, and an appreciation for the customer's position

➤ Anticipating a customer's needs and wants

➤ Ending a transaction or interaction so that the customer feels better than before it began

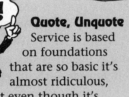

Quote, Unquote
Service is based on foundations that are so basic it's almost ridiculous, and yet even though it's simple, when it comes to consistently providing high levels of hospitality, it's easier said than done.
—Holly Stiel, former concierge in a fancy San Francisco hotel and author of *Ultimate Service*

Each of these many points deserves more explanation, and you will find the details throughout this book. For our purposes now, understand that providing good service means a lot more than muttering, "Have a nice day," to your customers. It means giving your employees the information, the authority, and the capacity to serve your customers as well as humanly possible. It means undertaking a very big job.

Great Expectations

Let's say you had a magic wand you could wave over your entire organization. (That would be a big wand, eh?) You wave the wand and *poof!* Everyone everywhere suddenly starts giving all your firm's constituents good service as defined earlier.

You still have a problem.

So what's the problem? Giving good service is not good enough in our service economy.

➤ All companies—service companies and manufacturing companies, even government agencies and not-for-profit organizations—are striving to provide excellent service to the people they serve.

➤ Consumers of every description—and that includes your customers and other constituents—are being exposed to lots of service from many, many service providers.

And all those organizations are trying to distinguish themselves by the quality of their service. That means organizations now compete on the basis of service. So customers—spoiled by all that service—can tell in a microsecond the difference between *outstanding* service and good, mediocre, or bad service.

Tales from the Real World

There's a sign you can commonly find in places like print shops and auto repair garages that says, "Speed. Quality. Price. Pick any two."

Sure, that's supposed to be a joke. (Didn't you laugh?) But today the joke's on those of us who would presume to win business from a demanding public. Now, we not only need to fulfill that happy trinity of customer demands—speed, quality, and price—but the market also demands that we provide those other characteristics along with a healthy serving of knowledgeable, custom-tailored, friendly service! Without question, the competitive battle will go to those companies that perform admirably in all four dimensions of customer value.

To compete on service today—and that's what you've got to do—you need to be really, really, *really* good at it.

There is a clear relationship between the level of service and customer loyalty (as measured by repeat business and profits).

Hierarchy of Service

Dependent on Company

Preferred Vendor

Satisfactory Service

Unsatisfactory Service

Copyright©1997 by Don Blohowiak

The higher the level of service you deliver, the more your customers want to do business with you, and the higher your profits are likely to be.

When your customers feel that your company exists to serve them and their uniquely personal needs, your company is on its way to realizing the competitive advantage we call The Service Difference.

And the Cure...

It's a lot less stressful for customers to do business with a supplier they know and love than to keep seeking out alternatives. Still, customers can be awfully fickle. You want them to give you their business time after time, to appreciate all that you do for them, to show a smidgen of loyalty.

Quote, Unquote
Companies are gauging their progress not just by return on assets, but also by the happy return of customers.
—*Executive Issues*, The Wharton School

Dream on. It's not happening. A silent, deadly disease is sweeping every segment of the economy: *Defectionitis*. A malady marked by the quiet, unassuming defection of customers who stealthily take their business from you and give it to somebody else. And there's a simple reason for this epidemic. Customers see no reason not to shop around to save a few cents here, a few bucks there, or to enjoy a little added convenience.

Defectionitis is a serious, infectious disease that can be quickly terminal for your organization unless it's immediately treated with massive doses of industrial-strength customer focus at all levels of your organization.

Customer focus therapy cures ailing sales and profits by mobilizing your business to do everything it can to encourage customers to come back and spend more money with you time after time.

Do you want to do business with a customer:

a) Just once

or

b) Over and over again for as long as he still has a couple of bucks in his pocket.

Did you answer *b*? Very good! That investment in your education is paying off handsomely.

Repeats Repeats Repeats

It takes a lot of investment in promotion, product design, operations, and lots of other stuff to attract and be ready to serve a new customer. Then, when you actually attract a new customer, you may have to educate him or her about your products, sales, and business policies. You may have to do a credit check, set up a new account for the new customer, create a new file with a new label just for that new customer (ugh), and gather lots of information about that customer in order to provide them with the service they expect.

Add up all that effort, and you can see that adding a new customer to your business can take quite an investment in time, money, and energy. Business experts who study this kind of thing figure that it costs something like five times more to serve a new customer than a repeat customer.

Here are two very important truths about why creating repeat customers through outstanding service is worth the trouble:

1. It costs your business a heck of a lot less to serve repeat customers—those who already know what you offer and like buying from you—than what it costs to chase a whole bunch of strangers and try to convince them to spend their money with you.

2. Steady repeat customers generate far more profit for you than customers who buy from you just once or just once in a while.

Repeat = Lower Expense

Most organizations spend much of their time and energy acquiring new customers. They advertise. They promote deep discount sales. They run contests for their sales people to land new accounts. They spend lots of time, energy, and money trying to convince someone to make a single purchase. Certainly, a business can grow by adding new customers. But it might be much more profitable by spending more energy encouraging *existing* customers to buy again and again and again.

Here's why. Existing customers already know your company. They have an idea of what it stands for. They have sampled the quality of its merchandise. So it should cost far less—maybe even *nothing*—to encourage satisfied customers (you did satisfy them, didn't you?) to return time and again. To cajole great masses of the uninitiated to try your company for the first time costs far more. They don't know about your business and they certainly don't care about it. So in order to get their attention and motivate them to give you a try, you often need to buy ads, send countless mailings, offer steep discounts, and increase sales compensation.

Would you rather spend $10 on ads, mailings, special discounts and the like to attract a new customer for their first $50 purchase, or 50¢ to mail a customized reminder letter to your repeat customer who may well make two or three additional $50 purchases with nothing more expensive than some heartfelt words of encouragement and appreciation?

> **Watch It!**
> While it takes considerable effort to win a customer for life, it is pitifully, effortlessly easy to lose a customer for life. You cannot overstate the importance of this with every employee whose work impacts on customers.

Repeat = Revenue

An associate of Don's goes every morning to the same convenience store for a large coffee. He spends about a dollar on it. To the clerk completing the transaction on any given morning, this is a $1 customer.

But this same customer also makes a habit of returning at lunch and buying a prepared sandwich, a soda, and a snack for the afternoon. About a $6 transaction. Sometimes he brings his friends in the store and they each spend a few dollars for lunch, too. Then, on his way home at night, he often stops at the store for another cup of coffee and maybe picks up a half-gallon of milk. So in an average week, this "$1 cup of coffee customer" actually spends somewhere around $30 to $50 in that convenience store, not to mention whatever his buddies spend on their lunches.

So in an average year, this $1 transaction guy is actually visiting the store two or three times a day, about four days out of the week, and dropping upwards of $1,500 per year! Imagine if this same customer continues to return day after day, year after year for as long as he lives in the area (like 15 or 20 or more years). That $1 cup of coffee customer may be worth some *20 grand* to that store.

If you owned that store, wouldn't you want each of your employees to understand that each $1 customer could represent a whole lot more potential revenue. And wouldn't you want to make sure that no $1 customer, potentially worth 20 grand to you, was ever driven away forever by a sour cup of coffee or a sour employee?

And while the products and the numbers are different for your business, isn't the principle of creating a repeat customer equally true—and important—for your business?

Repeat Calculation

What's a repeat customer worth? $_____

Do you give up? Well, don't—because you really should know the value of creating a customer for *life*. Fortunately, it's easy to calculate.

Lifetime Value calculation.

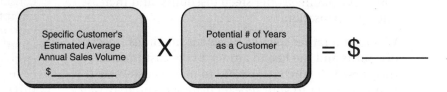

Business experts who study this kind of thing have determined that if you keep something like just five percent of your customers who otherwise would take their repeat purchases to the competition, you can double your profits. Whoa!

From Their Mouths to Your Wallet

When you were looking for a reliable, honest auto mechanic, how did you find him? Before you went into that restaurant you recently tried, how did you know that it served great food? If you're like most everyone on the planet, you wanted to lower your risk of a big ugly surprise so you asked people you trust to refer you to a business they trust.

We all rely on our friends and associates to recommend going—or not going—to a particular business. Marketers call this friend-to-friend endorsement of a business "word-of-mouth advertising." It is the most powerful form of advertising. It is also the most difficult to create.

Whether you do a great job for your customers or a rotten job, people are going to talk about your business. Unfortunately, because we humans seem to feel negative emotions more intensely than positive ones, we're more inclined to tell more of our friends about bad experiences with a business than positive ones. Admit it, you do that, don't you?

Understand this: Customers believe their own experience. You can't make them believe that your company is wonderful when they just felt like they were treated mediocre or rotten by it.

So, to get positive word-of-mouth going for your business, especially from your demanding customers in this service-based economy, you've got to do a really outstanding job. For everyone. Consistently.

And when you do, you build a great reputation. That takes time. But it forges a bond with your customers and prospective customers in a way that no slick advertising campaign, and no promotional coupon ever could.

The good news is that because there are so many different businesses chasing after your customers' money, people *want* to know who they can trust. So people are going to be talking about you.

Create a free sales force for your business—an army of delighted customers who tell everyone they know how good your company is to do business with. That's a great antidote to *Defectionitis*.

Quote, Unquote
One word of praise from a satisfied customer is worth a thousand words of product description.
—Jeffery Gitomer, Business Marketing Services, Charlotte, NC

At Your Service
Customers have come to expect good service. So they tend not to notice or appreciate merely competent service. To get them talking about your business and recommending it to all their friends and associates, you need to do an outstanding job. The answer is to consistently create enjoyable experiences so that people *want* to tell all their personal contacts about how great your company is.

The Least You Need to Know

➤ Customer service distinguishes your business from others.

➤ Customers are all the important people your firm serves.

➤ Customers are both demanding and fickle; to win their loyalty, you have to provide truly outstanding customer service.

➤ To serve your customers in a way that meaningfully distinguishes your firm from others, you need to provide customers with Personally Pleasing Memorable Interactions (PPMI).

➤ Sustained profits come from serving customers time after time for a lifetime of business.

➤ You generate more business and stay both more competitive and more profitable by building a reputation from positive word-of-mouth recommendations.

TROUBLE IN AISLE TWO...

CLIFF

Chapter 2

Service: It's a Mission

In This Chapter

➤ Getting past lip service

➤ Making service a *Mission*

➤ Making the Mission real

➤ Testing the commitment to make the Mission real

➤ Doing what *you* can

"The customer is King." "We love customers." "The customer is always right."

There's no shortage of lip service concerning customer service. Everyone seems to know the right words to say.

So why does it seem that you actually encounter great service so rarely?

Too many organizations that brag about their service do so because they think they should (it is the rage, you know). Or, just as dangerous, they really believe they already give the kind of service that creates loyal customers—even though their customers don't think so.

Watch It!
Companies can fall in love with concepts and forget why the latest craze was appealing in the first place—to improve and increase business! Remember to focus on the job of creating loyal customers.

A great experience leaves a customer wanting more. It leaves a customer eager to have an interaction with your firm again.

And, as discussed in the previous chapter, profits come from repeat business. The more repeat business you get, the more profits you get.

Remember: your business is not your physical assets, your stock, or even all your employees. Your business is nothing more than the collection of interactions you and your colleagues have with your customers. Period. Without those customer interactions and transactions, you have nothing.

Mission: Mission

It's fashionable for companies of all sizes to have a Vision and Mission Statement. Mission Statements should:

➤ Express why the organization exists.

➤ Give employees and customers alike a clear sense of what the organization stands for.

If you don't yet have your Mission plaque on the wall and you want to scrap the current one and start from scratch, here's a simple process you can use to create a meaningful Mission and Values Statement.

Think about the *big questions*: Why does the company even exist? Why is it in the business it's in? What does it hope to accomplish?

1. Get input on these issues from people significant to the company's future: customers, owners, employees, suppliers.

2. Review the ideas. Combine them. Shape them.

3. Begin drafting a few simple sentences:

    Our firm exists to _____ .

    We are committed to _____ . (This might be several items, for example, what products you'll make or services you'll offer, the kind of customers you'll serve.)

    We will distinguish our company from others by _____ .

    We will achieve our objectives by _____. (Here you describe the values your company stands for: such as product innovation and quality; opportunity for all employees; fair value for customers and profits for your company; and so on.)

4. Get feedback from people on the draft:

    Does it really sound like your company? Does it capture the true personality or sound too ideal, abstract, or "textbook-ish"?

    Is it specific enough?

    Can you envision the company really living up to the statements?

5. After incorporating the comments, revise the draft. Create a final. Adopt it.
6. Publish the statement. Widely. To your employees, owners, suppliers, customers.
7. Commit to living by the Statement. Truly incorporate it into how your company does business:

    Use it as a guide for daily operations.

    Use it as a touchstone for difficult decisions the way the U.S. Supreme Court uses the Constitution.

    Make it part of your training program.

    Refer to it when using it as a basis for policies and decisions.

Tales from the Real World

Publix Super Markets, a ten-billion dollar-a-year employee-owned chain in the Southeastern U.S., has won numerous awards for its caring customer service.

Its mission statement is wonderfully ambitious and succinct: "To be the premier quality food retailer in the world."

And likewise its promise to customers: "Where shopping is a pleasure." And Publix customers think it is!

Proof Is in the Paging

One of our favorite Values Statements is from Ram Mobile Data, an aggressive nationwide paging company owned in part by BellSouth. The statement was created by a group of employees from various parts of the company, and reads as follows:

WE OWE EACH OTHER a working environment characterized by trust and respect for the individual, fostering open and honest communication at all levels.

WE OWE OUR CUSTOMERS AND PARTNERS the highest quality of service possible, characterized by responsiveness, accuracy, integrity and professionalism. We will continually strive for quality improvement.

WE OWE OUR COMPANY our full professional commitment and dedication. We will work diligently toward maximizing the company's profitability and long term success. We will always look beyond the traditional scope of our individual positions to promote teamwork and business effectiveness.

WE OWE OURSELVES personal and professional growth. We will seek new knowledge and greater challenges, and strive to remain on the leading edge of our professions. We will expect to change and continually self renew.

A copy of the Values Statement sits on every desk at Ram Mobile Data—a constant reminder to employees as to what the company is all about.

> **At Your Service**
> You can create a Mission Statement for a department within a larger organization. It gives employees a clear idea of what their priorities are and how they fit into the larger organizational picture.

Involve Employees

Get your employees to participate in creating the Mission Statement.

> **Watch It!**
> Getting employee involvement in the Mission Statement creation process is great. But don't try to have every employee working away at it in meetings (as we have seen some well-intending but naïve companies do). That can create a communication and logistics nightmare.

Here is a suggested process:

➤ Invite employees to volunteer to serve on a Mission task force of ten or fewer employees (if you need to involve more, create subgroups at your various locations and have them submit idea summaries to the main steering group).

➤ Ask all employees to submit ideas for the Mission Statement to the task force.

➤ Have that task force work closely with a top management group to create a Mission Statement that reflects top management strategy and employee insight.

Involve a wide cross-section of employees in the Mission Statement cooking process. Top management needs to set the strategic direction for the company. But employees from all areas and at all levels can make a significant contribution in defining *how* the company achieves its Mission.

Keep the Faith

Reciting or pledging allegiance to the ideals on the wall—like "serving customers beyond their expectations"—isn't the same as *behaving* in a way that assures your customers of a satisfying experience.

Put It to the Test

Answer these tough questions to test whether you are putting your Mission Statement to work for your customers:

➤ Do all your employees know, really know, what your organization stands for?

➤ If you've gone to the trouble of creating a Vision/Mission/Values statement, can you honestly say it guides day-to-day behavior of most (any?) of your employees?

➤ How many of your employees even know what it says?

➤ Could they recite it, or at least capture the essence of it?

➤ Would they say they work in harmony with it day-to-day?

➤ Are the principles integrated into their job descriptions and part of their performance evaluations?

If your Mission Statement doesn't score well on this test, scrap the darn thing and replace it. Or get about the business of making those words meaningful in guiding on-the-job behavior (and your assessments of it).

Watch It!
News flash: customers don't care what your Mission Statement says. They care about how you treat them. And how you treat them should spring from your organization's core values—if those are clear enough, and felt deeply enough by everyone in the organization.

At Your Service
Make your firm's mission and values clear to your employees so they know what the organization's true priorities are. (And if it's only to make the most money possible, at least be honest about it.)

Prove It!

Meaningful customer service is about demonstrating your appreciation for the people who placed their trust and confidence in you. And we mean demonstrating in very fundamental ways that you truly care about what the customer values.

If you have a poorly designed and unreliable product, being nice to customers won't make them believe that your Yugo is a Porsche.

And even the fanciest of talk and the slickest of slogans about customer service doesn't impress any customer. Do you think a sports team boasting about its commitment to winning convinces fans to overlook its losing record?

Yeah, Right

Don bought an electronic gizmo that was supposed to come with a rebate coupon in the box. Only it didn't. He discovered the coupon was missing on a Sunday afternoon. Even though he figured it was a total waste of time to do so, he called the retail store, an electronics chain in the Northeast U.S. called Nobody Beats the Wiz.

The helpful salesman explained that the store didn't have the coupons on hand, but their customer service center—available through a toll-free number—could likely send it. Don experienced one of those "yeah, right" moments. Still, he tossed caution to the wind and dialed the "800" number.

To his surprise, not only was it staffed on a Sunday afternoon, the call was answered in just a couple of rings. The helpful person at the other end promised to locate the rebate coupon, even if she had to contact the manufacturer. And she'd have it in the mail within a few days. Another "yeah, sure" moment?

Don thought so. Until three days later when the coupon arrived, as promised.

The store backed up its customer service slogans with real (and fast) action. Since that experience, and in light of the chain's 7-day no questions asked return policy, as well as its 30-day price guarantee policy, Don has purchased thousands of dollars of equipment from Nobody Beats the Wiz.

Acid Test

Here's one way to test your company's commitment to customers. Ask any of your colleagues you hear preaching about how much the organization values service, "When was the last time you actually had a meaningful interaction with a customer?" Like talked to one, not just eavesdropped on the customer service department's phone monitor, or watched a customer from a distance, or through the glass at a focus group interview.

Organizations that truly care about customers have:

➤ Management that is in close contact with customers.

➤ Compensation for management based on the level of customer loyalty (which is more than just a simple percentage of people who say they are satisfied; see Chapter 15).

If you know that your top management hasn't really been face to face with a customer for many a moon, suggest, gently, that they get back in touch with the reason your firm exists.

While it's best to interact with customers where they purchase or use your product or service, consider this alternative. Set up an *event* that has customers and your senior management group interacting. It could be something like a lunch discussion where an independent moderator helps customers and managers discuss items of mutual interest. Of course, this isn't ideal. But it could be the first step in easing ivory tower management back down to the trench level—where they really need to be on an on-going basis.

Beyond Greed: Why Service Gets Bad

When your employees give bad service, or less than great service, which is nearly the same as bad service today, they probably do it for one of the following reasons:

1. They don't believe that giving good service is really expected by management.

2. They don't know how to give good service.

3. They aren't service-oriented people (and really shouldn't be in a service job).

4. Your organization is not set up to support providing good service. (You have flawed policies, inefficient procedures, inadequate support systems, unclear priorities, confused employees, excessive bureaucracy, etc.)

5. Your organization treats its employees with little respect. Employees who feel like they are a necessary evil, who don't feel valued or respected, tend to treat customers the same way.

All five reasons can and must be addressed by management. Each of these service-squashers is addressed fully in this book. None are solved by putting up a poster or circulating a memo declaring "The customer comes first." Bleccchh!

Some managers say they can't afford to deliver good service. Horse feathers! This is a self-deceiving trap. Good service isn't any more expensive than bad service. The award-winning, and lesser-known, organizations we feature in this book don't pay their people far more than competitors. And they don't make less profit than their less enlightened competitors. In fact, they tend to make more. Delivering great service is not about either spending more money or saving money. It's about profiting from leadership.

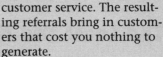

Quote, Unquote
The cheapest way to run a business is to provide the highest-quality customer service. The resulting referrals bring in customers that cost you nothing to generate.
—David Steinberg, president, Sterling Communications, a Cellular One retailer, Silver Spring, MD

Small Ambition

Suppose you say "amen" to all the stuff above about a company-wide commitment to great service. Then in the next breath you say, "This all great. But you guys don't understand. My bosses do not get it! What then, smarty pants?"

Quote, Unquote
Across America, the bulk of businesses look at customer service as an expense. If you establish a tradition that views customer service as an expense, every good manager knows what to do: minimize it. But if you see service as an asset, it takes on a completely different aspect.
—George Heilmeier, president and CEO, Bellcore

Well, you wouldn't be the first person to have wrestled with this problem. Here's our advice:

1. Don't get discouraged. At least *you* know what needs to be done. And that's a good start.

2. Do everything you can to create The Service Difference in your domain, your corner of the organization, no matter how big it is.

3. Control what you can control. Influence what you can influence.

4. You can always buy another copy of this book and secretly slip it onto the Big Cheese's desk with a cryptic inscription on a sticky note: "JB, Great stuff. How about a copy for all managers?—R." That'll do wonders for your company's progress and our kids' college funds.

Not Just a Department, a Way of Life

Concern for the competitive impact of customer service has encouraged its evolution from simply managing "customer contact tasks," like responding to customer inquiries or complaints, to a company-wide, consuming passion for pleasing customers.

Naturally, reading this book helps you to build a superb customer contact/customer service function in your organization. But just as importantly, it presents you with many ideas and techniques for building the Customer Service Organization where the whole company is thinking about and organizing work to make great customer service the top priority.

The Least You Need to Know

➤ Giving your customers great service doesn't come from slogans; it must be a top priority in the organization.

➤ The sense of Mission must be clearly stated and understood by all employees.

➤ The Mission becomes reality when top management becomes personally involved with customers.

➤ Even if you don't have the ideal total organizational commitment, you can still make progress in your part of the company.

Chapter 3

Just Who Serves the Customer Around Here?

In This Chapter

➤ Creating cohesive customer contact

➤ Developing a culture of superior service

➤ Making customer satisfaction everyone's job

➤ Demonstrating service by management

➤ Cooperating beats internal competition

➤ Seeing the signs of success

Depending on the type of business you work in, lots of different people in different functional areas may interact with your customers. Those customer contact functions might include:

➤ Sales   ➤ Shipping

➤ Telemarketing   ➤ Technical support

➤ Credit   ➤ Collections

➤ Order processing   ➤ Customer service

That's a lot of people who might reach out and touch customers. And with all those possible contacts, there's plenty of opportunity for confusion.

The Great Debate

Whose job is it? Who owns the customer? That sounds like a question only for people concerned with organizational politics. After all, if you were to poll your customers and ask them, "Who at Amalgamated Enterprises owns you?," chances are pretty darn good that 99.95 percent of the respondents would reply, "No one owns me; and I don't really care very much about Amalgamated Enterprises!"

Still, the issue of "who owns the customer" gets even nonpolitical people's juices flowing. That's because at the heart of the question is the complex issue of how to truly deliver on the *belief* that your company should provide outstanding service.

From Fragments to Process

Customers can get lost in the shuffle, or worse, caught in the cross-fire, when dealing with many different departments in a company. That's especially true if the different departments don't communicate well—or at all. The following diagrams show the old and new views of customer contact departments, where work was "handed off" from one department to another.

In the old, fragmented model of customer service, each customer contact was handled by a separate department with little or no coordination. No one was sure what was going on.

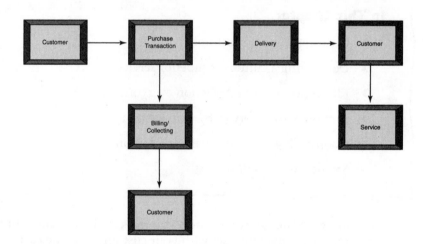

Think of customer service as a coordinated system, a process that integrates a wide collection of tasks. When that is a truly collaborative effort between different functional groups in the company, no one has to worry about whether the Marketing department or the Sales department or the Operations department or anyone else "owns" the customer—because everyone does.

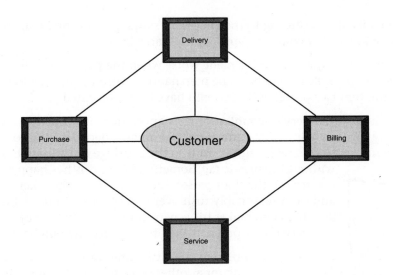

In the new, cohesive model of customer service, communication and information flow between the customer and all the customer contact functions. Everyone knows what's going on.

How Are You Operating?

Below are signs of an integrated, coordinated commitment to customers. Use this checklist to assess whether you're operating in the new cohesive model, or back in the fragmented one:

❏ Customer needs and requirements are clearly understood in every corner of the organization

❏ Work is viewed in terms of the whole process not just one department passing work from it to another department

❏ Work groups with employees from several different functional areas jointly take responsibility for making sure that all work activities 1) are coordinated, and 2) serve the customer, not the company

❏ Information is shared between work teams and functional departments

❏ Technology supports information sharing

❏ Policy and procedure changes are made only after consulting other functional groups to assess unexpected impact on customers

❏ Problems that arise are viewed as opportunities to improve the process of serving customers; there is no blaming, only working together to improve things

Who Is the Convenience for?

Don buys some office supplies from one of those humungous discount warehouse clubs. Printer cartridges are displayed in a glass case. To buy a printer cartridge, you are supposed to pick up a numbered plastic tag corresponding to the numbered print cartridge on display. Then you take the plastic tag to the check-out stand, pay for the item, and then take your receipt to another counter to pick up the cartridge.

At best, this is not an elegant system. But it's made worse when the tags are missing from the display, making it impossible to purchase the merchandise without chasing down an employee to find a solution to a problem that should have been prevented.

When Don goes to the customer service counter for assistance, the contact people are very friendly and very eager to help. They immediately summon a department floor worker to write up a note with the item number on it so the cartridge can be purchased without the plastic tag. Sometimes (yes, this has happened a few times), the floor person is busy selling a big ticket item and can't reasonably rush over to scribble out a note. Eventually, the clerk makes his way over to the small display case and very nicely prepares the little chit for the purchase.

Don has grown tired of this little time-wasting exercise and has begun looking for another place to purchase his printer cartridges. Morals of the story:

Watch It!

Turf battles and empire building are destructive forces in a company. When managers start fights over who owns the customer, they're usually looking to gain political power.

Sometimes it's the opposite: managers don't want to be bothered, and shirk their customer responsibilities, saying it's not their department's job.

The question that should be central to every management team: "How can we maximize customer value and satisfaction by working the most effectively together?"

1. Customer service springs from a well-designed system that prevents creating problems for customer contact people to solve.

2. People who stock shelves or replace little plastic tags or do other seemingly minor tasks need to understand how important their little part of the process is to the whole objective of satisfying customers.

3. Even the nicest, friendliest, most helpful customer service people cannot compensate for the inconvenience caused by an uncoordinated or poorly conceived service system.

Make sure your system is convenient for the customer, not just your company and employees.

Community Property

No matter how many internal groups have responsibility for customer contact, truly great customer service comes from everyone in the whole company working as though their job is to please customers. Because it is!

Believing that is one thing; making it part of the way your company works day after day is another. Let's look a little closer at how you can make continually great service a reality.

Culture and Style

When you try to make everyone in the company feel that they have responsibility for giving your customers great service, you don't just issue a memo saying, "Effective January 1st we will all start giving great customer service." Great service needs to become part of the company personality.

Companies, like individuals, have a distinct personality. That personality comes from your company's unique history, the customers you serve, the people on the payroll, and your firm's values and traditions. Management gurus call this stuff *corporate culture*.

Your company may make and sell exactly the same product as several other companies. But no two companies will be alike in the way they make and sell a product, even if they use very similar physical processes. An important difference is in the company personality or culture. You need to know a few important things at this point:

➤ Every company has its own unique culture

➤ Providing great service to customers must become an essential part of your company's corporate culture

➤ Evolving a corporate culture to greatly value service is a huge, on-going job requiring the commitment of top management, and the cooperation of everyone else

Giving your customers great service is impossible if your corporate culture doesn't support it. So you have to build a culture that does.

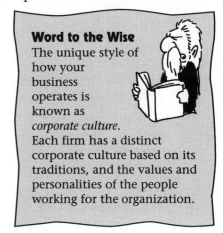

Word to the Wise
The unique style of how your business operates is known as *corporate culture*. Each firm has a distinct corporate culture based on its traditions, and the values and personalities of the people working for the organization.

Make Customer Service Everyone's Job

Do your employees have job descriptions? That's how everyone knows what they're supposed to do, right?

Have you read a job description lately? What does it say? Does it list tasks and duties?

That stuff is okay, but it's incomplete. It doesn't clearly tell your employees *what's important* about their jobs. And that, of course, is creating happy customers who want to come back again and again to your business.

You need to put customer service in everyone's job description. Add a sentence or two at the beginning of every employee's job description that says: "The [describe job] exists to help Our Company serve customers better. The really important outcome of this job is [describe whatever it is]. That helps Our Company to prosper by satisfying and delighting those wonderful people who make your job possible—our customers—by [describe]."

Let's see how this approach works for a couple of real jobs away from the front line of customer contact.

Example 1. The overnight sanitation crew member position exists to help Our Company serve customers better. The really important outcome of this job is to provide a clean, sanitary, and inviting work atmosphere for your fellow employees at Our Company. That helps Our Company to prosper by satisfying and delighting those wonderful people who make your job possible—our customers—by providing a physical working environment that encourages everyone at Our Company to do their very best work.

Example 2. The financial analyst position exists to help Our Company serve customers better. The really important outcome of this job is to provide well-researched, well-reasoned, and inspired thinking to assist intelligent decision-making at Our Company. That helps Our Company to prosper by satisfying and delighting those wonderful people who make your job possible—our customers—by putting Our Company's precious financial resources to their very best use.

By putting the customer service connection into all job descriptions, you help to create the link between every job in the company and a service culture. You strengthen that link when you show employees how their job—no matter how far removed from actual customer contact—impacts customers in some important way.

Make Customer Service Part of Pay

You need to put your money where your slogan is. Do you really care about customers? Make that service commitment part of every employee's performance evaluation and compensation. At the periodic performance review do the following:

➤ Ask, "How did your work impact our customers in the past quarter?" (You *are* doing quarterly or monthly performance reviews aren't you?)

➤ Tie compensation to the answer you get to the above, or more importantly, to the *actions* you've observed that employee taking to back up the answer.

Management Model

Does your corporate culture come with an "owner's manual"? Even if you have a big old Policy & Procedures manual, it probably doesn't describe "how things really work around here."

Corporate culture is communicated in many ways even if it's not written down anywhere. One of the most powerful ways of creating and communicating an organization's culture comes from the way company managers behave. Employees learn a lot about what an organization truly values from the way their bosses behave.

Word and Deed

Employees learn by example. Let's say they read a memo that says, "Treat your customers with respect." But they feel management doesn't treat them with respect. Guess what they believe the true culture is?

If the company newsletter says, "We must get to know our customers as individuals and establish a relationship with them," but employees never see top management anywhere near a customer, they conclude something else about the company's true culture.

Imagine that a manager gives a speech to employees and tells them to be warm, friendly, and inviting to customers. But this same manager barely knows the names of her employees and rarely talks to them at all. That tells employees something very different about the real culture at the company.

Tales from the Real World

T. Scott Gross, an author who gives seminars on customer service and sales, points to Herb Kelleher, chairman of Southwest Airlines. "On Thanksgiving weekend, one of the heaviest travel weekends of the year, Herb Kelleher can be found at an airport. Not directing operations," Scott says, "but handling baggage. By working side-by-side with his employees, he shows that he knows and appreciates that his employees have to be there on the holiday."

Other top executives deomonstrate how to show commitment to good service by staying in touch with customers and employees. Bill Marriott is often found at his Marriott hotel properties talking to front-line workers. The late, great Sam Walton loved nothing better than touring his Wal-Mart stores and surprising employees, to their delight, with his visit.

When top management shows a keen interest in the operation, everyone else tends to pay attention, too.

In education, they call it modeling. In management consulting, we call it monkey see, monkey do. Whatever you call it, a corporate culture grows out of employees mirroring the actions of their managers. How you behave as a manager shouts to your employees what you really value.

Setting the Example

To create a service culture, show employees what it means to serve. Think of your employees as your customers. Treat them that way. Let them learn from your example.

No matter what example you set, you are communicating what you expect and value.

Creating a Culture of Cooperation

There's nothing more powerful than a whole company mobilized to deliver great service. Individual employees create great service when they work collaboratively with employees in other departments to please customers.

Depending on your current corporate culture, getting people to move across functional boundaries to work with their colleagues in other departments may seem as natural as breathing or as uncomfortable as trying to squeeze into jeans three sizes too small.

Getting It Going

Here are a few simple ways to promote, demonstrate, and celebrate a culture of cooperation:

➤ Encourage your employees to share information across department lines. Better yet, erase the very idea of department lines. Suggest that your employees view the company as, in the words of a client of Don's, "one big team made up of many smaller teams."

➤ Urge your employees to participate on cross-functional teams (more on this in Chapter 17).

➤ Create opportunities to meet people from other parts of the company. Try shared staff meetings with work groups from other functional areas. Maybe some joint pizza lunches. Get people talking informally in a neutral, stress-free environment.

➤ Use the company newsletter, bulletin board, voice mail, or whatever communication media you have available to you. Spread the good news about people in different functional areas working together to please customers. If you get any letters or positive comments from customers, promote the collaboration behind the success stories. Hold up good examples of cooperative behavior for all to see.

Watch It!
When the big boys and girls don't play well together, everyone knows it and that trickles down. An enthusiastic espirit de corps at the top becomes a role model for everyone else. Make sure you don't forget to demonstrate cooperation at the senior executive level.

Strike a Deal

Back in the Dark Ages, when political turf wars and power struggles were more important to executives than customer satisfaction scores, Don faced a difficult dilemma. He was responsible for the promotional launch of a new software product at a company he had just joined. The problem wasn't the major project. That's simply hard work. The problem was his new boss prohibited him from having any contact with key people on the product development team. Apparently, shortly before Don arrived, the folks in development crossed swords with the folks in marketing. Executive feud. Stand off. And that was that.

But not quite. Taking career in hand, Don took a brave, secret trip down the elevator and walked into the development director's office. After the executive warned Don that he risked his new career by being there, they shut the door. After some tense initial moments of distrust, they struck a deal to cooperate and share important information. They did exactly that and helped to create the most successful product launch in the company's 100-plus year history.

21 Ways to Know It's Working

When you've created a culture of service, and your internal departments are working together to serve customers, something should happen. Actually, several good things should happen.

Here's a list of 21 positive outcomes to watch for:

- ❏ Favorable letters and comments from customers increase.
- ❏ Customers stay with you, even if your prices are higher than competitors.
- ❏ Customers who leave come back within a year.
- ❏ Customers are referring friends, family, and associates to the business.
- ❏ Other managers are asking, "How do you do it in your department?"
- ❏ Customers are more open about telling you what they really want.
- ❏ Customer complaints are less costly; they don't escalate to higher levels.
- ❏ Customers often suggest ways to improve your service.
- ❏ Many sources of customer complaints seem to have gone away.
- ❏ Customers are leaving competitors to use your service.
- ❏ More customers are paying their bills on time.
- ❏ When you get press coverage, it's generally favorable.
- ❏ Employees are staying longer; turnover is decreasing.

continues

---

continued

❑ Employee absenteeism is down.

❑ Employees are involved in process improvement.

❑ Operating costs are going down relative to income.

❑ Competitors are copying what you do.

❑ You're spending less time and money on rework and recovery (fixing customer problems to their satisfaction).

❑ Your stock price is going up (corporations).

❑ You got a rate increase (regulated industries).

❑ You got re-elected or re-appointed (government or non-profit).

Reproduced with permission. Copyright © 1997 Kaset International (a Times Mirror Training Company)

The Least You Need to Know

➤ Great service comes from coordinating customer contact departments without fragmentation or political motivation, and from creating a corporate culture that supports service and insists on it.

➤ All your employees must understand that customer satisfaction is the first and most important part of their job description, and a key part of their compensation.

➤ Managers must model good service behavior by the way they treat employees and the interest they show in dealing with customers.

➤ Encourage all employees to share information and to work together to please customers as their top priority; celebrate when they do.

➤ When you create a culture of service, the results present themselves in visible, measurable ways.

Chapter 4

Standardized—Spelling Out Good Performance

In This Chapter

➤ Experiencing make it or break it service

➤ Facing "The Instant of Absolute Judgment"

➤ Determining what you should set standards for

➤ Setting standards

➤ Making standards a daily reality

➤ Measuring up against standards

Imagine that your company picks up the tab for you to eat lunch at a particular restaurant every day (that does take some imagination, doesn't it?). Now, this restaurant is a nice place with table service. So far, so good.

Some days, the host warmly greets you by name and seats you immediately at your favorite table in the sunny corner. Other days, you stand at the entrance for ten minutes, get a grunt from the host and get seated after waiting another ten minutes. Then you find yourself right smack dab in front of the swinging doors to the kitchen. Even worse, on other days, no one greets you, and you have to go find an empty table, and probably end up at one you have to wait to be cleaned. Then you learn the kitchen is out of most items you like. No wonder no one was eager to seat you.

What's good about this restaurant? It's free! Remember?

But if it weren't, wouldn't you be a lot more likely to spend your own money there if it treated you well all the time instead of making your lunch hour some kind of culinary Russian roulette?

Consistently good service isn't an accident. It comes from standardizing your approach to it. That means leaving nothing to chance or to the mood or whims of employees.

You're about to discover how to assure consistently great service through standardization, which basically breaks into:

➤ Determining the service standards you should have

➤ Setting the standards

➤ Implementing them

➤ Assuring you meet your standards

Before leaping into how you can create the standards that assure your customers great service, let's take a quick look at why standards are so critical.

The "Instant of Absolute Judgment"

Customer service is often provided in brief interactions that only last for a few seconds at a time. Just seconds! But the impact could last a *lifetime*. That's because customers make emotional judgments about a company. Any single interaction can create an impression that will forever color a customer's attitude toward buying from your company.

Some people call this spontaneous evaluation a "moment of truth" (a phrase coined by Jan Carlzon of Scandinavian Airlines). We don't think that term goes nearly far enough in describing the potential impact on your business. We prefer to call it "The Instant of Absolute Judgment."

It can take years to build a reputation, but only a second to destroy it. Crushingly sad but amazingly true.

If you please a customer over and over again, she'll probably keep coming back. Disappoint her now and then, and the loyalty bond begins to erode. The customer drifts away a little bit at a time.

Upset a customer, make her angry, or let her down with a big disappointment, and you'll likely lose her business for the rest of her life.

Standards to the Rescue

You can dramatically increase the odds that your business will deliver consistently good service when you set *service standards*. They describe precisely how your business should achieve certain measurable service levels.

Examples of Service Standards

Standards should be unique to your industry and to your business in particular. To help you understand what we mean by standards, here are some examples:

➤ The toll-free helpline will be staffed 20 hours a day by certified technicians.

➤ Every caller to the helpline will get through to the help center on their first call (no busy signals) at least 97.5 percent of the time.

➤ After connecting with the telephone help center, a caller should wait no more than 3 minutes to speak to a live technician.

➤ Callers should receive a satisfactory solution to their problems on their first call at least 93 percent of the time.

Five Initial Questions

Interested in setting standards for your own organization? Great! Here are five questions to stimulate your thinking.

1. What work do we do that customers care about?
2. How might we do a better job at that work?
3. Ideally, to what level of perfection would we like to perform that work?
4. What are the expectations of our customers on how we should perform the work?
5. How can we ensure that customers *enjoy* dealing with us?

At this point, don't worry about having the answers to all those questions for all your work. Right now, we're just setting the stage for creating standards for your business.

Using Your "SMARTS"

To have a meaningful impact, service standards should meet certain, uh, standards. When you do actually start creating standards, they need to operate in a certain way to really have the impact you're looking for. We've created a helpful acronym to describe effective service standards, SMARTS.

S—Specific

Issuing instructions to employees that say, "Be friendly to customers," is not specific. (For example, friendly to one person could mean merely not hanging up on someone.) It is vague, broad, and open to many different interpretations. So is, "Generally, answer the phone as soon as possible." An example of a specific standard is: When answering the phone, answer it by the second ring and say, "It's my pleasure to serve you today. How may I help?"

Effective standards are specific as to:

➤ Who the standard applies to

➤ What actions are expected

➤ How you'll know if you're meeting the standard (see "M—Measurable" immediately following)

M—Measurable

You need to know if you're achieving the goal or not. Measurable means quantifiable, like in numbers. "Credit representatives will answer incoming customer calls by the second ring 96 percent of the time," is a specific, measurable goal.

The specific goals you set for your organization need to flow from your customers' expectations and your current level of performance. Later in this chapter, we give you a step-by-step process for setting your specific standards.

A—Achievable

It's fashionable to talk about "stretch goals," but employees need to believe they can achieve the standards. Or they won't even try. Setting standards means far more than merely identifying the goals. Just as importantly, it means designing and supporting the work process so you can achieve the standard on an on-going basis. This could involve a major structural change to the way you currently do your work.

R—Relevant to Customers

This is the most important characteristic. While there are a million operations you could set standards for in your company, your priority focus must be on the things that matter to customers and influence their buying decisions. Set standards for things that customers will notice and appreciate. The more relevant your standards are, the greater the likelihood your employees will implement them.

T—Timely

Good service is more than just the actions you take to assist customers. It's also the *time* you take to serve them. Solving a problem *during the customer's first call* has infinitely more value for most customers than the same outcome a month from now. Your service standards should include a goal and measure for time performance. (You'll find an extensive method for determining the right standards for your organization later in this chapter.)

S—Supported by the Organization

Service isn't just the activities of customer contact people. It's the tools, systems, and processes that support those efforts. Employees can't be better than the system allows them to be, no matter how much the boss carries on about improving service. The standards should become an essential part of employees' job descriptions and evaluations. Every employee, from the CEO on down, must be held accountable to these standards. If any employee is not held accountable, the standards will fall apart.

Fill In the Blanks

Want to create a service standard? Keep all the SMARTS points in mind, and then just fill in the simple formula that follows the example below.

To give you an idea of what the finished product looks like, we'll start with an example from a grocery store, followed by a format you can use to create your own standards.

Example

We will serve our customers with quick check-outs by cashiers in our express line, with a performance measure of having no more than three customers waiting in any cashier line and a target maximum wait time of under two minutes for any customer at any time. We will accomplish this objective by:

1. Refresher training sessions for all cashiers on efficient check-out procedures, with follow-up sessions every quarter.

2. Operating additional express lanes during peak times for express customer loads.

3. Increased staffing during peak times for express customer loads.

4. Friendly monthly competitions for speed and accuracy among all cashiers, with token rewards for winners and all participants.

At Your Service
Even the best-intending employees may not consistently deliver great service if you don't define what it is. Standards are not rigid rules meant to constrain behavior. Instead, they are guidelines that remove uncertainty and assure consistency. Employees can more fully invest themselves in delivering great service—with less stress and more creativity—when they know what's expected from them.

Create Your Own

Objective: We will serve our customers with _____{name the specific task goal related to customer requirements}.

Performer: By _____{identify who's performing the work}.

Measure: With a performance measure of _____{the time, dollar, or other measures you are trying to achieve}.

Support factors: We will accomplish this objective by _____,_____, and _____ {the organizational support that will make the performance improvement possible}.

When you create specific standards, you make your expectations for performance clear to your employees. You define great service in order for them to deliver it consistently.

A System of Information

Don was shopping for office supplies in one of the nation's largest retail dealers. He saw a "Sale" sign over the brand of transparencies he uses to make color overheads for his management development presentations. The attractive savings made an impulse purchase virtually certain. One small catch. The sign said the savings came from an "Instant Rebate."

What is an "Instant Rebate"? Don didn't know, and neither did the friendly but not knowledgeable staff at the "Customer Service" counter. One thought it meant there was a rebate coupon tucked "somewhere in that rebate display over there." Don wandered off to plow through scores of manufacturer rebate coupons strewn about the display. Finding none for the transparencies, it was back to the Service desk (and we use the term loosely here).

After three employees pleasantly said the customer service-speak equivalent of "duh," finally the store manager was summoned. He confessed that he didn't know what an Instant Rebate was either. But at least he had the good sense to authorize ringing up the sale on the spot with a credit for the Instant Rebate, whatever it is. Then he went down the aisle and removed the sign from the shelf.

Lesson: Good service requires a system of information, procedures, and systems. If the people charged with implementing your slogans, deals, or objectives don't have a clue as to how to deliver on them, then they can't please your customer.

What Should You Standardize?

To show you how service standards can impact an operation, let's take a little trip together. Picture this. You're going on a business trip to a distant city. You're going to fly there.

In playing out this scenario, you'll encounter several opportunities to receive great customer service or big-time disappointments.

Taking Off

As you read the following account, watch for the many places where the airline might want to standardize service to meet your expectations as it flies you from here to there. Follow along:

➤ A taxi drops you off at the airport. How long should you wait at the curb before a skycap welcomes you to the airline and checks your bag?

➤ Should the skycap tell you your flight's assigned departure gate? Should he write it on your ticket? Should he enter your arrival into the computer so you don't need to check-in at the gate?

➤ Should the skycap give you explicit directions to the gate?

➤ When you get into the airport itself, how far should you walk before you see a monitor with the gate assignments so you can double-check the departure gate?

➤ How far should you wander before seeing a sign pointing you in the right direction?

➤ When you get to the gate, how long in advance should you be able to check-in for your flight?

➤ Even if you're just allowing the bare minimum time to make your flight (doesn't everybody!), even at peak time on a very busy travel day, how long is the maximum time you should have to wait in line before being greeted, welcomed, and checked-in to your flight?

➤ How long should the boarding process take?

➤ If you are a very frequent flier, what special treatment—if any—should you receive?

➤ If you hardly ever fly, how can the airline make you feel welcome and special, too?

➤ When you board the flight, should you be greeted, welcomed, and offered directions to your seat *and* assistance with your carry-on bags?

➤ Once you're seated, should you be offered something to read? How about a pillow and blanket?

➤ If you ordered a special meal to accommodate your new, "Strictly Cabbage" diet, should the flight attendant confirm that the meal is onboard and ready for you?

At Your Service
Every aspect of a customer's experience might be improved by a service standard. Take nothing for granted. Physically walk through the entire customer experience and note every step, every part of the process, that could potentially disappoint or delight a customer. Great service is no accident. It results from close scrutiny—and careful management—of the total customer experience, detail by painstaking detail.

Once you are comfortably settled in your seat (it is comfortable, isn't it?), the captain announces his appreciation for your business today. After the safety demonstration, you begin reflecting on the service you received today but never really thought about before. Unless, of course, you are in the airline business or fly more than a human should.

Back on the Ground

When you were reading about that little imaginary flight, could you see how many places service standards could come into play? Were you surprised at the many points at which the airline had an opportunity for your "Instant of Absolute Judgment?"

Could you imagine good and bad service performance levels? We'd bet that you'd have no difficulty at all in assessing the ideal level of service you should receive from an airline you fly.

Well, now that you're all warmed up, let's discuss creating service standards that can assure *your* customers receive first class service all the time. We cannot overemphasize the need for consistency here. Every negative "Instant" wipes out one or more positive "Instants." Standards of service greatly enable you to consistently provide positive experiences.

Implementing Standardized Service

We have shown you how to write a service standard, but there's quite a gap between having a written standard and putting it to work in your business.

To implement your standards, follow this simple nine-step process (explained in greater detail in the sections that follow):

1. Determine what your customers value.
2. Decide which services to improve.
3. Set measurable standards, and write them down.
4. Make achieving standards part of the culture.
5. Train people to achieve the standards.
6. Measure regularly.
7. Inform employees of your collective progress.
8. Reward success.
9. Reevaluate your standards.

Step 1: Determine What Your Customers Value

It takes a lot of effort to design service standards, train employees to achieve them, make them part of your standard operating procedure, then measure and evaluate performance against those standards. *So*, you want to be sure that all that time, effort, and trouble is worthwhile.

Ask the following questions:

➤ What are critical areas where service standards will make a difference to your customers in choosing your business over another?

➤ What level of service should you provide your customers to create a great service experience?

Here are four factors to consider when choosing tasks to standardize:

1. *What your customers tell you they want.* Naturally, most people would like to receive a million dollars in value for their hundred-dollar investment. You need to have a clear understanding of what really matters to them in making a buy/no-buy decision, today and the next time. (Chapter 14 goes into detail on effectively surveying your customers.)

2. *What your competitors are doing.* You shouldn't do everything your competitors do, but you need to be aware of how they do things. Have their practices impacted customer expectations to the point that you need to respond to them in order to be competitive?

3. *Your observations of customer behavior.* Customers may not fill out survey forms complaining about the ambiance of your dry-cleaning store, but if you see them wince when they walk in and they're holding their noses waiting for the clothes to make the journey around the track, take a hint. People may not complain that your french fries are soggy, but if three out of four are throwing them away uneaten, take a hint.

> **At Your Service**
> In your business, there may be many service interactions that you take for granted because they're so routine. Try to see your business through a totally fresh pair of eyes. With the help of some coworkers list every point of contact your business has with a customer. Every interaction is an opportunity to impress a customer positively or negatively. The list you create can form the foundation for your service standards.

4. *The "best practices" of companies outside your industry.* Customers form expectations based on every business they deal with—not just by you or your competitors. Stay aware of what state-of-the-art service is. You don't necessarily have to provide that level, unless your customers insist, but you should try to get close enough so that your performance remains acceptable to your customers who are dealing with many, many vendors in all aspects of their lives. The biggest mistake is paying attention only to what your industry is doing. Innovation comes from looking at ideas outside the vacuum you tend to operate in on a daily basis.

Step 2: Decide Which Services to Improve

Now take the information from step one and do the following:

➤ Isolate a group of practices in your business that if you improve, your customers will both notice and appreciate.

➤ Rank those in importance for affecting customer perceptions.

➤ Assess the readiness of the organization to tackle and support a change in those areas.

➤ Prioritize the list and determine which services you will improve in the next three, six, nine, and twelve months.

Tales from the Real World

When Marriott, which had a good reputation for service, wanted to serve its hotel customers even better, it asked them what was really important to them. Based on the customer feedback, Marriott set new standards. Example: Faster check-ins. Check-in time went from an average of just under three minutes to half that, with 98 percent under two minutes.

To achieve that standard, Marriott overhauled its job classification and training systems. The goal: less specialization of people in the lobby for more help at peak times. They developed more well-rounded players through cross-training.

When the dust settled, the hotelier needed far fewer people in the lobby, cut overhead costs 40 percent, and improved both employee and customer satisfaction.

Step 3: Set Measurable Standards, and Write Them Down

Answer the following questions:

➤ What does desirable performance look like, exactly?

➤ Can we measure it? How will we know if we achieved it?

➤ By what process will we measure it?

Then write the standard using the format we showed you in the section "Fill In the Blanks."

Step 4: Make Achieving Standards Part of the Culture

Next you need to do the following:

➤ Formally reorganize work to support the standard.

➤ Create the systems (administrative, technical, managerial) to support achieving the standard.

➤ Integrate the standards into employee job descriptions.

➤ Evaluate achievement of the standards as part of an employee's performance review; reward performance.

Step 5: Train People to Achieve the Standards

Standards mean nothing if the people responsible for delivering them aren't capable of doing so. Do the following:

➤ Determine what skills you need to implement the standard.

➤ Assess what skills are lacking and need to be taught.

➤ Determine the means by which you'll teach those skills. (There's more on training in Chapter 20.)

➤ Budget time and money for employee education.

Step 6: Measure Regularly

Standards that aren't measured are nothing more than a wish list. Before you release the standards, let people know that you intend to monitor performance against the standard. Also, determine the method for monitoring. It's not practical to measure everyone's performance to standards every day. You'll need a system for spot checking. Before you publish the standard, be clear about who is going to assess progress. The managers responsible for meeting the standards? A staff person? Outside consultants? How often will you take measurements?

At Your Service
Educating employees is not free; just ask those of us who provide such services! At the same time, understand that employee development is not merely a cost center. To the contrary! A better way to think of employee education would be to consider it an *investment* that pays dividends—in greater customer satisfaction, greater sales, and greater profits. The more skilled your employees, the better they can serve your customers and build the kind of loyalty (and resulting profit) that flows from positive customer experiences born of great service.

Step 7: Inform Employees of Your Collective Progress

Because the standards are important to your business performance, let employees know how they measure up. To not tell them is like asking people to play in a ball game where the score is a secret. People lose interest in meeting standards when they don't know how well they're performing.

In addition to publishing performance-to-standard statistics, show the link to important business indicators such as customers retained, new customers acquired, overall sales, profits, stock price, customer satisfaction scores—whatever helps your frontline understand that their contribution makes a big difference.

Employees must clearly understand the positive impact they will have on the company's success by implementing the standards. *And* the negative impact they will have by not implementing the standards. No one wants to feel responsible for being the reason behind a failure.

Step 8: Reward Success

Recognize performance achievement: throw compliments with abandon, throw a party, or even throw money at people. Make some noise, have some fun. Thank people for what they've done. Encourage them to keep at it. More motivation ideas appear in Chapter 20.

Step 9: Reevaluate Your Standards

Don't ever think you've finally fine-tuned the business. Just when you get it the way you thought it should be running, your customers will want something else. People's needs change, their tastes change. Stay in touch with your customers and the market. Never be satisfied. Never stop trying to please.

Can You Standardize "Niceness"?

Let's briefly go back to your airplane ride. There you are, back in your seat. As you relax—all snug in your warm blanket, head propped up on the nice clean pillow—you close your eyes (but not too long, you can't read with your eyes closed), and replay all those service interactions detailed earlier.

Watch It!
Service standards work when they are paired with training, support, measurement, and reinforcement through rewards. Don't cheat your organization by just devising and publishing standards. That's going less than halfway. You won't achieve your standards. You'll have wasted your time and made your workforce cynical.

Evaluate the quality of the experience by thinking about the following questions:

➤ Were the greetings you received genuinely warm, or did the airline people seem to simply go through the motions?

➤ If the curbside baggage handlers were not airline employees but contractors instead, did you notice any difference in their level of service? Because in the end, you will either blame or compliment the airline on the service. After all, it was given in their name.

➤ Did you get the feeling that all the people you dealt with appreciated your business and were genuinely glad you were there that day? Or did you feel like somehow you had interrupted their other, really more important work?

➤ Did the way the airline people conducted themselves give you confidence? Were you given the impression that these people really knew what they were doing?

➤ What kind of treatment, based on what you experienced for this ordinary, routine flight, do you think you'd receive from this airline if the plane were delayed for a mechanical problem? Or how about if the flight were cancelled?

So much of the impression that customers form about your service comes from how they feel about your individual employees. So, naturally, you want your employees to come across as friendly, likeable, helpful, and knowledgeable. How can you specify a standard for *that*?

You can standardize *behaviors*.

Setting Standards for Behavior

While it's not possible to measure "niceness," you can specify the behaviors that add-up to being nice. For example:

➤ *Greeting customers.* Ever walk into a retail store where no one acknowledged you? Or you couldn't find help in the store if your life depended on it? Might as well buy by direct mail. A standard could specify, "All customers will be welcomed to our store within a minute of arriving, with a friendly greeting of, 'Welcome to Our Store! How may I help you today…'"

➤ *Smiling.* Does this require explanation? By putting a smile into your service standards, you make clear just what you mean by words like "friendly demeanor." (Smile even on the phone. Your customers will see your bright shining face through your words.)

➤ *Using a customer's name.* Dale Carnegie said the sweetest sound in the universe was the sound of your own name. People who use people's names seem friendlier than those who don't. So a standard could suggest that service people use a customer's name as soon as is reasonable in a conversation, and to close every conversation with "thank you, Ms. Customer Name."

Watch It!
The most common greeting we all hear in entering a place of business is: Can I Help You! Never, ever, ever, say this line. When Ron hears this, he responds, "I don't know, can you?" If you don't know whether or not you can help someone, how should the customer know? Of course you should be able to help the customer. That's what you are being paid for. Instead, you should be asking "How may I help you?" There really is a difference.

Watch It!
While everyone appreciates the personal attention that comes from calling people by name, some prefer you call them Mr. or Ms. So&so rather than by their first name. Calling people by their first name is considered too casual or overly familiar. Better to start more formally. If your customer would rather be addressed as Ms. Rodriguez, don't risk offending her by calling her Maria.

➤ *Escorting customers.* Organizations widely acknowledged for their outstanding service like the Ritz Carlton hotel chain and Publix Supermarkets specify that employees give directions to customers with their feet. As in walking. As in, "Let me take you there."

Why Else Set Standards?

Here are four important reasons why setting standards improves your company:

1. Offers a consistent experience to your customers. They know what to expect from you and so are more likely to keep coming back.

2. Helps you examine how you do your work. Going through the standards setting procedure gives you a great opportunity to reevaluate how you get the work done.

3. Improves employee morale—they know exactly what's expected from them and can work to achieve it. Everyone likes to know the rules of the game and how to keep score.

4. Guarantees your quality. You cannot have quality without consistent standards. Quality results from consistency over time. It is not a one shot event.

The Least You Need to Know

➤ Customers make decisions about buying from your company based on how they feel treated by it at any time. The slightest offense or disappointment in any moment can forever sour a customer on your firm. Such a moment is an Instant of Absolute Judgment.

➤ When your firm defines good service and sets service standards, customers will have a great experience with your organization.

➤ Service standards direct your operations. They define how your service will be performed. They have characteristic SMARTS: specific, measurable, achievable, relevant to customers, time-based performance, supported by the organization with adequate resources and systems.

➤ Your company has a personality, which can be reinforced by setting standards for employee behavior at all levels.

Who's Your Valued Customer?

Look at the title of this chapter. Sounds like a goofy question, doesn't it? Your company depends on all your customers for its very existence. You appreciate the confidence they place in your company with their business, so they're all valued and important.

Hey, a customer is a customer. Right?

Here's another odd question: Should you treat all of your customers the same?

You don't need to have a poster proclaiming "We love customers," over your work area to remind you that every customer deserves respect and helpful, courteous, and fair treatment. But should you treat all your customers equally—offering all of them the same exact treatment?

Exactly Alike Only Different

When you see or speak with your customers you are probably aware that they're all different as people. (In Chapter 7, we show you how to identify and relate to distinct personality types.) What you may not be aware of is that each of your customers is also very different *as a customer.*

While they are all important, some are more *valuable* to your business than others.

Some customers may do a lot of business with your firm, demand little extra attention from you, and make your business lots of money. Other customers may spend relatively little with your company, demand a lot from you, and actually *cost* your business more to serve them than the value of their purchases.

Do you know which of your customers *contribute* most to your profits or which actually *cost you* money to take their money?

Word to the Wise
Your *customer base* is all the customers you serve. Within that wide collection you might have many different types of customers. Customers can be divided into *segments*, groups of customers that have certain characteristics in common.

Every business should segment its customers into distinct groups in order to serve their specific needs more effectively.

Divide and Serve

Peel an orange. See all those orange wedgy-things? Notice how they're not all the same shape or size? Some are juicier than others. Some are sweeter than others. Your customers are like that. Collectively, they're your *customer base*, the orange.

At Your Service
Grouping your customers into meaningful segments requires good information about each customer (such as purchase history, buying patterns, payment history, and so on). To understand what your customers have in common—and the important differences between them—you must maintain a customer *database*.

Within your total customer collection are different groupings of customers (which we'll describe in a moment). These are the orange wedgy-things. Let's call the customer groups *segments* (you can call the orange wedgy-things anything you want).

Why Segment?

Dividing your customers into groups gives you two basic advantages.

1. You can serve customers better
2. You can improve your financial performance

Sounds pretty good so far, eh?

The 80/20 Principle

You can serve both your customers and your business better by separating customers into classes because of an economic rule of thumb. The concept was devised by an Italian economist and sociologist named Vilfredo Pareto. One day over some pizza and Chianti, ole Villy came up with the principle you probably know as the 80/20 rule. It roughly suggests that 80 percent of the results come from 20 percent of the causes.

How does that relate to your customers? How about:

➤ 80 percent of your profits come from 20 percent of your customers

➤ 80 percent of your recurring trouble calls come from 20 percent of your customers

➤ 80 percent of the time you get recognized for only 20 percent of your great work (Wait. That's in Chapter 20. Onward.)

Now, don't get stuck on the percentages. Of course, every business is different. But Villy had the right idea. No matter what part of life you look at, it's usually a small number of factors driving the majority of results.

As an example, Don worked with a large, profitable business where a detailed analysis showed that only about two percent of the customers drove nearly ninety percent (yup, 90 percent!) of the profits. As dramatic as that startling relationship is, it was not apparent until someone poked through the data lurking around the company and really got a handle on how different customer groups influenced the fate of the company.

Who's driving your success? And your problems?

Secret Relationships

How do you put this 80/20 stuff to work for you? Analyze your customers to discover hidden relationships between certain customers and their impact on your business. (We'll tell you how a bit later in this chapter in the section titled, "Segmenting Customers.") The goal is to identify the customers who:

➤ Account for most of your sales

➤ Buy specific products or services

➤ Require the most, and the least, follow-up servicing

As you gather this information, certain patterns will begin to present themselves. You might find that:

➤ Your most time-consuming (and therefore most expensive) service contacts come from your smallest customers

➤ Your greatest volume of sales and profits come from a relatively small group of customers

Some More Equal Than Others

When you learn how certain customers affect your business differently than others, you can make better decisions about how you use your limited support resources.

Golds Over Here, Silvers Over There

You might divide your customers into groups that receive different levels of service. Some companies use a simple scheme to label the groups, such as one of the following:

➤ Platinum, Gold, Silver, and Bronze

➤ Ultra, Plus, Standard

➤ Premier, Preferred, and everybody else

At Your Service
When is a dollar not a dollar? Well a dollar is always a dollar, silly. But...some dollars are worth more to you than others, when they come to you from more profitable customers. Not every customer is profitable, and so some customers are worth much more to your business than others. Treat everyone well. And make sure your most valuable customers are very well cared for.

You might decide to provide your most profitable, and therefore most valuable, customers with special services. Such as:

➤ Special toll-free number with no, or vastly reduced, wait times

➤ Special privileges, the way airlines give early boarding rights to their most frequent fliers

➤ Awards for different levels of business attained

➤ Assigned contact people who can be reached directly

➤ More choice in when they receive their bills

➤ Special advance information or sneak previews of new products

If your customers come to your facilities to do business, you can create special areas for your higher value customers. Here are some examples:

➤ Airlines have lounges for their most traveled customers

➤ Banks have special reception areas for their biggest accounts

➤ Some restaurants have a casual-serve area and a fancier sit-down dining room (and they may offer complimentary desert to their frequent patrons)

Simple Segmenting

Say you work for an office supply company. Your firm deals in volume with some medium-sized businesses and government agencies based in your area. Your firm also carries several nicer, higher-end products than those huge chain stores. You sell these products typically to professionals in the area—doctors, accountants, dentists, lawyers.

The volume of business that your customers do with your company can range from about $50 a year to tens of thousands of dollars.

Most customer service contact is by phone with customers who call your local number to check whether you have certain items in stock, the status of their order, or to discuss a bill. The government agencies pay painfully slowly (but they're good for it), and require little in the way of anything other than routine service. Most of the other large order customers are "low maintenance." They routinely buy their big shipments (of copy paper, pens by the gross, etc.), pay their bills, and don't require much hand-holding.

The same isn't true for some of the customers who make relatively small purchases of the upscale items (fancy pens, desk sets, and so on). Some of them complain about everything, question invoices, and have a much higher level of product returns. In short, they're more trouble to deal with.

You don't want to stop doing business with most of the people in the second group, because their money is green, and even with the extra care and feeding, they still are profitable. But, and this is important, you want to make sure that they don't suck up all your service resources and prevent your large, quiet accounts from getting through to your support staff because they're on the phone with a small dollar whiner.

You might consider giving a special number to your high-dollar, low-maintenance customers so that they sail right in, past the others. The extra line is likely a small incremental expense. And given that these large, low-profile customers don't call much anyway, you aren't likely to disturb the operation by asking your staff to attend first to the calls on the priority line.

> **Watch It!**
> Large accounts may require large amounts or small amounts of service, depending on their needs at any given time. However, all large accounts expect preferential service when they need it.

> **At Your Service**
> When you segment your customers, you aren't saying, "This group is good, and this group is bad." Your goal still is to provide *all* your customers with great personalized service. By segmenting your customers and providing different service levels, you are simply trying to assure your more valuable customers of a relevant, tailored, and memorable experience.

Special Teams

Consider assigning a team of experienced service specialists to give very personal attention to your most valued customers. Not only might they staff a special "hotline" for your top customers to call, they might also take a more active role in servicing your most critical accounts.

At Your Service
Some companies also group service specialists by product type, with a group of specially trained people to field calls. Such specialization is especially appropriate when detailed technical knowledge is required to adequately support certain products.

For example, they could:

➤ Review account status on a scheduled basis, looking for any signs of potential trouble—returns, abnormal call activity, drop in purchases, slower payments.

➤ Contact customers a few times a year (yes, actually calling the customer *instead* of waiting for the customer to call you). In that call, you could find out if service has been maintained at an acceptable level, if the customer has any concerns or questions, and if there are other ways that your company might be of service.

Segmenting Customers

Segmenting customers means that you intend to serve them differently. Sometimes those differences may be slight. For example, the service on your Spanish language line is identical to the service on your English and Korean lines.

Other times, the service difference may be more pronounced. For example, a preferred customer at a bank with substantial assets in the bank's care receives counseling and other services that a minimum checking account customer may neither know about nor value.

Slicing & Dicing

There's no one right way to segment customers. You might decide to slice your customer base in many different ways:

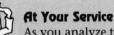

At Your Service
As you analyze the information you have about your customers, you're bound to find that you don't have all you'd like. Keep notes on what you don't have that you'd like to have. Use this list as an agenda for discussion with your other management colleagues. Rule to live by: *You can never know too much about your customers.*

➤ Where they're located
➤ The kind of products they buy
➤ Their total spending with your company
➤ Their income (consumers)
➤ Their age (consumers)
➤ Their preferred language
➤ How often they buy from your company
➤ Total amount of business they do with your company
➤ The type of business they're in
➤ Any other way that makes sense to you

How do you get at the information you need to decide who qualifies for what level of service? Start plowing through data.

Start the Data Dump

Your firm probably already gathers a lot of the information you need to examine your customers with a fresh pair of eyes. Ideally, you have a central database where you can grab lots of different information and manipulate it to see relationships between factors like:

➤ The number of purchases in a year

➤ The number of calls to your service center

If you don't have a tidy central database where all the information is just waiting for you—like most places in the world, you can still get what you need. It just takes some work. There are many places you can gather information from:

➤ Sales reports

➤ Service records

➤ Billing records

➤ Credit records

You might have to get many of your colleagues into the effort. And you might have to begin your analysis without all the information you need. But get started anyway.

What You're Looking for

The goal in slicing and dicing information about your customers is to see relationships between This and That. For example:

➤ Do your largest dollar customers use your service resources in proportion to their purchase volume? What about customers who buy a certain product? Customers who buy from a certain sales person?

➤ Do you get more billing inquiry calls from one region of the country or another? Or one customer classification more than others?

Watch It!
Two cautions for you. First, revenues from a particular customer don't always tell the whole story. Large dollar customers may have such a great price discount or receive such added benefits that they aren't as *profitable* as smaller customers who are paying more or receiving less. Work with your financial wizards to delve into segmenting by revenue. There's often more than meets the eye in the financial realm.

Second, don't assume that a customer doing a small volume of business with your company isn't important. That small customer may be sampling your wares while considering a switch away from another major supplier to your company. On the other hand, today's small volume customer may be about to become an industry giant.

A small customer today could be your best customer next year. Treat all customers with respect and gather as much information about every customer as you can.

Fire Some Customers!

Ever deal with a customer you'd just love to tell, "Take a hike, pal!"

Oooh. That many, huh?

Well maybe you should do that now and then. Not use those exact words, but fire some customers.

As we pointed out previously, not every customer has the same value. Some, upon close inspection, may cost you more to serve than their business is worth. And some may cost you more aggravation than they're worth.

Tales from the Real World

We don't know if the following story really happened or not. But when we heard it, we wanted to pass it along.

A very crowded flight was cancelled at the Denver airport. A single gate agent was trying her best to accommodate a long line of inconvenienced, disappointed customers. Suddenly, a passenger pushed his way to the head of the line. He loudly declared, "I *have* to be on this flight and it has to be in First Class."

The harried but calm agent, replied, "I'm sorry sir. I'll be happy to help you but I've got to help these other people first, and I'm sure we'll be able to work something out."

Mr. Obnoxious wasn't satisfied. He asked in a loud, demanding voice for all to hear, "Do you have any idea who I am?!"

Without missing a beat, the gate agent smiled, got on the public address system and announced, "May I have your attention, please. We have a passenger here who *doesn't know who he is.* If anyone can help him find his identity, please come to the gate service counter."

The line of upset customers broke into a hearty laugh. Mr. Obnoxious wasn't so amused. He tensely scowled at the clever gate agent and blurted out an even more impolite version of "Screw you."

Unflapped, the gate agent replied, "I'm sorry, sir. You'll have to stand in line for that, too."

The delayed passengers broke into applause. Mr. Obnoxious slinked off.

Thanks, Kick Me Again?

When Don was giving a presentation to business executives in Croatia, members of the audience wrote questions which were then translated. Two different questioners asked about dealing with "abusive" customers. In post-war Croatia, the number of people with any money to spend is a small minority. Apparently, some of the well-off are using their powerful position to antagonize business people who are desperately trying to get a piece of that wealth.

As you know, you don't need to travel to a war-ravaged economy to find abusive customers. Or those who make unreasonable demands.

Most customers enjoy being served well. A few want you to lick their boots. Some treat you like a slave. Or worse.

Make clear to your employees that they absolutely do *not* have to take abuse from a customer, no matter how important the account. Hostile customers should be treated respectfully but firmly. Try the following possibilities:

➤ Suggest to the abusive customer that your company values their business but insists on civility.

➤ Request that they speak with you later regarding the matter that has them so upset. Often, someone who has really lost his cool comes back quite apologetic and feeling quite in debt for his embarrassing behavior.

Whatever you do, stick with the facts and do not join in the battle of emotions. In that battle, there is no winner.

> **Quote, Unquote**
> There is a difference between giving good service and being subservient. No customer has the right to abuse one of our employees.
> —Roger Conner, Corporate Vice President, Marriott hotels

"See Ya!"

Not everyone fits the profile of being an ideal customer for your products and services. Yet, no matter what you say or do, some customers still insist on doing business with you even though you cannot service them to their satisfaction. You may reach a time when enough is enough and you decide to segment a customer right into the "out" basket (or maybe the waste basket). How can you tactfully tell a customer good bye?

It's a tough call. And it might be quite painful financially. But there is a time to sever ties. Even golden ones.

Here are some words you can use in person or by letter to wish your soon-to-be-former customer *bon voyage*:

➤ You deserve a level of performance we seem incapable of meeting to your satisfaction...

➤ Your needs appear to have outgrown our capacity to meet them...

➤ Obviously we're not meeting your needs, rather than continue to disappoint you...

➤ We tried, but it seems we're not measuring up...

Yeah, we know, these pretty much are still in the kiss-up department, but why burn a bridge? Maybe someday your least favorite customer will leave his company and that nice #2 person will move up and you can rekindle the relationship. Or that nice woman whose husband was such a jerk—she finally leaves him and decides to do business with you again.

Watch It!
A pattern of abuse by a customer indicates a problem deeper than what even the most attentive customer caregiver can address. There is a time when you should ask a customer, even a valuable one, to take his account somewhere else.

If you think the customer has been a particular stinker, you might just send a terse letter saying something like, "We appreciate your business over the (years, months), but regrettably, we can no longer serve you. May we suggest you take your business to one of the following companies...." Then you can stick one of your competitors with this pain in the anatomy.

Successful businesses realize they cannot be all things to all people. They pick the market they want to serve and they serve it well. If you're receiving too many complaints from a certain market, it means you are not serving it well. It may also mean that it's not the market you should be serving to begin with.

The Least You Need to Know

➤ All customers are not created equal. Decide which are more valuable to you.

➤ A small percentage of your customer base may account for the vast majority of your profits.

➤ Analyze information about your customers to group them into meaningful classes.

➤ Consider factors other than just the number of dollars a customer spends when you segment customers.

➤ Grouping your customers allows you to provide different support services to them.

➤ Some customers are not worth keeping. After serious reflection and investigation, gently (or not) encourage undesirable customers to take their business elsewhere.

Part 2
Service Is Communication

Communication is what makes us human. It's the sharing of ideas and feelings between minds and hearts. And the process that is absolutely central to providing great customer service. In this section, you'll learn how to communicate more effectively to deliver The Service Difference.

Improve your communication with customers by better managing your own communication skills. We look at how you can read your customers' behavioral style to speak to them in "their language" and handle complaints and problems effectively through better question-asking.

You'll learn how to assist an angry customer without getting sucked into the emotional storm. Plus discover how to use written communication to win friends and influence people. And even create instruction manuals that truly help your customer and reduce customer service intervention.

Wow. There's a lot of really good information here. We can't wait for you to jump in and soak it up.

NEED A HAND, CHUCKLEBUTT?

Chapter 6

The Pleasure of Your Business...

In This Chapter

➤ Playing your vocal chords

➤ Understanding what your gestures can say

➤ Avoiding negative words

➤ Using a very powerful word for service

➤ Making sure you follow up

Have you ever been in a situation where if the customer would only listen to you, his problem would be solved? You probably wondered what prevented that customer from paying attention to your words. Many times, the most important thing is not what you say but how you say it.

Researchers have discovered that in actual face-to-face contact, the success of the communication is broken down into three components—words, tone of voice, and gestures or body language.

When you're speaking to customers, are you mostly concerned with what you are saying, or are you equally, if not more, concerned with how your customer perceives the way you are projecting your message? In the game of influence, many times it's how you play the game that counts. Influence is about perception, not reality.

Words are a very small percentage of how we really communicate.

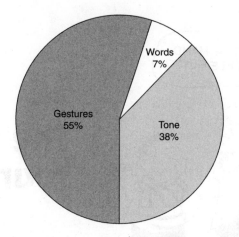

Words 7%

Gestures 55%

Tone 38%

If you're providing customer service in person, the numbers in the preceding figure are accurate. They do change when your service is limited to the phone. On the phone, gestures cannot be seen (unless you are using a video phone or are speaking to someone on a psychic hotline). So the tone of your voice becomes more important, to the tune of 86 percent. Let's take a look at this important piece of the pie called "tone."

Name That Tone

Think of your voice as being the music played by that marvelous instrument known as your vocal cords. The tone of your voice is like the tones in music. Just by hearing your tone, customers will be able to identify the mood you are in and the message you are trying to convey. As with any musician, you must clearly practice the piece of music you want to play for your customers. If it is not done correctly, your customers will not be pleased with the concert they came to hear.

The elements comprising the overall tone of your voice include:

➤ Pace   ➤ Intensity

➤ Volume   ➤ Attitude

➤ Inflection

Keeping Pace

How you pace your speech helps to paint a picture in your client's mind. Speaking too fast is an indication that you want to get off the phone and that you really don't care whether or not the customer understands what you have to say. Of course, what you may consider as speaking too slowly may be considered as too fast by people from different parts of the country and world.

Ron, being from New York, always has to work on his pacing when speaking to people from the South. In fact, he sometimes speaks too fast for people who are from New York! But Ron understands that the success of communication depends not so much on what is being said, but whether or not it is being heard. So it's important that you match your pace to the pace of your customer. If you and your customer are both communicating at different rates, the communication probably isn't going to be successful. And no matter how passionately you sing your song, the customer definitely is not going to enjoy the concert.

Pump Up the Volume, or Down

Did you ever call somebody in a different country and find yourself yelling into the phone so your voice would carry over the ocean? Why? The truth of the matter is the phone equipment you are using is good enough for the person on the other end of the phone to hear you no matter where they are in the world, even when you speak at your normal speaking volume.

Many times, it's easy to mistake appropriate volume for clarity of the message as you try to communicate through the cultural and language barriers. Remember the old joke from the TV sitcoms? The goofy American meets someone who doesn't understand English, so the American tries shouting.

Your volume needs to be adequate for you to be clearly understood, but it must not be over exaggerated or you'll create the wrong listening environment. Yelling can be an indication of anger and frustration. And for the person on the other end of the yelling, it is an assault on one's sense of hearing that can lead to both physical and mental damage.

> **Word to the Wise**
> A good customer service representative adjusts his pace or speed of talking to match the pace of the customer. He adjusts the volume to ensure the message is heard, uses *inflection* to signify highs and lows, maintains intensity to give the highs and lows the proper effect, and makes sure his attitude is proper at all times.

At the very least, the receiver of the message will do whatever she can to tune out your message and protect her senses. On the other hand, raising one's voice—modestly—at certain times serves as a tool for helping to reinforce a theme or express enthusiasm for a certain idea.

Make sure the volume you're using is commensurate with the selection of music you're playing for your customer. The volume is critical for creating the listening environment you want your customer to be in.

Paint with Inflection

If you are listening to music where the musicians' chords are the same all the time in every song, wouldn't you be bored? Of course you would. Just as a songwriter would never dream of writing song after song that sounded exactly the same, you shouldn't speak to a customer in a monotone (the same tone). Your words can only paint pictures for people and convey reassurance or helpfulness through your voice inflection—the highs and lows in your voice.

Imagine hearing this phrase with all the words being communicated the same way....

I really like you.

Now, imagine hearing the same phrase with the word *really* being said in a manner that reflects a stronger sense of urgency....

I *really* like you!

The inflection used here paints a picture of someone who is highly fond of you, while in the first example someone liked you, but without the intensity. Do you see and hear the difference?

Watch It!
While you should display a caring emotion for your customer, we're not suggesting that you get caught up in your customer's hysteria. When you have an attitude of calm grounded in concern and a willingness to help, your calm won't be mistaken for lack of concern.

Use a variety of inflections to adequately paint the picture you want your customer to see. And like a satisfying song, your message will find its power in its highs and lows.

Levels of Intensity

Different situations call for different levels of emotion. If you're answering a call from a customer who has just had a catastrophic experience with your product, the customer's probably showing a great deal of emotion. If your answer is really low key, your customer may perceive your response as lacking a great deal of care or concern. Just as you must match the volume to the situation, you must also match the emotion to the situation. Otherwise, you're singing a different tune from the one your customer is giving you.

Tales from the Real World

Ron, a former volunteer medic in Fair Lawn, NJ, was crew captain on a call involving a heart attack victim. Racing from the ambulance, up the stairs, and into the house, Ron inadvertently shot right past the patient who was sitting calmly in a chair, having a heart attack. Seeing the patient frightened by his too intensive entrance, Ron concluded that he must remove himself as the primary first aid giver in order to create a calm atmosphere. He immediately relinquished his authority to his second-in-command. Ron never lost sight that the most important thing was the well-being of his patient (customer).

Watch Your Attitude

Olympic skater Scott Hamilton once said that the only debilitating disease is a bad attitude. If you are on the phone without the proper attitude of acting in the spirit of service and understanding, then you will not be projecting the proper pacing, volume, inflection, and intensity called for by the situation.

If you are feeling down for whatever reason, take a sanity break and get some fresh air. When the phone rings, always smile when you say hello. The difference in the position of your lips will greatly affect your perceived attitude. A smile helps you say hello in a relaxed manner that acts as an invitation for the customer to come into your world. A terse hello represents a small crack in the door through which the customer must squeeze if he has any chance of really communicating with you. Your attitude will set the stage for the entire interaction and will play a large part in its overall success.

Actions Speak

Like the tone of your voice, your gestures also play a tremendous part (55 percent) in your overall success as a customer service representative. Your gestures will give the customer a picture of how you really feel about her and the situation. Take a look at the following table that lists some common gestures and how they're commonly perceived.

Common Gestures to Avoid

Gesture Type	Gesture Implication
Arms folded across chest	Closed, unreceptive, suspicious
Hand covering mouth while speaking	Lack confidence or belief in solution
Leaning backwards/against an object	Not interested
Avoiding eye contact	Feeling of negativity, not listening, wanting to limit interaction

Your actions also paint a picture for your customer. For instance, remember the time you walked into a store and went to the counter where the sales clerk was on the phone and failed to look up immediately to greet you? You probably felt unwanted. Unfortunately, this happens all too often.

How about when you walk in for service and you hear employees bad mouthing the company or the product. Now that must give you a good feeling about the company you're dealing with, right? Not!

Or, how about when you are constantly being interrupted by the sales person or customer service representative who has to pick up another line, or speak with someone else, say, a fellow employee about something of great urgency and importance, like last night's date. How do you feel then?

The best way to cure all of these indecencies is to treat each and every customer like your boss. After all, if your boss is on the phone, would you put her on hold to speak with someone else? (The right answer should be yes, if the person is a customer who's waiting to speak to you because in the great pecking order of things customers should be regarded as having higher priority than your boss…. fooled you!). If you treated your customer as a boss, would you chew gum while speaking to him, or not look up when he approached you? Of course not!

The bottom line is that the customer deserves the same treatment and respect you would give your boss. Because in the end, without customers there would be no jobs.

Watch Your Mouth!

Okay, we said that the words you use only represent 7 percent of the overall story you are telling your customer. While this is generally true, a certain group of words can dramatically change the image you're trying to give your customer.

"I Can't, I Won't, I Shouldn't"

When you say I can't do it, the customer focuses on the question that pops into his mind, "Why not?" rather than what you have to offer.

Watch It!
Using words like don't, won't, can't, shouldn't, and wouldn't all tell the customer how you cannot help him. Customers don't want to hear how you cannot solve their problems. They are only interested in the solutions you can provide.

Talk about what you can do for them. It will help you create a positive environment from which to handle the service interaction.

Turn it around and say "Let's see what we can do." This focuses everyone's attention on possible solutions.

When you say I won't do it, the customer focuses on the negative emotion revolving around your resistance versus listening to what you have to say. You want your customer listening to you, not turned off.

Turn it around and say "This is what I can do for you…." Your customer is now listening to your solution.

When you say I shouldn't, you convey the feeling that what you are offering isn't proper (or that you are working against your company), or that the customer doesn't deserve the solution you're giving. Either way, the solution isn't viewed favorably by the customer.

Turn it around and say "I would be happy to do the following for you…." Now you're presenting a solution with enthusiasm and desire. And that should encourage your customer to embrace your solution.

"I Don't Think I Can Do This"

When you say the word don't, you immediately put the conversation in a negative atmosphere. If you and your company don't do certain things as a matter of policy, or if you simply don't *want* to do certain things, then why draw attention to them by focusing the attention of your customers on these issues? You need to turn the tables and focus positively on what you can do or want to do to assist your customer.

Turn it around this way. Say, "This is what I can do for you." As you have probably noticed by now, it's the same strategy you use in substituting for the words *won't* and *can't*.

"Not!"

If you want to really tick-off a complaining customer, tell her that what she has told you did not, could not, would not, or simply did not happen. Talk about totally rejecting someone. All you have to do is say the word *not* and watch your customer turn into a raging bull or an escaping prisoner. The rage quickly presents itself as her yelling that you do not believe her. The angry, dumbfounded customer will experience a most negative Instant of Absolute Judgment (remember this from Chapter 4?) and vow to never do business with you again.

Turn this potentially disastrous situation around. Here's what you say: "I have not come across this problem very often. Please tell me more so I can help you."

By asking for additional information, you begin to turn the customer into a willing participant in helping to solve the mystery—and right the wrong.

"But..."

Did you ever hear someone give you a compliment followed by the word *but*. Oh that dreaded word *but*. The word *but* is a clear indication that you doubt the story of your customer. When you say, "I know what you're saying, but couldn't it have happened this way...?" you are telling your customer that something else really happened, and she just isn't telling you.

Turn it around by simply leaving out the *"but."* Instead, end your first statement by assuring your customer, "I hear what you're saying."

Then, continue with this as your next statement, "Tell me, is there anything else that happened I should be aware of?" Or you can ask closed ended questions like, "Was the lever ever touched?"

Word to the Wise

When you show an understanding of, and an appreciation for, another person's situation or point of view, you are *demonstrating empathy*. That simply means you can identify with how another person feels. Psychologists tell us that most people have a deep need to feel understood (don't you?). So when a customer service representative shows a customer that they appreciate how the customer is feeling, this can affect the customer at a profoundly deep level.

Whatever you do or say, the word *but* more times than not leads the customer to feel you are now negating whatever was said prior to saying the word *but*. So here's our advice, *"Say whatever you want but just don't use that word!"*

A Most Powerful Word

Did someone ever cut in front of you on the checkout line at the supermarket and not say anything to you at all? You probably experienced a state of anger, frustration, and amazement at how someone would dare do such a thing.

Now, has anyone ever cut in front of you with a statement like:

> "Excuse me, would you terribly mind if I cut in *because* I must be home in 5 minutes to relieve my baby sitter?"

Granted, you may not really care about the man's personal life and commitment to his baby sitter. However, since he gave you a reason to justify his request, you probably would let him in, no matter how reluctant you might be. People need justification and reasons as to why they should accept your requests and solutions.

The following are sample scenarios where the word *because* plays a powerful role.

Getting Someone to Help You

Sometimes, you might need your customer to cooperate by giving you the information you need to help solve their problem. For example, if you ask your customer for his computer's serial number, he might rebel at the inconvenience and wonder why you are making him go through the hassle of crawling under his dark desk to find it.

To turn this situation around and get your customer to cooperate, you can say, "Please give me your serial number because that identifies your account. When I have the serial number, I will then be able to locate your record and proceed with assisting you." No one wants to look for serial numbers, yet everyone wants to move towards a solution. Help your customer help you do that.

Justifying Your Solution

It may seem weird, but in order for a customer to accept what you're suggesting, you need to provide the proper justification. Just telling the customer not to overload the system in the future may not be good enough.

However, you'd have a much greater chance of preventing future problems if you empha-sized the positive outcome of cooperation, and said something like this, "To keep your equipment running without interruption, be sure it isn't overloaded. We can help you determine how many programs can safely run at one time." Now the customer under-stands why he shouldn't overload the system and should be motivated to avoid an overload if he cannot afford to have his system shut down again.

Justifying Your Limitations

Many times, you may not be able to provide the request your customer is seeking, such as a total refund. How you respond to this request is vital to your customer's perception of how you are handling the situation and whether or not he will want to do business with you again. Remember each interaction you have with the customer results in an impression that can win or lose a customer for life.

Let's suppose a customer wants a refund for a product that was taken out of the box and your company has a policy against refunds on opened merchandise. Telling a customer refunds are not permitted will not mollify your customer. She will want to know *why not*. You can avoid this by saying up-front "Refunds are not permitted on open products because the manufacturer will not take it back and we cannot re-sell it." Your customer still didn't get what they wanted, but at least they received a justifiable reason as to why you cannot honor what seems like a reasonable request to him.

Don't misunderstand us. In the above situation, we suggest offering a refund to the customer—if the request is within reason—to keep the customer happy. But many times you will be facing strict corporate guidelines to which you must adhere. Following the guidelines isn't as important as how they're communicated to the customer. Get to like the word *because* because it will provide you with power in explaining your reasons to your customers.

1 Capital Offense

To promise something to a customer and not follow-up, is the #1 capital offense for anyone providing customer service. In order for any company to succeed with its customer service program, it must make every employee accountable for their promises, even if the responsibility moves out of their hands. Even when you cannot provide the total solution, you can follow up to make sure the ball hasn't been dropped—and that you have a customer who is pleasantly satisfied even in the face of initial disappointment.

This is crucial because lack of follow-up provides the customer with a number of perceptions, none of which are good. Lack of follow-up tells your customer that you don't care whether or not his problem is fixed. It depicts you as being irresponsible and ungrateful for your customer's business. And with all the choices out there, your customer—the provider of your beloved paycheck—will simply take her money somewhere else.

People want to be recognized and appreciated for their actions. They will give their business to companies that make them feel good about spending their money

Watch It!
When you don't follow up to make sure a customer's needs have been met, you leave your customer with one or more undesirable impressions: 1) you don't care; 2) the customer can't trust your company; 3) your company is irresponsible; or 4) your company doesn't want the customer's business.

there. And today, there are plenty of options for your customers to choose from. They will go to the places that are more than happy to show your customers how much they appreciate their business. The choice is yours.

The Least You Need to Know

➤ The tone of your voice is a dead give away as to how you feel about the customer and his complaint. Successful communicators know that what you say is not as important as whether or not it's heard.

➤ Your gestures and actions will also give the customer a clear picture about how you feel about her. Treat each customer like a boss and give her the same kind of respect and attention. Your customer does have the right to fire you by taking away her business. When this happens, you have no job.

➤ Words can help you and words can kill you. Never use any words that focus on negative energy or on what you cannot do. Use words that focus on positive attitudes and actions; emphasize what you *can* do. Paint pictures that motivate your customers to join you in moving forward toward a solution.

➤ Customers usually will comply with whatever you say as long as they understand why you're asking them to do it. For solutions to be acted upon, customers must buy into the justifications.

WHAT DO YOU SAY GRANDMA? YOU IN, OR OUT!

WHAP

Chapter 7

What's the Customer's Style?

> **In This Chapter**
>
> ➤ Responding to the Demanding customer
>
> ➤ Relating to the Influential customer
>
> ➤ Appealing to the Steady customer
>
> ➤ Working with the Compliant customer
>
> ➤ Understanding what your style is

Ever notice how people react differently to things?

You can actually say the same exact words in the same exact tone and manner to several people and get many different reactions.

Everyone has a different approach to the world. Call it an operating style, or as the psychologists put it, a behavioral style.

Since people see and approach the world differently, to communicate effectively, you need to use different methods in communicating with different people. Now, we know the world is inhabited with billions of people, and each of them is a unique entity. But we're not suggesting that you have to know billions of ways to communicate with your customers. (You can breathe now!)

Different Strokes for Different Folks

There are many models for classifying behavior. Behavioral scientists building on the work of people such as Dr. Carl Jung and Dr. William Marston developed a model that highlights four basic styles of behaving. We've adapted the model and customized it to apply specifically to customer service.

Model Behavior: DISC

All of us, to one degree or another, have some elements of four different styles in our personality. An individual's uniqueness comes through in their distinct mix of behavior. At the same time, all of us are dominant in one behavior style. By dominant we mean that people prefer to behave more in keeping with one style than the others. We all give clues about our dominant style by how we walk, talk, and generally behave. Here are the four styles as applied to customers, summed up by the acronym DISC:

D = Demanding Customer

They want it now and don't care about the details.

I = Influential Customer

This person loves relating to others. They want to be accepted and they like to talk a lot.

S = Steady Customer

Very interested in how things work. This is a reserved person who doesn't like change.

C = Compliant Customer

Interested in the quality of things. A stickler for making sure everything is in order and that the rules have been followed.

We tend to react to others based on our own behavioral style. Often we fail to understand the behavioral styles of others and how they view the world. To give customers quality service at the highest level, it's critical that you understand the behavioral dynamics behind most human communication.

That sounds like a mouthful. But don't worry. We're going to cover this vitally important area in a simple, easy-to-understand way. Heck, you might even have some fun with this stuff!

Quote, Unquote
We see the world not as it is, but as we are.
—Stephen Covey

Tuning In

The success of any communication depends not so much on the actual words conveyed but on whether or not they're really heard and understood. Are you communicating in a style that coincides with the frequency your customer is tuned to? If not, you're in for lots of static and probably some trouble—even if the solutions you're trying to give your customer are right on.

Let's take a look at four channels you can tune into and communicate on for successful customer service.

The Demanding Customer (D Style)

The demanding customer is no doubt the most vocal customer. When things go according to his expectations, he will be the first one to buy something or accept an answer from someone trying to help him. Yet, if service is, in his opinion, done incorrectly, or if he feels challenged, he will be the first one to engage you in an argument. This type of customer can be perceived as being belligerent in service situations involving conflict.

"Whaddya mean you can't honor this rebate coupon that expired two years ago? That's outrageous! I'm a loyal customer, and actually shopped here twice in the past five years. Now I expect some satisfaction, and I mean now!"

Research shows that 18 percent of the population exhibits a mostly D Style. Typical demanding customers are driven people who push for results and expect the same from others. They are bottom-line oriented. They do not like a lot of detail and get bored very easily. If you service a D and give a long-winded explanation on how technically something went wrong, you probably lost that person's attention after your second sentence. They don't care how things happen or work, they just want them to work. And they want it now!

Tales from the Real World

Ron is probably one of the most demanding customers of all. Always in a hurry and not one for taking his time while shopping, Ron prefers the laser approach to shopping. Like a surgical maneuver, he wants to go into a store, pinpoint what he wants, secure it, and leave. All in ten minutes or less.

Meet Jami Cohen, a very successful sales clerk at the Casual Male. When Ron walked into the store, he immediately identified his needs and wants. Jami immediately pinpointed the styles of pants and shirts Ron wanted; she pulled them out and encouraged him to try them on. In a few short minutes, Ron had what he came for and was on his merry way. Naturally, Ron was thrilled. And so was Jami, as she had just rung up a few hundred dollars in sales. Moral of the story: Don't fault customers for their behavioral styles. Adapt to them and watch the money fly in.

Recognizing a D Style Customer

D Style customers tend to be demonstrative in their talk and tastes. They are status conscious, usually looking for the best in products and services. Their offices will contain large desks and walls filled with plaques, awards, and mementos.

Their style of dress represents an expensive taste and they're always ready for action. They are highly competitive people who want to win. Since they don't like a lot of detail, they are excellent candidates for products like executive book summaries.

Based on our perception of how they act in public, here are some famous examples of D Style Dominant Personalities: Ross Perot, Michael Jordan, Madonna, Barbara Walters, and Hillary Clinton.

Since D Style people perceive themselves as being the center of the universe, they tend to take up a lot of room. Ever notice someone sitting at a table with their arms stretched across the chair next to them? That's a D Style of behavior. Their walk is often brisk and bold, clearing away anything in their path. If a D Style is walking toward you on a mission, move out of the way or expect to be bumped aside. To D Style people, their mission or issue-of-the-moment is the only thing that counts. At least in their minds. Ds tend to stand with their weight on the forward foot ready to spring into action.

On the phone, you can recognize a D Style very easily. She is the one who does not have time for your questions as you dutifully seek information to be helpful. Yet Mr. or Ms. D wants the answer *now*.

Your Body Language for the D Style Customer

If you are servicing a D Style customer in person, greet them with a strong handshake. Maintain direct eye contact with them, lean slightly forward in your stance while keeping your distance. D Styles don't want to deal with weak people. They want to deal with strong, confident individuals who know what they are talking about. So provide that perception by how you look and act.

Speaking with a D Style Customer

As you can guess, you will only succeed in speaking with a D Style customer if you are direct and to the point. Your tone of voice must be strong, clear, confident, and direct. Your pace should be fast—give your impatient customer the impression that you are quickly heading toward results. The same goes for your actions. Look like you're making something happen, like you're taking definitive action on the important D customer's behalf.

Words and phrases you can use to successfully communicate with D Style customers include:

➤ Fast

➤ Immediate

➤ Now

➤ Today

➤ New

➤ Let's do it

➤ Unique

➤ Benefits

➤ Bottom line

➤ Leaders in the field

➤ Win

➤ Make it happen

➤ Results

Here's what you need to know if you want to get your point across to a D Style customer.

Dos and Don'ts of Communicating with D Style Customers

Dos	Don'ts
Be clear, specific, to the point	Ramble, waste their time
Be prepared and organized	Look disorganized, lose things
Stick to business	Chitchat, idle gossip
Present facts logically	Cloud issues, leave loopholes
Ask specific (What?) questions	Ask rhetorical, useless questions
Take issue with facts only	Personalize issue
Provide Win/Win Solution	Force D into losing situation
Provide choice of options	Make decision for them

(Reprinted with permission from copyrighted material from Target Training International, Ltd.)

The Influential Customer (I Style)

The I Style customer is the person who needs and wants to talk. She has a need for interaction with people and social recognition. Therefore she will be optimistic, inspiring, persuasive, and trusting in her approach to you. She often speaks with enthusiasm, has a smile on her face, and is hoping for the same from you.

Research shows that 28 percent of the population exhibit I Style behavior. They want their problems resolved, but want to have them resolved by people who are friendly toward them. The I Style customer isn't a big fan of voice mail since it eliminates the element of human interaction. If you service an I Style customer, accept him and be friendly. With this type of customer, relationships are extremely important.

Recognizing an I Style Customer

Based on our perception of how they act in public, examples of I Style Dominant Personalities might include: Bill Clinton, Robin Williams, Oprah Winfrey, Steve Martin, Rosie O'Donnell, and Bette Midler.

I Style customers tend to smile and talk a lot. As with Ds, appearance is everything, especially physical appearance. They like to wear designer label clothes and jewelry that signify social affiliation.

I Style customers are into people-related products like *People Magazine*, *Success*, and *Psychology Today*. They appreciate funny cards and collect memorabilia from friends. They appreciate a happening, contemporary atmosphere.

You can spot an I Style very easily. They are the ones who stop to talk with everyone and look at everything on their way to the rest room. They might bump into you only because they were paying attention to other things or people.

The I Style customer is often late. Bill Clinton had to work on his inability to keep his schedule on time in the early years of his presidency. As an I, he was always talking to people and never on time. I Style customers also tend to get off the subject and talk about things irrelevant to the problem at hand. Not because they're ditzy, but because they just love the interaction more than the subject.

On the phone, the I Style customer will be bubbly, enthusiastic, and engaging.

Your Body Language for the I Style Customer

I Style customers respond well to expressive gestures. You need to smile at them and either stand or sit next to them to provide an atmosphere of acceptance. Close is fine with I people; they like you and want you to feel close to them. On the phone, you definitely want to smile while you speak with an I. Your smile will come through in the words you use and your tone. Remember, I Style customers are oriented and driven to people and relationships.

Speaking with an I Style Customer

Since I Style customers are expressive, you need to be expressive and animated in return. That's how you get their attention. Your tone of voice should be energized, enthusiastic, friendly, persuasive, and filled with high and low modulations.

You should also sound colorful. I Style customers love images and word pictures. Your pace should be fast and animated. Your actions should be fast and filled with gestures. These behaviors communicate your aliveness that I Styles want to experience.

Words and phrases you can use to successfully communicate with I Style customers include:

➤ Fun

➤ I feel

➤ You'll look great

➤ Put you in the spotlight

➤ State-of-the-art

➤ Everybody

➤ Picture this

➤ Recognition

➤ Exciting

➤ The latest thing

➤ Wonderful

➤ Awesome

➤ Fantastic

Here's what you need to know if you want to get your point across to an I Style customer.

Dos and Don'ts of Communicating with I Style Customers

Dos	Don'ts
Allow them to discuss dreams	Legislate or muffle actions
Allow time for socializing/relating	Be curt/tight lipped
Talk about people/their goals	Concentrate on facts/figures
Ask for their opinion	Be impersonal
Provide ideas	Waste time in "dreaming"
Put details in writing	Leave decisions up in the air
Be stimulating, fun, fast moving	Be too businesslike
Provide testimonials	Talk down to them
Offer immediate and extra incentives for them to take risks	Get trapped and spend too much time

(Reprinted with permission from copyrighted material from Target Training International, Ltd.)

The Steady Customer (S Style)

The S Style customer is an accommodating individual. This is the person who, when he is inconvenienced by your product not working will make sure he doesn't upset you with his complaint. The S Style customer is patient, relaxed, logical, and systematic. He is adverse to change, since he doesn't want anything to upset his process. In servicing an S Style customer, it's important to keep this need for stability in mind. If your solution requires a great deal of change on the part of the customer, you are in trouble, especially if you don't soften the perceived impact of the requested changes. S Styles need to be secure in the fact that the solution is going to work and bring closure to the issue.

Research shows that 40 percent of the population represent the S Style customer. The S Style customer is a person who works hard to finish a great amount of work, even taking on the work of others. In fact, you may be servicing an S Style customer who may not be the real customer, but rather someone taking care of the problem for the real purchaser.

Recognizing an S Style Customer

Based on our perception of how they act in public, examples of S Style Dominant Personalities might include: Mother Teresa, Gandhi, Barbara Bush, Walter Payton, Tom Brokaw, and Kevin Costner.

Since S Style customers are loyal and service oriented, they are likely to dress with clothing emblazoned with their employer's logo, and jewelry they received for years of service to their company. They are casual in nature and dress modestly. They like to come back to familiar, reliable places. The moment an S Style customer buys from you, you could have them for life unless you screw up or forget to meet their emotional needs and wants.

If the S Style customer must wait while you provide service, have on hand magazines such as *Reader's Digest*, *National Geographic*, and *Better Homes & Gardens*. These magazines often have articles on how things work and the order of things in the world. Remember, S people are concerned with the how comes and how to's.

Your Body Language for the S Style Customer

Since S Style customers are relaxed in nature and weary of change, you should lean back when standing in front of them and don't rush with your actions. You should appear to be relaxed and not too close for comfort. Use small hand gestures and maintain an atmosphere of calm.

Speaking with an S Style Customer

To facilitate a calm atmosphere, your tone of voice should be warm, soft, calm, and steady. Your volume should be on the low side. Your rate of speech should be relaxed and thoughtful. Your actions should be well paced and relaxed. Think of a baby. If you do something unexpected out of the blue, or suddenly move with a jerky motion, you'll startle and frighten the baby. The same holds true for S Style customers. Now hold on, we aren't saying that S Style customers are babies. What we are saying is that you can most effectively communicate with them when it's with the same tender and calm manner as you would use with a baby.

Words and phrases you should use in communicating with S Style customers include:

➤ Think about it	➤ Comfort
➤ Take your time	➤ Assure
➤ Trust	➤ You can expect
➤ Guarantee	➤ Conservative
➤ Promise	➤ Certain
➤ Security	➤ Here's what's going to happen
➤ Reliable	➤ Step-by-step explanations
➤ Help me to help you	

Here's what you need to know if you want to get your point across to an S Style customer.

Dos and Don'ts of Communicating with S Style Customers

Dos	Don'ts
Start with personal comments	Rush right into business
Show sincere interest in them	Stick coldly to facts
Listen patiently and be responsive	Force a quick response
Present your solution logically, softly, and non-threateningly	Threaten or demand
Move casually, informally	Be abrupt and fast
Ask specific (How?) questions	Interrupt them
Avoid hurting their feelings	Mistake their acceptance of your solution for satisfaction
Provide personal assurance and guarantees	Promise anything you can't deliver
Give them time to think	Force quick decision

(Reprinted with permission from copyrighted material from Target Training International, Ltd.)

The Compliant Customer (C Style)

The C Style customer is your everyday perfectionist. She wants it precise, orderly, and accurately. She is meticulous by nature and diplomatic in behavior. If you are going to satisfy a C Style customer, you better be armed with all the facts, figures, and supporting data you can get your hands on. They want all the Ts crossed and Is dotted before they will accept your ideas. C Style customers are sticklers for following the rules. If you deviate in any way from your policy or the law, they will let you know.

If you have been keeping score all along, you will know that research suggests that 14 percent of the population exhibits this style of behavior. While you may be thanking someone above for only giving this trait to 14 percent of the population, the C Style customer plays a pivotal role in keeping the world working with some measure of precision, and in keeping all of us honest.

If you're trying to cut corners in the service you provide, forget it. The C Style customer will spot you a mile away blindfolded.

Recognizing a C Style Customer

Based on our perception of how they act in public, examples of C Style Dominant Personalities might include: Ted Koppel, Jack Nicklaus, Clint Eastwood, Diane Sawyer, and Spike Lee.

C Style customers are great poker players. They always have the same look and you never know what's going on in their minds. They are conservative in nature, as exhibited by their clothing, which is often of good quality. Their jewelry symbolizes professional affiliation and is the "real thing." They love do-it yourself-projects. In fact, they always will ask you questions concerning how they can do it. They love to decorate their offices with charts and graphs. The magazines they want to read in your waiting room include *Consumer Reports*, *Discover*, and technical journals.

The C Style customer will reluctantly move out of the way of an object in his path, at the last possible moment and only after having theorized, strategized, and analyzed numerous possible solutions on how to overcome the obstacle. When they finally stand aside, they're likely to have their arms crossed with one hand resting on the chin as in a thinking position. Hey, they are *always* thinking.

C Style customer's style of humor, when you can find it, is dry wit. Do not expect them to say anything unless they're convinced you have the right solution or they are annoyed. Especially on the phone. Forget about engaging them in casual conversation. It won't work. They called for information or a solution. Anything else is a silly waste of time. Even downright irritating.

Your Body Language for the C Style Customer

Don't touch or get too close to a C Style customer. Sit or stand across from them where they can see you. If standing, stand firmly with your weight planted on the back foot. Maintain direct eye contact and use little or no hand gestures. Remember, these are extremely analytical people, some to the degree you might consider as being suspicious. Do nothing to suggest you're trying to avoid them or take advantage of them.

Speaking with a C Style Customer

C Style customers are wary of what you have to say. Therefore, you must keep your tone of voice controlled at all times with little modulation. They are suspicious of hype style responses. You must be direct and precise in what you have to say. Your pace should be slow and thoughtful. Your words, vocal tone, pacing all should convey: Here are the facts you need to get what you want. Nothing more.

Your actions should be slow and deliberate. C Style customers fit two old sayings, "Just the facts ma'am," and, "Nice and easy."

Words and phrases you can use with C Style customers include:

➤ Proven/proof

➤ Guarantees

➤ No risk

➤ Research (or data) shows

➤ Take your time

➤ Supporting data and analyze

➤ No obligation

➤ Here are the facts

➤ Information

➤ Analysis

➤ Think it over

Here's what you need to know if you want to get your point across to a C Style customer.

Dos and Don'ts of Communicating with C Style Customers

Dos	Don'ts
Be prepared	Be disorganized or messy
Be straightforward and direct	Be casual, informal, or personal
Look at all sides of an issue	Force quick decision
Present specifics of what you can do	Be vague and not follow through
Create time line and measurements	Over promise
Take your time, be persistent	Be abrupt and fast
Use data and facts from respected people	Use emotions or feelings
Give time to make decision	Close too hard
Give them space	Touch them

(Reprinted with permission from copyrighted material from Target Training International, Ltd.)

What's Your Style?

Besides identifying the behavioral style of your customer, it's important to recognize your own behavioral style. Only then will you know how to temper your approach as you deal with the different style of customers. If you are demanding styles like us (Don and Ron), you may need to calm down and be more patient with people, especially those who are S and C Style customers.

At Your Service
To make it easier to identify the four styles of behavior, keep in mind that the Ds and Is tend to be expressive and outgoing. Ss and Cs tend to be reserved and introverted.

Watch It!
Keep in mind that when a customer calls you to complain, their behavior is affected by a stressful situation. In stressful times, people often act differently than in calmer, "normal" times. Their behavioral styles may change in relation to the stress they're feeling. The stress can exaggerate the extreme characteristics of their style. And that can make for some strange behavior! If you follow the methods of communication we suggest for each style, you'll help prevent the situation from getting more stressful for both you and the customer.

If you are of an I Style nature, you may talk too much when it comes to dealing with Ds. And don't forget, Cs don't want to have idle chatter with you and Ss are looking for security, not social recognition like you.

If you are an S Style individual, you must be prepared to change your way of communicating to be heard by the other styles. While you are slow in your pace of speech and low in volume, Is and Ds want you to pick things up, both in speed and volume. They want to move faster than you are prepared to move. And while you are steady in nature and look for guarantees, the C Style customers want no risk at all in employing your solutions.

If you are a C Style person, show others some emotion. The Is want relationships and smiles. The Ds want decisions and action. The Ss want a stable, relaxed atmosphere with friendly faces all around them.

As a caring, responsible service provider, you are quite valuable to your customers in wanting to make sure your solution is really appropriate. However, you must communicate the solution with some feeling—appropriate to the individual you are interacting with at the moment. Remember, your success depends not only on the accuracy of your solution, but also on whether or not it is heard and understood by an *individual* customer. Great service is specific to the one person you are serving at any given moment.

We hope by now you will have an appreciation of what it means to communicate effectively with others. To ensure you are communicating properly with your customer, focus more on their words, actions, and body language. Think less about your situation. The more attention you pay to your customer, the better both of you are going to feel. And the more effectively you will serve and *please* your customer. By tuning into your customer's individual behavior style, you will gain a deeper appreciation for and understanding of your customer and his problems. He in turn will want to listen to you since you will be communicating on the same frequency he is tuned to. Your service interactions will be personal, pleasing, and memorable. And that's what it's all about!

The Least You Need to Know

➤ Customers come with various styles of behavior. Quality service organizations know how to treat and deal with each style of behavior.

➤ The demanding customer wants it now with no hassles and doesn't care about the details.

➤ The influential customer wants to talk about their problems, be accepted, and stay happy.

➤ The steady customer wants to keep things as is, and if change is necessary, he wants to be assured that your solution is logical and will work.

➤ The compliant customer wants as much detail as possible in order to make a decision and wants to be sure that everything is working according to specification.

➤ Successful customer service representatives adapt their style of communication to the behavioral style of their customers.

Chapter 8

So What's the Problem?

In This Chapter

➤ Understanding that time can be more valuable than money

➤ Using the power of questions

➤ Asking the right kinds of questions

➤ Taking the bite out of your questions

➤ Listening to your customer

➤ Remembering to ask, listen, and comprehend

Imagine that you had an account that provided you with $1,440 every day. The only thing is, if you don't use all the money on a given day, the unspent dollars are lost forever.

You probably wouldn't have too much trouble spending $1,440 every day, now would you?

But what about time? Do you think much about how you spend the 1,440 minutes you get every day? That's how many all of us get. And since we can't store those minutes, we're forced to spend them on something. Did you use your free gift of 1,440 minutes productively yesterday? The day before?

They're gone now. To avoid losing those precious minutes in the future, now is a good time to spend a little time thinking about the concept of time.

Time Is of the Essence

You see, in customer service today it's all about time. Time is a precious, limited, non-renewable resource. It's important to you because you're on a fixed budget of 1,440 minutes a day, and it's important to your customers because they get the same allotment of 1,440.

Unlike money, you know you can't get more time. And your customers know they can't get more. Because we can't bank time, borrow time, beg time, or steal time, no one wants to waste time. And so, you probably find yourself feeling time pressure on the job. Just about everyone we know does.

At Your Service
Haste makes waste! Remember this phrase? It adequately describes what happens when you don't take the necessary time to solve your customer's problem in the first call.

Quote, Unquote
Once you become conscious of the questions active in the moment, you always get some kind of intuitive direction of what to do, of where to go. You get a hunch about the next step. Always. The only time this will not occur is when you have the wrong question in mind. You see, the problem in life isn't in receiving answers. The problem is in identifying your current questions. Once you get the questions right, the answers always come.
—James Redfield, *The Celestine Prophecy*

Have you ever heard this old saying, "We never have time to do the job right, but we always seem to find time to do it over again?" Strange, but many people under time pressure believe they don't have enough time to invest in doing a good job or handle a problem well. It's a good bet that the people operating in the "get by" or "do it over" mentality never really resolve the problems they help to create.

Dealing with a customer's problem twice is a double waste of time, for you and the customer.

If you are sacrificing "quality time" with customers in an attempt to help more customers, you're probably not properly handling the complaints of the customers you speak with. Spending more time with customers up-front in their initial call—to properly diagnose their situation and uncover their needs and wants—will save you time in the end because you will have solved their problems properly to begin with. And you won't have to waste time trying to appease an angry customer. So how do you do this? You ask questions.

The Power of Questions

Questions are without a doubt the most powerful tool you have as someone providing service to customers. When you ask questions, you wield the ultimate power in a moment of influence. As Ron is fond of saying, the answers to your success lie in the questions you ask. Questions provide you with:

➤ Information you need in order to service your customers appropriately and efficiently.

➤ Control over the conversation. Simply ask a question on a particular issue, and the conversation is now centered on that issue.

Asking questions isn't good enough. You need to:

➤ Know how to ask the right questions

➤ Ask enough questions

➤ Listen to the response

➤ Acknowledge the responses and act on them

Before we dive deeper into how to ask questions, let's see what stops us from asking questions to begin with.

Why Aren't You Asking Questions?

Based on our research and our experiences working with customer service personnel, we have uncovered the following common reasons for what prevents people from asking questions. After each reason, you will find our response.

As you read this part, check off the reasons that affect you and your employees' ability to ask the right questions and enough questions.

❑ The customer pressures you to stop asking questions and just give her the solution.

Response: If you don't ask the questions and get the information you need, you might end up giving the wrong solution, which will turn out to be no solution. And then you'll waste time *doing it over again*!

❑ The customer will think you are not very knowledgeable if you need to ask so many questions.

Response: Doctor's are very knowledgeable. Yet they ask tons of questions because they know that if any information is missing, they won't be empowered to prescribe the proper cure. Do you want service from the fastest doctor in town, or the one whose patients live long enough for a few return visits?

❑ The customer may give you an answer you don't want to hear.

Response: Let them! You need to hear the good, the bad, and the uncomfortable to get a proper feel for the situation. And if the answer is nasty, think about how you have the power to turn this nasty situation into a successful intervention.

❑ The customer may feel the answers are so obvious that there is no need for your questions.

Response: Never assume anything. It's when you think you know what's happening that you are vulnerable to making the biggest, easiest-to-avoid mistakes. And the most embarrassing.

❑ You don't ask questions because you fear the customer will feel you are interrogating them.

Response: If done properly (and we will show you how later on in this chapter), this won't be an issue. It's better to ask the questions and solve the problem than to have a customer who is still unhappy.

Tales from the Real World

As Don was writing this book, he had problems with his computers, including an all-out hard drive crash on one machine and bizarre failures on a replacement PC right before deadline. Can you say heart palpitations?

Gino Tosolini, a wonderfully patient and empathetic service technician on IBM's technical support line, probed ever-so-gently, asking for diagnostic information he could use to restore Don's machine and his fragile state of mind. Even when the process—which took well over an hour—bordered on torture as Gino went to get help from more senior level technicians, he always explained what he was going to do, and why, and asked for Don's permission to take the process to the next step in order to help solve the strangely mysterious problems.

P.S. Turns out that the brand-new machine that appeared to have a highly-unusual power system problem was simply conflicting with a fax device made by Xerox. Don made the discovery quite by accident after several calls to the PC maker offered no hint of a solution, as the conflict had not yet shown up in the IBM technical database. The incompatibility between PC and fax nearly forced replacing the PC and totally wiping out many hours of installing and configuring software before the problem revealed itself. Still, the care, interest, and patience that Gino demonstrated made the horribly disappointing and time-wasting experience almost bearable. He even called back to check on the problem after thinking about it over a four-day weekend break. Gino helped to restore confidence in a company that initially appeared to build a very sour lemon for a guy in desperate need of a sweet solution.

❏ You tend to talk too much and keep others from participating.

Response: Shut Up! It's not important what you have to say. The important words will be uttered by your customer. If you don't let them talk, how will you know what to do or say? Sometimes the better part of being friendly and helpful is silence.

❏ After asking a question, you're thinking about what your next question should be instead of listening to the customer's response.

Response: You're thinking too hard. Turn off the busybody part of your brain and listen. When your customer finishes her thought, think about the customer's response for a moment; that'll trigger your next question. If it works for you, take notes as your customer talks. That may free you from having to remember all the details.

❏ You don't have time for questions. You need to move on and take the calls on hold, or you will lose your job!

Response: Guess what? If you consistently fail to solve your customer's problems, you will definitely lose your job. In fact, if fast-slamming customers is how you operate, you should quit now because you're making a lot of people miserable. Yes, time is important. And we aren't suggesting that you waste time on calls. But there's a big difference between frittering away time with idle chit-chat and task-focused discussion. If you don't take the time required to solve the problem, you're failing your customer, your company, your family, your nation, and most importantly, yourself!

If you checked off any of the boxes above (and believe us, you'll not be alone), consider what leads you to such actions limiting your ability to give great customer service. The actions themselves may only be symptoms of a much deeper problem. Find out what causes you to stop asking enough of the right questions. Otherwise, you will be severely handicapped in trying to help your customers.

> **At Your Service**
> If you take notes during an interview with a customer, simply jot down key words that will trigger your mind. Avoid writing down every word that is said. Otherwise, you will be concentrating too much on what you're writing instead of what you are hearing.

What Types of Questions Are You Using?

Now that you understand why it is to your advantage to ask questions, you're probably wondering what questions you should be asking. Let's take a look at the types of questions you should be asking on a regular basis. First, we'll look at two different question formats—open- and closed-ended questions—that direct how the customer provides you information. Then, we'll look at different types of questions that are best suited to requesting specific kinds of information from customers.

Open-Ended Questions

Open-ended questions don't require specific answers. They're used to get the customer talking. An example could be:

"Mr. Customer, what happens when you turn your machine on?"

As you can see, the open-ended question is used to obtain detailed information. It's a common type of question to ask, especially at the beginning of the service call.

Closed-Ended Questions

Closed-ended questions require specific yes/no type answers. They are not for acquiring a lot of detail. Their primary focus is to determine very specific information or to clarify a customer's perceptions, wishes, or responses. Using appropriate closed-ended questions

At Your Service
Many times customer service departments will request information from the customer to help build their databases for future use. A post-service follow-up call may be scheduled to be certain the customer remains satisfied. The information may also assist the company in figuring out who buys their products. The database also might be used for future marketing campaigns. In other words, information about your customer is golden. The more you know, the more powerful you will be in servicing and marketing products to meet the future needs of your customers.

gets you further in the discovery process, instead of taking up valuable time sifting through long-winded or incomplete diagnostic information. For instance:

"Mr. Customer, was your machine on or off when the problem occurred?"

Note that this closed-ended question requires a specific answer of on or off. If you don't get an answer here, then you know to ask more questions to get to the heart of the problem.

Closed-ended questions usually come in response to details provided in open-ended questions—except for the first few seconds of the call, when you might be asking status questions seeking specific information.

Now, let's turn to another category of question types—these could be either open or closed-ended depending on the situation. The question types we define below relate to the *kind of information* you're asking your customer about, and should help you get the information you need to provide great service.

Status Questions

These are the questions you ask at the front end of the customer service call to obtain information necessary for resolving a problem. For example:

"What is your name, phone number, serial number, and account number?"

While this information is important, most everyone in the universe finds them more annoying than speed bumps. So the way you ask the questions can have a negative or positive impact on the overall customer intervention. Remember to give a reason as to why this information will help you help the customer (because…). That makes the questions a tad more tolerable.

Illustrative Questions

These questions are open-ended questions that require a customer to paint as complete a picture as possible about their experience. This is vital for your understanding of what their interest, problem, or concern is. A sample illustrative question can be:

"Please describe for me what happens when you turn the switch on."

Without answers to such questions, you are in no position to help your customer.

Clarification Questions

These questions are probably the least asked and the most important. Whether or not you ask these questions at the right time dictates whether or not your solutions are accurate. For example:

"Mr. Customer, when you say you want your machine to run faster, please describe for me what speed you would consider to be fast."

How many times have you been a victim of or were the supplier of a solution that did not work because you didn't clearly understand what your customer was really talking about? In your business, you probably hear the same words many, many times a day, day-in and day-out. Yet, if you fall victim to thinking that you understand what your customer means by inserting your definitions for the words they use, you're going to miss something important.

Even if the customer is an expressive I Style, whatever meaning he has in mind is unclear if you don't ask some clarifying questions. Just because you may have finished a call in which another customer's machine didn't work because the switch was broken doesn't mean that the next customer's machine with apparently the same symptoms is not working because of a faulty switch. It may be another problem altogether.

At Your Service

People don't necessarily use words that fit the definitions found in a dictionary. They use words that they think best describe their feelings, experiences, and biases. For instance, suppose a customer tells you his machine is not working. Does not working mean that the machine does not turn on at all; or can it mean that the machine isn't performing to specification; or can it mean that the machine keeps shutting down at the wrong times? And after you get past that first level of detail there surely are a few others, so clarify, clarify, clarify.

Ask, don't assume. Clarify your customer's words, no matter how many times you hear them. It is your customer's definition and explanation that counts, not the one you initially think you hear.

Tales from the Real World

Ron is known for the "ketchup story" he tells in his programs. The short version is that Ron stopped at a McDonalds with his wife Cindy and daughter Amanda for something to eat. Cindy gave Ron her order and requested a lot of ketchup with her french fries. Ron came back to the table with the food and at least 20 packages of ketchup. Cindy immediately wondered why Ron didn't bring back a lot of ketchup as she had requested. Bewildered, Ron looked on in amazement as his wife left the table, went to the counter and came back with her version of what "a lot" of ketchup looked like. It was a little cup filled with ketchup.

Immediately Ron realized what happened. When he heard the request for "a lot of ketchup," he thought quantity in terms of number of packets. His wife's perception was getting enough ketchup that was free-flowing in a cup in which she could dip her fries. The plastic packages, no matter how many Ron brought, didn't solve the problem. Ron knew if he had clarified what she meant by a lot of ketchup, he would have provided it the way she wanted it.

Tales from the Real World

As Ron was writing this book, his laptop all of a sudden stopped holding a charge. This was unacceptable because Ron relies heavily on his laptop battery as he spends a lot of time on planes. He called his computer dealer, Integrated Designs, Inc. Dave Rawley, Service Coordinator, realizing the problem was in the computer itself, asked Ron what would be the consequences if he had to ship it back to IBM for servicing. After hearing that the laptop was also Ron's main computer, Dave had Ron bring the laptop to him for troubleshooting. After one hour, he called IBM for the parts and gave the laptop back to Ron to use in the meantime. Four days later, he called Ron back to install the parts. Throughout this entire time, Ron never lost the services of his laptop and got the problem resolved. Now that was excellent customer service.

Consequence Questions

These are questions that tell you how the problem is affecting your customer. For instance:

> "Mr. Customer, what will happen if you need to send us your computer and not have it for a while?"

This is critical because your role is not only to provide service to your customers, but to do so in a manner they will appreciate.

This focus on really clarifying what your customer is after is what separates people who provide excellent customer service from people who provide ordinary customer service. And excellent customer service is what brings your customers back for more.

Desires Questions

This is the question asked at the end of the customer service intervention that tells your customer you really care about him. It asks whether or not you can do anything else for him to be completely satisfied. For example:

> "Mr. Customer, is there anything else we can help you with today"

The Desires Question takes the customer service call to the next level. You may be thinking that if the customer does not bring it up, why should you—especially when you have other people on hold waiting for your help.

Think about it. Your customer calls. You fix his immediate problem and he leaves. Or, your customer calls, you fix his immediate problem, and before he leaves, you ask him if he has any more desires so that you can help to the maximum. Which method do you think will make you memorable in the mind of your customer?

You want to be memorable. For all the money you and your company are investing in customer service, you want your customer to remember your efforts the next time he goes to buy. If you are pro-active and asking a desires question, you have a better chance of having your customer remember you and your company as caring for their business when its time to make the next purchase.

Taking the Bite Out of Your Questions

Earlier, we told you we would give you ideas about how to ask questions that would not be perceived as being interrogative by your customer.

A question doesn't have to be a statement followed by a question mark. It only has to be a statement that verbally requests feedback from the customer. In the preceding illustrative question example, you will note it started with the words "Please describe" and didn't have a question mark at the end. It was a statement seeking more information. Using the words "Please describe" is an excellent way to take the bite out of questions you need to ask.

Sometimes, all you have to do is make a statement or repeat your customers response. For example, your customer may say:

> "It's not working."

You reply:

> "It's not working."

Your customer will be automatically prompted to provide additional information. Try it. It works like a charm.

Give your customer a reason for the questions. In Chapter 6, we talked about the word "because" being one of the most powerful words in the English language. As a refresher course, the word "because" is powerful *because* it provides a reason, a justification for why you are doing certain things. In asking questions, the word "because" will turn any resistant customer into a participating customer.

Watch It!
Remember that questions are a powerful tool that help you uncover the information you need to help your customer. As far as your customer is concerned, questions may be considered inconvenient, unnecessary, and accusatory. Be sure to frame your questions in a friendly manner and give your customers a valid reason about why they should answer them. You can't solve your customer's problem if they're unwilling to help you.

Tales from the Real World

In a presentation before a group of customer service representatives at a computer company, one of the participants asked Ron how to get customers to cooperate by giving their serial numbers. Customers are always reluctant to take the time to find it and don't understand why it's important. Ron suggested that the participant give uncooperative customers a good reason for the hassle. He said the next time a customer is stubborn, tell them that the serial number allows you to find their record faster and provide them with quicker solutions.

A few weeks later, on a follow-up visit, the participant thanked Ron because that tactic reduced the number of customers who were resistant to giving their serial numbers by 50 percent. The end result: his customers got faster service and he was able to markedly improve his productivity.

In addition, watch your vocal tone. The point of asking questions is not to point blame, but to uncover the necessary information you need to help your customer. Let your tone convey the honestly helpful nature of your questions (see Chapter 6).

Did You Hear What I Told You?

Okay, so now you have asked the right question, but did you hear your customer's response? There's a distinct difference between hearing and listening to your customer's response.

Hearing your customer is the physical act of taking in through your ears what is being said. Listening to your customer is the emotional act of understanding what your customer is really saying.

Customers know immediately whether you're really listening to them or just hearing their words. There is nothing more aggravating than having a feeling that you are not being listened to. In fact, if you were to offer a solution immediately without listening to your customer's complaint, the customer may think your solution isn't proper. Why? Because your customer may be thinking; how do you know the solution you're proposing is really going to help if you never took the time to find out what was really wrong?

Here are some helpful hints you can use to better hear what your customers are saying:

Be relevant—Is what you're saying or asking the customer relevant to the overall issue? If it is, you're more likely to tune into the response.

Be patient—Remember in Chapter 7 we discussed the behavioral styles of customers? Their style may not match yours. So be patient and let them tell you what's on their mind the way they know how. If you interrupt them, you may be missing some information that will force you to give the wrong prescription for the cure.

Avoid genuinely fake responses—Automatic responses like, "That's interesting," "I understand," and so on, can sound hollow and insincere. Responses that have the right words but lack true listening behind them are as useless as they are obvious. Your customers will hear right through them. And by saying such automatic responses you actually may shut down your listening process. If you tell someone, "I understand" before you really do understand, you may talk yourself into believing you understand when you really don't understand and therefore you will stop listening to your customer. You understand?

Take your time—Before responding back to your customer, take a few seconds to digest the information if you have to. We know that a few seconds can seem like an eternity. But if you don't fully comprehend what your customer just said, then it will severely limit your ability to respond appropriately. Just ask the customer, "Could you give me a moment to get the information I need to assist you?" That information is probably in your brain. Wherever it is, take the time to get it, so you can get it right.

A good rule of thumb to effective listening is that you should be doing 80 percent of the listening in the beginning, with your customer doing 80 percent of the talking. If your percentage of listening is below 80 percent at the beginning of the customer intervention, you're talking too much and you won't be of much help to your customer.

Remember Your ABCs

Some situations may make it difficult for you to follow all the rules and processes you're supposed to.

In the early 1980s, Ron was a certified Emergency Medical Technician (EMT) and volunteer medic. The certification test for being an EMT included a written test and a grueling skills performance part. In the skills performance section, Ron and his classmates had to carefully manipulate themselves around people acting as accident victims without sacrificing the ABCs of airway, breathing, and circulation. If they made one slight mistake in their maneuvering that could compromise the ABCs of a patient, they failed the test.

In real-life emergencies, they were sometimes forced to make modifications in their procedures. For example, it

Watch It!
If you don't mind your communication ABCs in dealing with your customers, you will jeopardize the customer relationship. The ABCs (Asking, Basic Listening, and Comprehension) are essential ingredients for satisfying your customers. They want to know you're interested, they want to be heard and they want to be understood.

became impossible to move a patient with a broken back in a crunched up Volkswagen Beetle the same way you would move a patient on a floor with plenty of room. However, the stringent training program left an indelible imprint in the EMT's minds that no matter what they did, they must not compromise the ABCs of the patient.

In customer service, the communication ABCs are Asking, Basic Listening, and Comprehension (understanding). No matter what you do in the customer service call, and no matter what the situation is, be sure that you have asked enough of the right questions, listened to the responses, and gained a true understanding of the customer's complaint and needs. If you do this, you will provide your customer with total satisfaction.

The Least You Need to Know

➤ Time can be more valuable than money. Make sure you spend it wisely in the beginning to understand your customer's complaint, wishes, and desires. Otherwise, it will cost you more in the end.

➤ Questions provide you with the information you will need in order to prescribe the proper solution for your customer.

➤ Understand the reasons why you might not want to ask the customer enough questions. Most of these reasons are excuses and not valid.

➤ The types of questions you use will dictate the kind of information you will receive. Make sure your questions address the issue at hand.

➤ Take the sting out of your questions by posing them properly. Questions will either help you or haunt you, depending on how you ask them.

➤ Asking questions without listening and hearing your customers' responses is a waste of time. Without truly listening to them, you cannot serve your customer.

➤ Whatever you do, make sure in each customer service intervention that you ask enough of the right questions, hear your customers' responses, and gain a true understanding of their issues. Only then can you prescribe the right cure.

Chapter 9

The Angry Customer

In This Chapter

➤ Learning to help the customer

➤ Making customer service a win-win situation

➤ Handling conflict resolution

➤ Understanding and solving customer problems

➤ Maintaining your overall mission

Imagine that someone breaks a promise to you. Or that a product you bought last week breaks down just when you really need it. Or that a company doesn't deliver the service you paid your hard-earned money for. Do you feel your teeth clenching, your fists tightening, and your blood beginning to boil? Relax! This imagining stuff is just a cheap ploy to introduce this really important chapter.

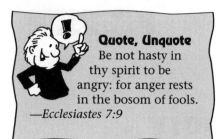

At Your Service
Anger is perhaps your most powerful emotion. And it's probably more contagious than kindness. One of the best ways to immunize yourself from customer anger is to focus on facts. Often, people get more and more angry because they're confused as well as disappointed. The more you and your unhappy customer focus on cold, hard facts, the less you'll get caught up in red-hot emotions. You'll have a happier customer sooner, and a less-stressful workday for yourself.

Everyone—even your dear old grandma—sometimes loses their cool when they feel like a victim of a dirty trick.

A few years ago, Ron was traveling through Dallas Ft. Worth Airport on American Airlines to give a very important speech in Kansas City. The winds of fate blew cold that day and his connection from Dallas to K.C. was canceled. Gripped by the fear of missing his talk, he frantically called the airline's frequent flyer Hot Line to make other arrangements.

Now most people normally describe Ron as a sweet, almost angelic man (some even call him by his nickname, St. Ron). But on that morning, even he admits he wasn't the most pleasant individual when he called for help. He was angry, frustrated, and scared to death that he'd disappoint *his* customer waiting for him to touch down and go to work.

Standing at a pay phone, covered in a cold sweat, Ron worked his way through the airline's mind-numbing phone mail options. (Push One if you want to hold forever. Push Two if you'd like us to transfer you to another busy extension. Push Three to speak to someone who totally has no idea what you're talking about....)

When he finally got a live customer service representative on the other end of the phone, Ron concentrated more on his emotional need to yell rather than finding a solution to his pressing problem.

However, even in the face of a screaming angel, the understanding customer service representative saved the day for both of them. She turned the initial conflict into a win-win situation. After patiently listening to Ron's frustrations, she gave him a choice of options to choose from. She told Ron she would be more than happy to listen to him complain some more, or, he could calm down and give her the necessary information she needed to get him on the next plane to K.C. in time to give his speech.

With this careful handling, Ron resisted his impulse to continue yelling. His rational side took over. He got hold of his erupting emotions and became more like his angelic self. A bit calmer, he gave information to the American Airlines Customer Service Representative that empowered her to provide a solution to get Ron off the phone and onto a plane to Kansas City.

Let Me Help You

The truth of the matter is that most people in customer service situations really do want to solve their customers' problems, even when the customers are whining lunatics. However, if you don't follow the basic model of conflict resolution, you're more likely to get sucked into the customer's tornado of emotions. When that happens, you have nothing but two out-of-control maniacs who aren't solving a problem. And that's a double shame since customer anger really is an easy issue to overcome.

The key is to bypass all the emotional issues using a technique commonly known as *Conflict Resolution*.

By the time you answer a customer's call for help, the person on the other end of the line or counter is feeling a lot of pain. Some of the pain was mental anguish caused by the performance (or lack of performance) of your products and services. Some of the pain may have been caused by your company's less-than-perfect method for delivering service.

People who get trapped in your system feel that they're caught in a maze—not only are they angry about their initial problem, now they're frustrated by the intended solution!

Most likely, you've had the experience of being lost in the "phone zone" of voice mail, getting your call forwarded to people who can't help, or simply not being able to find anyone who has both the information and the authority to solve your problem.

The bottom line is that the person on the other end of the phone, or across the counter, is really (and quite understandably) upset. And, like it or not, you're the target of their pent-up frustration.

At Your Service

It's easy for consultants or seminar leaders to give you advice such as, "Don't take it personally." Sure. Let's see how that works. Listen [*insert your name here*], "You're slow, confused, and totally incompetent. And your breath smells bad, too! But don't take it personally." Well, that last little bit of assurance made everything okay, right? Give us a break! Not taking personally another's criticism or outbursts of emotion requires a disciplined focus on task and technique. That usually requires training—and re-training—to teach and refresh those skills.

Tales from the Real World

A former colleague of Don's was once a high-powered attorney in Washington, D.C. who worked nearly around the clock constantly. He developed a terrible heart condition that his doctor said was caused by stress. The doctor told his distressed patient to rethink his commitment to his clients. "Remember," said the good doctor, "these are your client's problems, not your problems." Moral of the story: it's a good thing to care for your customers, and a bad thing to care so much that you take on emotional burdens that don't help you help your customers.

In reality it's hard to separate our personal feelings from a customer's attack on our products or company. However, there is one way of looking at a potential conflict that can take the edge off for you.

Milton Gralla, author of *How Good Guys Grow Rich*, claims that one of the reasons he was successful in building his publishing empire Gralla Communications was because he knew the value of upset customers. He realized that when someone calls to complain, you're guaranteed to have their undivided attention. Name any other time you are guaranteed to have your customer's undivided attention.

A customer's undivided attention allows you to re-establish the value of your company and enhance the relationship. It allows you to provide solutions that will never be forgotten. It allows you to strengthen the wall that keeps the competition out. Now, when you see an upset customer through this perspective, it kind of makes it easier to deal with the individual.

Let's Play Win-Win Customer Service

There are several possible endings you can have in trying to resolve a conflict. And only one ending you want to achieve all the time.

I Lose—You Win

No matter how well you run your business, your company is going to make mistakes and upset customers. And it's imperative that you turn a bad situation into a pleasant one. However, if by doing so you are putting yourself or your company at risk of losing a substantial amount of money without any real pay-off, then you're in trouble. You may have solved a customer's problem, but have created a huge one for yourself. Solve your customers' problems without giving away the store.

I Win—You Lose

In this scenario, you probably did what you had to do to get the customer off of the phone, but did you really solve the customer's problem? You may feel relieved because you no longer have to deal with the situation, but you will definitely feel the pain later on when the customer disappears for good.

I Lose—You Lose

Obviously, you want to avoid this scenario. But understand that even though you know this is a situation to avoid, this basically is the outcome when you lose your cool with the customer. The customer leaves upset, you're upset, and you have lost a customer. Now that's upsetting!

I Win—You Win

This is obviously the most desired outcome of the four. You manage to keep your respect and sanity intact, and your customer manages to get a solution in a manner that's considered a positive moment of truth. The overall relationship is left at a minimum undamaged, and possibly enhanced.

Three Steps to Resolve Conflicts

As we said earlier, Conflict Resolution is really easy to handle as long as you understand the basic needs and wants of your fellow human beings. The bottom line is everyone would love to have a solution to their total liking. However, in the real world many times this isn't possible. What's crucial is not so much that your customer totally likes your solution, but rather how well you have dealt with the overall situation. This is what determines whether or not your customer will come back for more. After all, we all know that mistakes do happen.

Are You Telling Me What I Told You?

The key to any successful conflict resolution is your ability to hear your customer. As mentioned in Chapter 8, there's a distinct difference between listening to your customer and hearing your customer. Since this is crucial to conflict resolution, we want to briefly stress the difference again.

Hearing your customer is the physical act of taking in through your ears what is being said. Listening to your customer is the emotional act of understanding what your customer is really saying.

If you don't take the time to truly listen to your customer, how can you respond with an appropriate question or statement? If you don't clarify the customer's perceptions and their definitions of words being used, how can you be sure that your solution will be adequate?

Oftentimes you might be pushed away from hearing your customer by the harsh attitude they display. It's

At Your Service

Getting to a mutually agreeable solution for your upset customer requires more than defusing explosive anger and soothing intense disappointment. You must provide specific solutions and make sure your customer both understands and agrees to those solutions. Before hanging up the phone, say to the customer, "Here's what's going to happen now," and then review with the customer the specific actions that will follow your conversation. Ask, "Does that meet with your satisfaction?" If the answer is "no," ask the customer what else you can do to make him or her happy.

At Your Service

Diffusing a customer's boiling temper is a pretty easy thing to do if you follow these three steps:

1. Listen and understand what your customer is saying.

2. Acknowledge to your customer that you heard and understand him, so he will understand that you understand him. (You understand?)

3. Act on what your customer is complaining about.

imperative that you find the inner strength to see beyond the emotions and identify the cold hard facts. Once the cold hard facts are addressed, the emotions will eventually subside. If you attempt to deal with the emotions without identifying the cold hard facts, you won't successfully resolve the conflict.

Customers are intelligent and intuitive. They know when you're trying to stroke them and when you're offering them substance. Listen and hear their complaint!

Acknowledge Me, or I Won't Listen to You!

After not listening to your customers, the next worst thing you can do to them is not acknowledge the pain they feel. Failing to acknowledge the pain is a clear indication that the customer wasn't being heard, resulting in a negative Instant of Absolute Judgement (discussed in Chapter 4).

At Your Service
Several studies conducted by business professors reveal that the vast majority of unhappy customers (more than 90 percent) never complain. But those who do complain and then have their complaint dealt with quickly and fairly tend to be *more* satisfied than customers who never even had a problem! Plus, get this, they are more likely to be a repeat customer! Moral of the story: make your customers unhappy and then happy? Well, not exactly. Welcome complaints and deal with them promptly and fairly.

When someone's really hurting they can't think of anything but pain. Think about the emotions that would go through your mind if you felt *your* pain was not being acknowledged when you suffered a wrong. Ouch! You'll be in no mood to hear anyone's solution to your problem as long as you're focused on the fact that your pain was not recognized.

Not hearing the solution results in failed communication. And that can be more disappointing than no communication at all. The customer service person you're dealing with may have communicated a solution to you. But your anger and frustration didn't allow you to hear it, so it really was never implemented. Since the solution was never put into effect, your problem was never solved and your resentment continues.

Always acknowledge your customer's complaint and pain. In Ron's story mentioned earlier, the first thing the customer service representative at American Airlines told Ron was that she was truly sorry he missed his plane and understood the severity of the situation. Hearing that, Ron knew this individual was truly in his corner and ready to help him. So he was ready to give American Airlines another shot at earning his respect and his repeat business.

So What Are You Going to Do About It?

Okay, you have heard—in the listening way—your customer and have acknowledged your customer's complaint and pain. So what are you going to do about it? Acknowledgment without action is still a clear indication that your customer was not heard.

Some people confuse apologizing with taking action. Apologizing for a situation is not action. It is justifying one's emotions. A customer might feel good about an apology. But an apology without remedy is like an empty gift box.

In management circles, there's even debate as to whether or not you should apologize. There are many stories where a vendor apologized for a mishap and wound up being sued because the apology was seen as an admittance of guilt. We know you have to do what's right for your company to protect yourself at all times.

For example, instead of apologizing like:

> "I am sorry we sold you a broken machine."

Acknowledge the issue and move on by saying:

> "I understand the inconvenience a broken machine is causing you. Let's see what we can do to get that thing working for you."

The key points here:

1. You acknowledged the situation.
2. You put the focus on taking action and moving toward a solution.

Action means:

➤ Clearly communicating how you're going to solve the problem.

➤ Doing whatever you can within your power to positively affect your customer's situation.

➤ Seeking a plan that links both your customer and your company to a common goal.

➤ Assuring that a solution is actually implemented for your customer.

Remember, you can't always give a customer precisely what they want from your company. You and your customer both know the world isn't perfect. The key to satisfying your customer who desperately wants a quick, fair solution is to get to work on it while showing *empathy* for the person.

Fine Arts: Conflict Resolution, Problem Solving

As with anything else, if you follow the rules, you will have a better chance of succeeding. Next we will talk about some rules for successfully engaging in the dual arts of conflict resolution and problem solving.

Understand It's Your Problem

You know that you didn't cause the customer's problem and the pain the customer is feeling. The customer may or may not know this. But guess what, the customer doesn't really care. All the customer wants is to be heard and have the problem attended to. Fairly, promptly, and courteously.

Since you are the one who answered the bell, then you're the one who has to handle the problem. As long as a customer has a problem, you have a problem. As long as a customer has a problem, your company has a problem. As long as your customer has a problem, you run the risk of falling victim to a negative public image. And maybe its aftershock: unemployment.

Take responsibility for resolving the situation to the customer's satisfaction. You will do no more important work in a day than that.

Clearly Communicate Expectations

It's imperative that you get the expectations of your customer out in the open, as well as making clear the kind of resolution your company can offer and stay in business. Clearly, in a friendly way, vocalize your expectations and needs. As the American Airlines Representative said to Ron, "I can only help you get to where you want to go if you give me the information I need."

Sometimes, when a customer feels particularly offended by your firm, or if the customer was expecting something more than what you can offer her, merely handling the original problem may not be good enough. Try the following:

➤ Tell the customer that your company really appreciates her business.

➤ Sincerely express to her you that you deeply appreciate the injustice she has suffered.

➤ Assure her that you have made available to her every remedy the company makes available to you.

If the customer still seems unsatisfied, ask, "What else could I possibly do to show our appreciation for your being our customer?" Sometimes, all the customer wants is to let off a little more steam and get a stronger dose of empathy. Sometimes they want a letter of acknowledgement from the company president. The good news is that uncovering and then satisfying the customer's real "want" may result in a happy and relatively inexpensive solution. And keeping an otherwise lost customer.

Solve the Problem

Every day you get up, you have a certain amount of emotional energy to spend. It's your choice as to how you spend it. You can spend it resenting someone for their actions towards you, or you can spend it helping to turn bad situations into positive ones.

Resenting a situation or person wastes a whole lot of energy. In the end, you are still miserable and you haven't positively influenced the situation. That's lose-lose! By using the energy to *solve* a problem, you will feel better about the situation, and your customer will feel better. The winds of peace blow away the stress accompanying the storm (okay, we're not poets). In fact, a positive resolution often leads to a feeling of euphoria, accomplishment, and self-confidence.

Never Take It Personally

As we said earlier, the irate or upset customer doesn't know you personally. So, the customer's actions and words aren't addressed to you personally. They are conveyed to you only because you are the physical target available for venting frustration and anger. You're getting hit simply because you happen to be there.

So never take the anger, criticism, and negativity personally. This is easy to say and hard to do when you're in the thick of battle. However, if you do take it personally, then you will wind up striking back and just antagonizing the customer more. As you'd expect, this will only lead to greater pain and frustration for both the customer and you.

Dr. Scott Peck in the hugely successful book *The Road Less Traveled* talks about the concept of growth and pain. He says that pain is the natural outcome and feeling of growth and change. And it is our choice to determine what pain we want to feel in our lives. We can feel the pain of change and growth up front, or we can feel the greater pain of not realizing our goals and dreams.

In customer service, you and your organizations will grow by dealing with the pain of listening to your customers' complaints, rejections, and criticisms. Many times, this leads to the additional pain of making changes to satisfactorily meet the needs and wants of your customers. While this is painful, realize it's not as painful as having your customers leave and give their business to the competition. When that happens, it can lead to unemployment for you. Now that's what you call pain!

At Your Service

You can solve customer problems using conflict resolution skills while keeping a few basics in mind. All you have to do is:

➤ Understand that the customer problem becomes your problem, while not taking the customer's anger or frustration personally

➤ Clearly communicate expectations

➤ Solve the problem

In the context of customer service, conflict resolution is nothing more than realizing you have a responsibility to understand and deal with people's problems. It need not be complicated. Only when people make it too complex does it turn into a nightmare. Keep the tasks in perspective, the emotions at bay, and watch your customer's problems get resolved to everyone's satisfaction.

Quote, Unquote
He profits most who serves best.
—Motto for Rotary International

The bottom line: to be human means to have emotions. To give good customer service we don't deny our humanity, we stay aware of it. We make every attempt to honor the customer's humanity with acceptance, empathy, dignity, and most of all, solutions to what ails them in the first place.

Two Commandments

Because we're basing the premise of this whole book on the notion that today customer service is a cultural issue versus a departmental issue, we would be remiss if we didn't hit upon the important subject of Crisis Management Communication and the two commandments you must adhere to at all times.

Acknowledge a Crisis at the Onset

History has served up important lessons that show what happens when a company or individual tries to dodge acknowledging the existence of a crisis. Look back to the Exxon Valdez oil tanker fiasco when Exxon chief Lawrence Rawl stonewalled journalists. All that official silence did was fuel the distrust of the public and cause a backlash where customers cut their Exxon credit cards in disgust. The opposite side of the coin is the classic Johnson & Johnson (J&J) Tylenol tampering case. In that instance, where some kook poisoned bottles of Tylenol, J&J's CEO James Burke acknowledged the crisis on its first night and ordered all Tylenol off the supermarket shelves until the situation was resolved.

 Watch It!
Recognize that there is a difference between an *incident* and a *crisis*. Not every problem that has received media attention ranks as a crisis requiring top management attention and an all-out "war room" approach. Deal with incidents using appropriate measures. Overreacting may indicate that a situation is more severe than it really is and cause undue alarm. That can do as much or more damage than the problem itself.

Now which corporate executive do you think came out on top? By acknowledging the crisis, James Burke was able to get everyone moving together toward a solution. With Exxon's refusal to acknowledge the Valdez oil spill, everyone was involved in pointing the blame versus working together toward a solution. Acknowledgment up front not only appeases your customers, but also eliminates the opportunity for your competitors to spread or capitalize on false rumors. You remove the competitor's trump card. By the time Exxon came around to acknowledging what happened with that oil spill in Alaska, it had to deal with the public-relations nightmare of dispelling all of the untruths that developed lives of their own before the company could effectively deal with the real problem situation.

Do yourself a favor and acknowledge a disastrous incident up front. Then get to work making things work better. Remember, by acknowledging a disaster, we aren't suggesting that you apologize and accept blame. Acknowledging the situation is merely an act of admitting that it does exist and creates an atmosphere conducive to moving toward a solution.

Tie Your Actions to Corporate Mission

Make sure that your crisis management strategy supports your corporate mission. To see how this is vital, look back at the Sears Auto Service Fraud Cases in California and New Jersey in 1992. Sears for years had spent hundreds of millions of dollars building a reputation based on trust. And the day the company was accused of systematically overcharging for car repairs in California, their initial strategy was to duck. They even went so far as to claim the charges were politically motivated and denied any fraud. Finally, after the state of New Jersey cited all six of Sears NJ Auto Centers one week later for conducting unnecessary repairs, Sears realized it needed to change course and implement a strategy supportive of its corporate mission, which was based on trust.

But the damage was done. Sears had spent years developing a tradition of trust with its customers, but a great deal of it vanished during that crisis creating a need for major repairs to the company's reputation. When a crisis hits, ask the following:

> "Is our strategy in line with the mission our customers and employees have come to believe and expect over the years?"

If it isn't, then change strategies immediately. Otherwise, all your years of goodwill and service surely will be swallowed up by the poisoned waters of the crisis.

The Least You Need to Know

➤ Customers who feel wronged or let down by your company can get pretty emotional about it. Good service comes from getting past customer anger; focus on facts and solutions, not emotion.

➤ There are always many ways to solve every problem. Search for ways that serve your customer to her satisfaction and that your company can comfortably live with.

➤ Resolve your customer complaints using the proven techniques of problem solving and conflict resolution.

➤ Realize that your business is healthier when customers complain and have their problem dealt with quickly and to their satisfaction.

➤ Make sure that your need for protection in times of crisis does not conflict with your overall mission.

Chapter 10

Writing for Service

In This Chapter

- ➤ Determining your goal
- ➤ Stating what's in it for the customer
- ➤ Expressing your call to action
- ➤ Writing for world class service
- ➤ Knowing which phrases to avoid—at all costs
- ➤ Utilizing elements of a good "Bad News" letter

Liar, Liar, your pants are on fire! Remember this phrase from your younger days? This is how your customers feel when they read letters that are sent in the spirit of service but are not written in the spirit of service.

The toughest part of sending a written communication is that many times you will not know how your customer reacts to the message unless they are driven to action. In most cases, their action can be broken down into two classes:

- ➤ Complaints
- ➤ Orders

Results Only

Only when you hear from the customer will you know whether or not your letter accomplished its goal. Otherwise, it's the great void.

The success of a written communication isn't based on how well the letter is written, but rather on how well it is received and acted upon.

Did the letter communicate the appropriate intentions and motivate the customer to take the appropriate actions? Even a letter of thank you should lead to a referral or continuation of business down the road if written properly.

Tales from the Real World

Ron was walking back to the hotel one night after dinner with a VP of Marketing from one of his clients. During the walk, the VP complained how the sales executives didn't respond to her recent memo and how she could not understand why. She claimed it was the best memo she'd ever written and that the salespeople were lazy for not reading it.

Ron gently informed her that the memo was not successful if it wasn't read, no matter how well it was written. The bottom line is that people read letters and don't think about whether they're well-written or not; they react depending on whether or not they feel the letter's message will benefit them. They simply don't much care about the writer.

Where's Your Destination?

Stephen Covey says you should "begin with the end in mind." When you think about it, this is really the golden rule for anything you take on. Say you want to fly from New York to Miami. Would you get there if the pilot's flight plan only called for going South? Probably not! But you're virtually certain to get to a specific destination when the flight plan calls for it. Ever hear of a major airliner landing in the wrong city? Pretty rare.

Only when you have the specific destination in mind can you figure out what you are going to need to reach that destination. Anything else is just motion.

Communicate whether the goal of your letter is to:

➤ Thank your customers for their patronage

➤ Handle complaints

➤ Respond to inquiries

➤ Communicate information regarding a transaction

If you start writing your letters before figuring this out up-front, there is a strong likelihood your intended message may never be communicated. That's because, even if you eventually get to the point you want to make, you'll have thoroughly confused or bored your reader. Net result: zip.

What's in It for the Customer?

In order for your message to be heard, it must grab the customer's attention. If you don't believe that, speak to anyone in direct mail marketing and ask about the power of headlines. Sometimes you can realize a tremendous jump in response to a marketing letter by changing only one word in the headline. Of course, you need to figure out what the magic word(s) is.

The Quick Scan Test

Think about when you read your mail. Say a letter happens to survive the initial cut—you know, to the trash or not. It makes it all the way to your kitchen table and you actually open it. How long would you give it before you decide if it's anything you want to be bothered with? For most people, it's a few seconds at best.

Get Their Attention

One of the best ways to grab your customer's attention is by starting your message with your purpose, either in the headline or in the first sentence. And make sure that your purpose is of benefit and interest to the customer.

For example, if you're writing to thank someone for doing business with you, you may start with:

> "Your recent purchase really honored us. Thank you from all of us at the Franklin D. Jones Company for the confidence you placed in us."

Or:

> "Thank you for sharing your concerns with us."

Or, for example, you may be sending instructions for a product update, such as:

> "The following information will guide you through the changes necessary to update your system."

> **At Your Service**
> People are bombarded with a lot to do and no time to do it. Add to the time pressure the habit most people have of channel surfing and it's easy to understand why it's a real challenge to make an impression on someone. In fact, statistics show that you have 18–39 seconds to make a favorable impression on a decision maker when meeting face-to-face—and that the average person spends only about 9–20 seconds reviewing sales-related materials, and a brief 4–11 seconds when reviewing a print ad. That's *if* they even stop to consider the message at all! So, if you don't grab your customer's attention fast, forget it. Your communication is wasted. And that's a fact!

People for the most part like being thanked, want to receive the latest information that could impact their lives, and want to know that their comments are being heard. If you start your letters out by stating these intentions from the top, there's an excellent possibility that your letter will be read.

Another key factor in grabbing and keeping the customer's attention up-front is to avoid using the word "I." If you're using too many Is (more than one or two is too many) in your letters, then you're probably communicating a self-centered message.

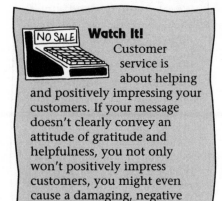

Watch It!
Customer service is about helping and positively impressing your customers. If your message doesn't clearly convey an attitude of gratitude and helpfulness, you not only won't positively impress customers, you might even cause a damaging, negative reaction.

Customers don't really care about how you feel or what you think. They want to know what you are doing to help them. Now this may seem a bit harsh, but it's the reality.

Out of the two opening sentences listed below, which do you think is more powerful?

"I enjoyed meeting you last night. I thought that what you had to say was interesting...."

"Your comments last night made quite an impact. Your thoughtful ideas came through loud and clear!"

As you can see, the first sentence is more focused on the writer, while the second sentence is clearly focused on the customer. When the message is focused on the customer, the customer *wants* to read it. And your message can only register when it's read.

Your Call to Action

Every letter you write should have a central purpose of enhancing the relationship with your customer. It could be to:

➤ Thank them for their business and to remind them to remember you when the need for your products and services arises in the future.

➤ Request that your customer spread the good word about your company to their friends and relatives.

➤ Suggest how they can get a hold of you in case of a problem.

Notice how every one of the examples suggests that the customer *do* something. Every letter you send to a customer should suggest that your customer do something. That's known as a *call to action*. A letter without a call to action is usually a wasted opportunity.

The following are some sample calls to action.

Thank You letters:

> "If there is anything else we can do, please call me direct at 201-555-5555."

> "Please call us with your future wall-covering needs. You already know us for our quality."

Responses to complaints:

> "Should you need any further assistance, please call us at 1-800-We Serve."

> "Please call us at 1-800-COMPLAIN with any other issues you feel we should be alerted to."

Survey requests:

> "By taking the time to fill out this survey and send it back to us, we will be in a stronger position to fulfill your future needs."

> "Your opinions count! Please fill out the enclosed survey and mail it back as soon as possible."

As with grabbing your customer's attention, the call to action must be centered on the customer, not you. Which of the following two sentences would be of more interest to you if you were the customer?

> "Our success depends on your comments…"

> "Your comments will allow us to serve you with products matched even better to your exact needs in the future."

The bottom line is if your call to action is not customer-centered, it won't be acted upon.

Word to the Wise

A *call to action* is simply a request for the customer to do something. It can range from asking them to call a certain number with any problems to filling out a customer survey and sending it back. No matter what type of letter you're writing, there should be a call to action that results in a stronger relationship.

At Your Service

Vanity phone numbers are great for getting a customer to remember your name, like Ron has: 1-800-423-KARR. But remember that your role is to make things easy for your customers, not hard and frustrating. Do them a favor and put the digits after the letters. There's nothing more frustrating or wasteful of time than having to translate letters into numbers. Ron lists his phone number as 1-800-423-KARR(5277).

Writing for World Class Service

Providing world class service isn't a reactive type of behavior. It is proactive. It involves taking the initiative and sending a communication to your customer telling her how important she really is to you and acknowledging her thoughts and comments. And sometimes it's merely a token of appreciation. But no matter how small the token may be, it will go a long way.

Tales from the Real World

In 1987, Ron bought a Honda Accord. Two weeks after driving home from the dealer in his new car, he received a package from Honda in California. Wondering what parts Honda forgot to put into his car, he carefully opened the package and was surprised (shocked) to find a tin of cookies inside with a note thanking him for his purchase. No car company had ever sent him cookies before, let alone a note of thanks.

Open All Hailing Frequencies

Providing world class customer service means keeping the lines of communication open. Never take your customers' feelings and gratitude for granted. If you do, they'll wonder what happened and why they never heard from you. And then, when it comes time to purchase the same kind of products again, they will return the favor by not communicating to you. In other words, they will go to the competition.

It amazes both of us how businesses spend incredible amounts of money trying to get new customers and not nearly as much as they should on trying to keep existing customers. Especially when it is a proven fact that it costs more to secure a new customer than it does to get more business from an existing one.

Look at Nordstrom, or better yet, go to Nordstrom. They know they will get a higher return on investment by mobilizing their resources to serve the customer as best as possible. Stories of customers receiving thank you cards and extraordinary service from their Nordstrom salesperson are legendary. When their customers think Nordstrom, they think world class service.

When you think about it, the success or failure of any business depends on its ability to effectively communicate with its customers: before, during, and after the purchase. Are you writing for world class service?

Phrases to Avoid

As with the words you use in verbal communications, there are phrases you should absolutely avoid in your written communication. Some of them are a complete waste of time, attention, and paper. And some of them totally detract from your overall message.

Let's take a look at some of these phrases:

It was a pleasure speaking with you! I enjoyed talking with you! What a useless line! Of course it was a pleasure speaking with the customer. And if it weren't, would you tell the customer? These are empty words with no meaning or impact unless you make specific reference to specific details from the conversation.

Please feel free to call us. Thanks. We are really glad you gave us permission to call you. Give us a break! If a customer has an issue or wants to call you for whatever reason, he is going to call, with or without your invitation. So spare these words and use the space to say, "Please call and tell us how we can serve you better."

As per our conversation.... These words are deadly to start a letter with. Remember when we discussed how your task is to capture your customer's attention in the first five seconds? These words won't do the job for you. They have no impact and waste those precious few seconds you have to grab the customer's attention. Start with some punch and get into the issue.

Common or Special

The words you use in a letter can be viewed either as commodities or precious gems. Words without impact in your message are mere commodities. They aren't even worth the proverbial dime a dozen. On the other hand, words that create impact, clearly state your message, and succeed in getting the customer to take action are precious gems indeed.

As with anything that is polished, you must take a few passes at it before you get the shine you're looking for. So on your first draft, forget about the words. Just get your thoughts on paper. Then read through your copy and strike out any superfluous words that have no impact or bearing on your overall mission. Make that letter shine!

> **At Your Service**
> Your written words represent *you*. They are a substitute for your interacting with a customer in-person. Just as you wouldn't leave the house wearing the first thing you blindly grabbed out of your closet, you shouldn't send off on paper the first words that pop into your mind. Take time to craft thoughtful, meaningful messages. If you keep "form" letters on your computer, add a personal touch to them. People believe you care when they get a clear sense that you care enough to communicate it clearly and warmly.

Elements of a Good "Bad News" Letter

Did you ever have to write a letter that you knew would not make the customer happy? Like telling the customer her suggestion is not feasible for whatever reason. Or, that the promised date of delivery is no longer valid. The point is that no matter how hard you try to give great service, sometimes things don't work out the way you want them to.

Whether or not a customer will continue to do business with you will sometimes be determined by how you communicate the bad news.

The following is some great advice on communicating bad news in the written form. The five elements were based on a model developed by nationally known communications expert Sue Hershkowitz.

The Cushion

You know the urge you have when you have to let someone down? To do it as gently as possible. That's what we call the cushion. The cushion is an opening statement that lays a soft landing for when you have to deliver the bad news. Here's a sample cushion statement:

Dear Mr. Jones:

We received your request for a full refund on the unused tickets and have carefully reviewed it in great detail.

The sample cushion statement above highlights the fact that the customer's request was important, heard, and acted upon. Whatever decision is made, the customer can at least feel somewhat better that a great deal of attention was given to his request. That's more comforting than believing your request was ignored.

The Transition

Now that you have laid down the soft blanket, it's time to position the customer for the let down. Here's a sample transition:

The tickets you purchased were based on a non-refundable fare.

The above transitional statement brings the conversation back toward the issue you are being asked to address in a manner that is not demoralizing. Telling someone "Now for the bad news" is what we would call a demoralizing statement.

The Bad News

Here it comes. Now you have to communicate the news you wish you didn't have to write about. The only way to do this successfully is to keep to the facts. Facts tend to neutralize the issue. Avoid inflammatory words and statements as discussed in Chapter 6 such as "can't," "won't," "don't," and "couldn't." These words will only turn the issue into a confrontation in which there are no winners. Here is a sample bad news statement:

Non-refundable fares are lower in cost and do have some limitations, including the unavailability of a refund for unused tickets.

All that was stated in the bad news statement above was the fact that non-refundable tickets carried some limitations, including no refunds. Nowhere was it stated that you don't, won't, can't give refunds. The neutral facts keep the emotion out of the equation.

Rebuilding the Bridge

So now you have knocked your customer down, even though you did it gently and properly. Now it's time to pick the customer up and rebuild the relationship. You must build a bridge that rises above the rejection and focuses on an acceptable solution. The following is an example of a bridge to a positive:

Please keep in mind that non-refundable tickets can be applied to any fare during the next 12 months.

The bridge above focuses on the solution that the customer can hold onto the tickets and redeem their value against a future purchase. In the end, the customer at least has some recourse.

Close with Action

As with any written communication, you want to end with a call to action and provide closure to the situation. Here's an example closing statement:

To apply this ticket to your next purchase, please call 1-000-WE-SERVE (937-3783) or your travel agent. We look forward to seeing you in the air!

In the above example, you see that the call to action was an invitation to call and make reservations on an upcoming trip using the non-refundable ticket. The letter ends with the perception that the customer and airline will continue to move forward together.

Give It a Shot

Here is a sample bad news letter with all the components strung together:

Dear Mr. Jones:

We received your request for a full refund on the unused tickets and we have carefully reviewed it in great detail. (Cushion)

The tickets you purchased were based on a non-refundable fare. (Transition) *Non-refundable fares are lower in cost and do have some limitations, including the inability to receive a refund for any unused tickets.* (Bad News) *Please keep in mind that non-refundable tickets can be applied to any fare during the next 12 months.* (Bridge Toward Acceptable Solution)

Watch It!

Any letter that smells of being a form letter immediately conveys an impersonal feeling. Now we are not saying don't use form letters. We live in the real world and know all about efficiency and productivity (we consult on those issues). When you do use form letters, at least write them in a conversational tone—not in the form of a speech that sounds like you're broadcasting to thousands of other customers. Remember that each piece of communication reaches but one customer at a time.

Likewise, every letter should come from a named *individual*. Don't sign the letter as from "the Customer Service Dept.," or "Acme Amalgamated Inc." The letter should come from a single individual. You can't communicate caring humanity by signing a letter as coming from a dehumanized, impersonal institution!

Watch It!
The New York Times has a great slogan; "All the News That's Fit to Print." When you're writing your next customer service letter, keep this variation on the *Times'* slogan in mind: "Only the news that's fit for your precious time." Your letter should only contain the words and news that's fit to print in relation to what your purpose is, what you need to communicate, and what result you want to achieve. Anything else is not fit to print.

Watch It!
After all the time you took to make sure your message was appropriate, be sure to take a few extra minutes to proofread your message. A message with grammatical and spelling errors is a clear sign that you did not value your message to the customer—and might get her to wondering what else your company skimps on.

To apply this ticket to your next purchase, please call 1-000-WE-SERVE (937-3783) or your travel agent. We look forward to seeing you in the air! Sincerely, (Call To Action and Closure)

Emphasize Empathy

When you're forced to write a letter to your customer containing bad news, write it in a way you would want to be told the news. Like everyone, you want to be given a solid reason for the negative answer. It must make sense, and be rational and non-combative. You want to feel like you have been treated fairly. You don't want to feel ignored or taken for granted. That's exactly how your customers want to feel. No one likes bad news. Even worse is feeling bad about how the news was communicated. You may not be able to control the news you have to communicate, but you can control how you communicate the news.

A Final, Personal Word

And one more thing! Regardless of the type of letter you're writing, please remember your audience is made up of fellow human beings, who, like you, want to be treated with respect—for both their feelings and their time. People want to feel that your letter is like a peer-to-peer conversation. So be conversational in your letters, not formal and not preachy.

Recall the objective of creating great experiences with your customers. When a customer receives great customer service, he feels that the solution was created just for him. It's true for your written communication as well. When a letter conveys a genuine appreciation for your customer, he or she feels satisfied and special.

Make sure your communication conveys feelings of warmth, genuine interest, and appreciation. Above all, don't hesitate to express your humanity. Your customers will recognize, appreciate, and value that more than you can imagine.

Tales from the Real World

Don worked with a large company whose customer service letters had all the charm of directives from the Soviet bureaucracy. No, those were probably friendlier. The irony? The client was a major communications company!

When writing to your customers for whatever reason, never decree, proclaim, or declare. And don't write to the unseen masses even when sending a mailing to all your customers. Similarly, if your company's customers are other organizations, remember that a company, institution, or agency can't read a letter. It's always a person at the other end.

No matter how many copies of your letter you send, only one, single person at a time will read your letter. So your written communication is always person-to-person communication and never institution-to-institution communication.

The Least You Need to Know

➤ A letter without a purpose may get delivered by the post office, but the message will surely not get through.

➤ Make sure your written communication is customer-centered, otherwise it won't get read.

➤ Every letter should have a call to action to further enhance the relationship.

➤ Delivering world-class customer service means letting your customers know how much you appreciate them and value their comments.

➤ Avoid using phrases and words that have no bearing or impact on the situation.

➤ Deliver bad news to your customer in a manner that softens the blow, provides the explanation based on facts, builds a bridge toward an acceptable solution, and moves the relationship forward.

➤ The power to succeed truly lies in communicating with customers, one person at a time.

Chapter 11

Look! It's an Instruction Manual

In This Chapter

➤ Understanding the KISS principle

➤ Reaping the benefits of clear instructions

➤ Applying the elements of good instruction manuals

➤ Choosing from the many types of electronic manuals

So you just got a raise and you go out and purchase that wall unit you've been waiting to buy. It's one of those pieces that you have to put together. You open the box expecting to see a manual of simple instructions. Instead, out falls a piece of paper with one or two crude diagrams that claim to show how to build the unit.

You stare at the diagrams in disbelief. You empty the box and climb in looking for the manual that surely got stuck in the box. Still no manual! But now you're stuck in the box.

You crawl out and once again look at the sheet with the crude diagrams and ask yourself if there's anything you're missing, like your sanity. You start questioning your level of intelligence as you realize you have no clue as to what the diagrams are telling you. You resort to calling a neighbor or friend and having to admit that you are really stupid and forced to ask if he or she—or better yet, their 12-year-old genius—could come over and do what appears to be a simple job. Does this sound familiar?

Watch It!
Your company may manufacture products overseas in a developing nation, but that doesn't mean your instructions need to be written there. We are absolutely baffled why companies insist on selling products with instructions written by someone who obviously doesn't speak the language they're writing in. A typical example goes something like this:

"Remove switch or put to on flat surfer. CAUTION! If case you finding switch or not, go now to on surfer place! Under no circumcisions touch there or hot may result. You am warn!"

Puh-lease don't force anyone to waste time trying to translate confusing, cumbersome, or crazy instructions!

Of course, if you ever found yourself in this situation, you weren't the stupid one. The company that provided the instructions really let you down.

Instructions are meant to make the job easy for the person installing, setting up, or using a product or service. They should not be an IQ or stress test.

When instructions confuse more than help, the customer immediately starts to resent the supplier. Buyer's remorse—that nagging doubt that maybe the purchase wasn't such a good idea after all—haunts most people anyway. Don't do anything to increase this potentially deadly feeling, such as make your customer feel like a complete fool.

Bad instructions can trigger a negative *Instant of Absolute Judgment* that we talked about in Chapter 4. Why lose a customer forever over a piece of paper?

Hello from Everyone in the Box

Instructions are probably the first contact many of your customers have with your products. They can shape a lasting first impression. Yet, as important as this communication is, instructions are too often taken for granted as nothing more than a necessary evil. That's a big mistake!

Instructions contribute greatly to a customer's perception of your product quality. When instructions are done well, you can vastly decrease the number of irate customers that your support personnel will have to deal with. Poorly written instructions, on the other hand, increase both the frustration levels of your customers and your costs to field their complaints.

Let's take a look at how you can use well-designed instruction manuals to increase customer satisfaction, and decrease both your support costs and merchandise returns.

The KISS Principle

If you want to make your customers happy, write your instructions with the KISS Principle in mind. KISS stands for Keep It Sweet and Simple. For instructions, like all other customer service communication, that means:

➤ Be clear
➤ Be helpful
➤ Be friendly

120

No Smarty-Pants

Just as poorly written or incomplete instruction manuals frustrate customers, the opposite can be true. Overly complex or detailed instructions can be just as annoying. Instructions aren't an excuse for your company to show off its intelligence, engineering prowess, or breadth of knowledge.

An instruction manual (video, CD-ROM, or any other media containing instructions) should be designed to take your company's collective intelligence and use it to simplify instructions to where the average person can easily understand what they have to do in order to achieve satisfactory performance from your product.

Tales from the Real World

A manufacturer of store displays for dairy cases developed an instructional video for $15,000. The developers were certain that the information was simple and easy to follow, even for the young store employees who were expected to put them together. After countless phone calls from frustrated store managers and a great deal of money wasted on needless customer support, a second video was developed, further simplifying the process. The second video cost an additional $24,000.

It took two videos at a cost of $39,000 and a lot of frustration on all sides before everyone was happy. If the first video had been done properly for $24,000, can you imagine how much money and frustration the manufacturer would have saved for its customers and itself?

What are your instructions costing you?

Kid-Proofing

In the movie *Big*, Tom Hanks played a boy transformed into an adult body. He had an adult's body and child's mind. He was discovered by a toy company as being a prodigy and given an executive position. One of his ideas was to put all new toys through a vigorous testing system. The system involved unleashing a crowd of children who used and literally abused the toys.

The adults were able to figure out from the kids' behavior if the toys were of interest and how well they stood up to child's play. Inspired, huh?

At Your Service

Create a manual that anyone who uses your product or service can read and understand. *Test* your manual for ease of understanding before you print thousands of copies. Make sure it satisfies all levels of intelligence and technical proficiencies represented in your market.

Watch It!
You're going to spend time making sure your customers know how to use your products and services. It will cost you less in time and money if you put the effort into the development of user-friendly instructions. Otherwise you're guaranteed to spend more in time and money following up on the complaints later on.

Consider the same kind of idea for your instruction manuals. Before you print your manual, give a copy of it with the product to a bunch of 8th graders and see how well they can follow the instructions for putting the product together and using it. If they're having difficulty following the instructions, consider them to be unclear or too difficult to understand. The instructions, not the kids!

Dumbing Down?

If you're concerned that simplified instructions may be too simplistic for some of your sophisticated customers, remember that the goal of this game is to achieve 100 percent satisfaction, even from those who aren't as quick in learning your products as others. Besides, your wise guy customers get a chance to feel intellectually superior when reading simple instructions. Hey, you're building their self-esteem. Good job!

Get It in Writing

The key to writing clear and easy directions and supplying easy to follow diagrams lies in the hands of your technical writers and artists. Being able to simplify technical information into an easy-to-understand form—meaning both the writing and the artwork of the form—is an art in itself. Make sure you surround yourself with qualified technical writers and artists. Ideally, these writers and artists shouldn't be involved with product creation. That would put them too close to the situation to view it.

Watch It!
Not everyone processes information in the same way. Each of our brains is wired differently. Some people have difficulty following word instructions even when they're written very clearly. Others, including Don, have difficulty following the most elegant drawings. Good instruction manuals accommodate everyone's comprehension style by using both clear words and pictures to communicate the information.

Like your customer, your writers and artists need to approach it from the outside in order to succeed in writing a manual that outsiders can relate to. There is a strong possibility of jeopardizing the huge amount of money you have invested in the overall development of your product or service by not employing the right artists and writers. Remember, a picture can be worth a thousand words.

A whole discipline has evolved for taking technical information and making it approachable for the non-technical folks in the world—most people! Find freelance writers and artists who understand your technical jargon and processes but who communicate for the rest of us. Find them in the phone directory under "writing services" and "graphic designers." Or you can contact the International Association of Business Communicators (see Appendix A) for a list of people you might want to contact. Good technical communication specialists are worth every penny you pay them.

Otherwise, you might have a Nobel winning piece of scientific literature on your hands, but a warehouse full of product that no customer can understand how to use.

Once the instructions have been developed, test them out on people representative of your market. If these people have no problems following the instructions, you're all set. If there are problems, identify them and redo the instructions. Then test again. Get it right before going to market to save you and your customers many hours of frustration later.

Benefits of Clear Instructions

Let's take just a moment to recap why good, clear instructions are worth the investment of time and money.

Avoiding Buyer Remorse

Poor and unclear instructions lead to a severe case of buyer's remorse. Feelings of inadequacy, re-thinking the need for the product, or refusing to go through a lot of pain struggling with unclear instructions might lead to the return of merchandise. That increases your costs and decreases your profits.

Developing Advocates

Poor and unclear instructions lead to the depreciation of good will in the minds of your customers. Their willingness to talk about your products and services in glowing terms decrease with every minute of frustration. Clear and easy instructions prevent any of this from happening. In fact, if the instructions are remarkably simple and easy, they might go out of their way to tell others.

Unclogging Support Lines

Watch It!
Some manufacturers try to break instructions into many pieces. Open the box and about 20 pieces of paper come falling out. There's the red one, the blue one, the yellow one.... The product maker is trying to save time and money by not printing an up-to-date manual. But all those different sheets flying all over the place only add to customer confusion and increase the possibility of overlooking or misplacing important information. If time pressures keep you from printing a consolidated set of instructions, invest in a STAPLER and assemble all the pieces into one unit so that your customer can at least keep all those pieces together.

Poor and unclear instructions lead to a severe case of clogged support lines. If the situation is dire, you may be forced to add support personnel and phone lines, all of which will cost you more than if you spent a fraction of that money and time simplifying your instructions from the beginning.

Understandable and truly useful instructions are as important as any other component in your customer service program in helping to deliver truly great service.

Elements of Good Instruction Manuals

There are several types of instruction manuals you can insert into your packaging. Computer products, for instance, often come with a fast start-up guide as well as a complete manual of instructions, and instructions that are loaded on to the customer's computer. If your product or service isn't as complicated as a computer system, then you can probably get by with one instruction manual.

As with anything else, there is a format you can use to write clear and concise instruction materials.

Depending on your product or service, you may not need to include all of the elements we describe below in the instruction manual. That decision should be based on the answer to this question:

> ➤ From the instructions alone, do your customers easily know how to use your products?

If the answer is no, you either must simplify what you have or add more instructions.

Tales from the Real World

Ron had a laptop computer made by a top computer manufacturer. When he developed a problem with his battery, he looked on the front and back for a support number. No number. Believing there had to be a number somewhere in the unit's 400-page manual, he spent 20 minutes leafing through the entire publication. Incredulously, he still found no number. Ron even called 800 directory assistance only to find out that no toll-free number was listed. He couldn't figure out why the company's phone number was considered to be top secret. But what he did figure out was when it came time to buy a new system he was going to buy it from another company.

On the flip side, when Don bought a new computer system, he was delighted to see the customer support number printed clearly on the inside flap of the box. Before he even finished opening the box, he was impressed with IBM's obvious commitment to supporting their product.

Accessible customer support is as important a component as anything you pack into a box and ship to a customer.

Support Services

In the first few pages, you should clearly point out where your customer can go or call if she needs additional help. People always look to the front or back of the book for this information. It is our recommendation that you put it in the front. Make sure you provide the phone numbers for all locations worldwide.

If you also provide support via the Web and Internet, supply your e-mail and site addresses. Be sure you provide all the steps one needs to reach your site. Don't take it for granted that your customers know all the steps. When you assume things, it is a good bet that your manual is starting to get complicated.

By the way, having a Web site for customers to reach you is increasingly a good service strategy, especially if you serve technology-savvy customers who expect instant answers to their questions. We discuss Web sites and other service technology in much greater detail in Part 5 of this book.

Table of Contents

The Table of Contents should clearly list all the parts and sections of the manual and what topics are covered in each section. Besides describing how to use your product or service, the first sections should describe all of the parts one should have received in order to properly use the product. If it is a system, all of the knobs, switches, and parts should be identified. If it is a service, then have a section that describes all of the tools one needs to use the service. For instance, if you're providing an online service, you probably want to list the system requirements for optimal performance, such as: Pentium processor, 12MB of RAM, 28.8 modem, and so on.

Troubleshooting

In the back of the manual, you should list the common types of problems one may encounter using your service along with the possible reasons and remedies. This list will save you incredible time and money by reducing the number of support calls to your help line. (Each line gives examples for different types of services and products.)

Sample Troubleshooting Listing

Problem	Possible Solutions
Machine doesn't turn on	Check to see if power cable is properly connected
No dial tone	Check to see that phone jack is properly connected

continues

continued

Problem	Possible Solutions
Computer battery loses its charge too fast	Manually bleed your computer battery (press function and F1 keys at same time) of current charge and re-charge the battery. When using the battery, always drain it completely before re-charging. If you still have problems, there might be a problem with your system board. Call dealer for further assistance.
Can't get through to reservation lines for tickets	Peak time for reservations are Monday–Friday, 10:00am to 2:00pm. If you are calling during these times, try to call later in the day if possible. Order your tickets at our Web site. Simply get online and type **www.ticketsforyounow.com**. There is no wait ordering tickets this way. Call your travel agent and let them earn their money.

To identify which problems might commonly occur, simply check your existing complaint call log. It will give you this information.

Index

The index should list every topic, word, title, and issue one can possibly have a question about. The index is the vehicle for someone to quickly locate the exact page where the subject they are searching for is located.

Make sure you test your index before you print your instruction manuals and ship them out. Sometimes professional indexers have never used your product—let alone had a problem with it that would require using the index. In addition, many people turning to the index to find something will look for different words to describe it. (One looks for "connection," another looks for "dial up," and another looks for "access.") Testing the index before publishing it should help everyone find all the good information that you've taken the time and trouble to assemble.

Warranty Info

All warranty information, exchanges, and return policies should be documented and listed in the manual. Addresses and all items of proof required should also be listed. Any regulatory statements that apply, cautions, and warnings should also be spelled out.

Glossary

It's always best to include a glossary at the end defining all terms and words relevant to your product or service. There's one in this book!

While you're not in the business of publishing dictionaries, you are in the business of making sure your customer completely understands everything there is to know about how to use your products and services. Do yourself a favor; define even the words that are simple to you. Remember, your reader may not find them to be that simple.

Electronic Manuals

In today's high-tech world, instruction manuals come in all forms. They aren't limited to printed media. Let's take a look.

Video

Video is a great media source for providing complex instructions. Printed diagrams can only show you pictures of before and after. Video can visually show you how to carry out the instruction. Video is a great tool for showing how to build things, put parts together, and perform certain techniques. For example, pharmaceutical and medical firms use videos a lot to show how their products work. Sporting goods manufacturers use videos to show their products in action, and some software makers do the same thing. Don's Jeep came with a video explaining how to use the anti-lock braking system; it really helped to make the point that ABS brakes work differently than conventional brakes.

Video is obviously more costly to produce than printed material. Depending on your internal resources and the type of video you shoot (ranging from studio shots to location filming), you can plan on budgeting anywhere from $1,000 to $10,000 per minute of finished footage. For budget purposes, you need to add your packaging and duplication costs, which vary depending on the length of your final program and the number of copies you make.

Watch It!
Video is great for telling a story or describing a process. But one major drawback with video in meeting a customer's expectation for answers fast is that it's linear. By linear, we mean that you must start at the beginning and go through all of the information until you hit the point that's of interest to you. Yes, you can fast-forward the video. But you still need to know where to stop. It isn't a clean method for people to quickly go to their points of interest.

CD-ROM

CD-ROM is commonly being used to help customers find and access certain information quickly. It can provide complex explanations and demonstrations in text as well as audio, animations, and even real action video. It's truly interactive. While videotape is linear, CD-ROM let's you bypass the information you don't want by allowing you to point and click to access the areas that interest you. CD-ROM has tremendous room to put lots and lots of data on, including pictures, videos, sound, and diagrams.

Here are some examples of how CD-ROM is used today in service:

➤ Auto Parts dealers looking up specs on parts

➤ Aviation repair personnel reviewing procedures

➤ Operation guidelines for complex mail machines, manufacturing equipment, electronic equipment, medical equipment, etc.

➤ Training companies supplying updates and continuing education courses

Watch It!
Clearly communicating instructions is not the only thing you have to worry about. You need to be sure the medium you use is one that your customer has access to and finds easy to use. Putting instructions on diskettes is useless if your customers do not have easy access to computers. Likewise, instructions on CD-ROM are worthless to a computer owner without a CD drive.

The list goes on and on. Look at your product or service. If it would take enormous amounts of disk space to adequately provide all of the information necessary (video, text, graphics, and sound), then it is a good candidate for CD-ROM.

CD-ROM's are cheap to duplicate but not cheap to produce. What we mean by that is that the actual cost of the physical disc can be about the same as a gourmet cup of coffee. But producing the content on that disc can cost as much or more as a gourmet coffee store.

From the simplest form involving text only to the more complicated formats, you can easily spend between $5,000 and $100,000 and up on development of the CD-ROM. Again, you need to add the cost of packaging and duplication to arrive at your total costs. Your decision to produce a CD-ROM will be partly based on the value of your products and services, the size of your potential customer base, and the intricacies of the instructions.

Audio Cassettes

Audio cassettes are a great tool for telling a story or giving instructions. They can be transported easily and listened to in remote places through portable cassette players. They cost far less to produce than videos. But they are also more limiting by not incorporating visuals. Some people cannot process information without visually seeing it. Still, you can create a hybrid by including a good printed piece to accompany the audio tape.

Diskette

Diskettes are great tools to disperse large amounts of text information. They are limited in that even with today's data compression techniques—there is not much capacity for color graphics and certainly not enough space to hold video. Disks are great for instructions and answers to frequently asked questions. They also serve as great tools for product and price updates.

They are cheap to produce. You can produce at will, even in small quantities, and save on printing and paper costs. Let's say one 1.44 MB diskette costs you a dollar and holds all the information your customer really needs. To print the pages in full color would cost you hundreds if not thousands of more dollars (especially in small quantities).

Disks offer your customers the option of printing only the pages that contain the information they need in print, and taking considerably less storage space than big paper manuals.

We do not suggest that you completely replace your printed manuals with diskettes. But diskettes certainly are great additions and possible replacements for massive print documents.

Tales from the Real World

A software developer was sending out a diskette to its customers, announcing new capabilities. On the face of the diskette was a set of instructions on how to use it. After giving it out to a few people, several complaints were received from people who couldn't figure out the instructions. The developers had the opinion that if the customer didn't know how to use it, then he didn't deserve it!

Fortunately, the president of the company knew if the customer didn't understand it, he would have no business in the future. He immediately inserted two additional steps into the instructions on the diskette label. These two new simple instructions also meant having to change the diskettes at some expense. Still, the greater acceptance in the marketplace far outweighed the inconvenience the company faced in implementing the changes.

Just because someone uses a computer doesn't mean he or she is a technical genius. We know. Many computers today are easier to use than they've ever been. But they can still be awfully complex and frustrating.

If you're using diskettes or other high-tech media, make sure you follow the same set of ground rules you use for writing printed manuals. Keep it sweet and simple!

Here's Our KISS

We've been saying keep your instructions sweet and simple and you will have little if any problems with customers not knowing how to use your products and services. Now, let's be honest. Just because you do this, it doesn't mean you won't get calls from customers who still don't know what to do.

Watch It!
If you start using a new technology to provide a faster and more efficient way of presenting instructions, remember to spell out the benefits to the customer for trying the new method. And give them simple, easy-to-follow steps of how they should proceed.

The bottom line to giving clear and concise instructions is: give your customers what they need and in a medium they want to use.

The volume of support calls to your help line can be directly correlated to the simplicity of your operating instructions. You really do have control over how many calls of assistance you will get. Giving good instructions is a classic example of where customer service today is a company-wide issue, not just a departmental responsibility. So go ahead, KISS your customer! (You know what we mean if you really read this chapter!)

The Least You Need to Know

➤ Provide your customers with clear and easy instructions to follow. Keep them sweet and simple.

➤ If you apply the KISS Principle, you will see your support costs decrease, customer satisfaction increase, and greater referrals from happy customers.

➤ Proper instruction manuals should include everything there is to know about your product and service. They should make it easy for your customers to quickly locate certain pieces of information.

➤ Instruction manuals today come in all types of electronic medium, including video, diskette, CD-ROM, and audio cassette. Select the electronic type that adequately supports your product and service.

Part 3
So, How Am I Doing?

To create Personally Pleasing Memorable Interactions (PPMIs) on a consistent basis, you need to be in touch with your customers—and stay in touch with them. You need to know their needs and preferences as well as or better than they do!

And that means getting feedback from your customers by asking them directly, observing them closely, and understanding them intimately.

How do you read customer minds? The next few chapters will give you some real world methods for delivering The Service Difference by practically becoming telepathic. Whether it be through their complaints, the questions they ask you, or surveys you take of them—you'll see how to get the inside scoop on providing continually better service.

YOU STINK STINK, STINK!!

Chapter 12

Complain, Complain, Complain

In This Chapter

➤ Learning valuable information from your complaining customers

➤ Reaping the benefits of complaining customers

➤ Establishing guarantees and warranties

➤ Turning complainers into champions

➤ Doing business for the long haul

The nerve of Mrs. Smith asking you for a refund. How dare she claim your product did not satisfy her needs. It must be her fault she didn't get any good use out of it. If she wants her money back, she's crazy. Once she bought it, she owns it.

Replies you might give Mrs. Smith:

Don't expect us to take it back. What? You expect us to turn around and resell this? Not on your life! It's unethical. Once you open the package, it's useless to us. It's yours forever.

If you're thinking of exchanging the product, forget it. It's not our fault you made the wrong decision. Hey, we just make and sell the products. We're not mind readers. You should know what you want.

What did you ask me? Do I stand behind my products? Of course I do. Every time I sell something, I stand behind it as I package it and watch it walk out of the place.

You know our refund policy is for only 30 days. Today is the 31st day. You don't qualify. (Did you ever have the feeling that some products were made with a built-in timer to fail on the day after the warranty is over?)

What's going on here? Well, clearly, Mrs. Smith is not having a good day. And there is a very good possibility that you've heard this story at least once in your life as a customer. How did you feel? Did you feel appreciated by the vendor? Or did you feel taken? After telling you to go and take a hike, did you feel an urge to be loyal to the vendor or did you feel the need for rapid and painful revenge?

Obviously, you want your customers thinking loyalty, not revenge. At the same time, you must be careful that in satisfying the customer you don't go broke by giving away the business. In this chapter, we're going to look at the value a complaining customer can bring to your organization. We'll also show you the methods you can use to deal with the complainers and turn them into loyal and satisfied customers.

Complaining Customers Are the Best

Studies show that most dissatisfied customers don't complain. They would rather stay silent and take their business elsewhere when there's something they don't like about your product or service. After all, there's a great deal of effort required to lodge a complaint.

To complain is a hassle. You need to take the time to determine who should hear your complaint, and then you need to communicate the complaint by writing a letter or making a phone call. Most people feel it isn't worth the trouble to go through this effort. After all, there are plenty of vendors out there who offer the same type of products and services. So most of your unhappy customers simply lodge their complaints by going to your competition.

> **Quote, Unquote**
> Some of our best service innovations evolved out of customer complaints. These innovations contributed to Hertz winning the J.D. Power Award for Car Rental Customer Satisfaction in 1997.
> —Bob Bailey, Sr. VP Hertz

This is why you must treat the people who do take the time and make the effort to complain as valuable customers. If one customer is complaining, there's a strong possibility that at least 20 other customers feel the same way but didn't bother to speak-up about it. It's the complainers who provide you with tips about what problems are brewing out there in the land where your customers use your product.

Complaints provide the early warning signals that allow you to fix problems you may not even know existed, and prevent your competition from stealing your customers. At the same time, some complaints may have nothing to do with defects. They may relate to customer expectations of your product; the unhappy customer may be communicating what she really wants from your product. Those kinds of complaints can give your product development efforts—and then your sales—a real boost. When you think about complaining customers in this light, you tend to have a totally different image about them than a bunch of whining malcontents.

For example, when it came to providing shuttle bus service at the airports, Hertz's focus was on driver training to deliver customer service: teaching drivers how to help with luggage, make correct announcements in sequence, and so on. The drivers were doing a good job. What Hertz wasn't initially aware of was that the most important thing to customers in busing service was bus frequency.

The company received complaints from people who felt like they were waiting for 15 minutes, when in fact the average wait was no more than 7–10 minutes. From these complaints, Hertz set a standard of 5 minutes maximum wait, when in most cases the wait now is between 2 and 3 minutes. To deliver this service, Hertz had to first listen to its unhappy customers and then invest a huge sum of capital on additional buses and drivers to please them.

> **Watch It!**
> You may receive a small number of complaints about a given issue. But if the small number of complaints come from your largest, most important customers (remember the 80/20 rule from Chapter 5), you need to respond. Volume alone doesn't always tell the whole story. Who's complaining can be more important than the number of complaints.

Profiting from Complaints

For Hertz, business people represent their biggest market for car rentals and their biggest priority is speed. What Hertz found out from customer complaints was that it excelled in speed of service in picking up the car, but failed in speed of service in dropping off the car. Business people didn't have time to go inside to a counter and wait in line to turn in their cars. It would have been cost prohibitive for Hertz to staff the counters appropriately to limit the desired wait to less than a couple of minutes.

Hertz came up with their Instant Return solution. With Instant Return, the moment you pull into the Hertz lot, an attendant punches the vehicle identification number on the windshield into a hand held wireless computer hooked up to a mainframe computer. By the time the customer gets out of the car, to many people's amazement, he or she is greeted by name. Only two questions need to be answered: how many miles did you drive? Did you buy any gas?

After the information is entered into the portable computer/transmitter, it prints out the receipt. The close-out transaction is complete in less than a minute, versus up to 10 minutes in line. The system ensures the customer does not miss his plane and provides Hertz with estimated labor savings of 20 percent. A classic win-win situation evolving from customer complaints.

The examples in the Hertz story did not come about by accident. Hertz had to do more than just answer the phone when the complaints came in. It had to truly hear the customer and turn those complaints into profitable value-added services guaranteed to make its customers happy. Let's take a look at the steps you can take to turn your customer complaints into profits.

Beyond Listening

Besides listening to a complaint, it's imperative that you ask the customer what the expectations are for an "acceptable level of service." Without this information, you won't be in a position to adequately solve your customers' complaints.

Determine the Scope of the Problem

Using the general rule that about 1 out of 20 unhappy customers will complain, keep track of all complaints. If 100 people make the same complaint, there is a good possibility that *2,000* people feel the same way.

Watch It!
Dealing with complaints on a piecemeal basis and not on a cumulative basis is a recipe for disaster. One complaint on an issue is an inconvenience. Several complaints on the same issue are the tell-tale signs of a major problem. Don't mistake a major problem for being an inconvenience. Keep a record of the number of complaints you receive on a particular issue. The numbers can only tell you a story when you're collecting them and paying attention to them.

If the number of complaints on a single issue represents a sizeable portion of your market, you need to take action. If an insignificant percentage of the market complains about something, then you may decide not to take any action at all. It could be that the complaints came from a section of the market that you aren't capable of or looking to service.

Developing Actions

When the number of complaints about some aspect of your product or service is significant, you need to identify actions to address the issue. The simple process to follow is:

1. Identify the desired results.
2. Evaluate your current results. (The difference between 1 and 2 represents the ground you need to make up in providing a solution.)
3. Create a plan to improve performance to satisfy and delight your customers.

Utilize All of Your Resources

Solving complaints doesn't always center on throwing more bodies and money into the battle. As Hertz found out in its close-out transaction procedures, that would have been too cost prohibitive, and perhaps even less desirable than the technology-based solution it created.

Your goal is to achieve maximum customer satisfaction and profitability. Evaluate every resource in your arsenal and at your disposal. Today, technology is an excellent source of achieving efficiencies with good returns on investment. Keep in mind that technology still requires an appropriate balance of high tech and high touch. World Class Service will always involve the appropriate touch of human interaction. Hand-held computers in a parking lot are useless without the right people implementing the transaction between the customer and the computer.

Turn Your Solution into a Sales and Marketing Tool

Now that you have increased your level of customer satisfaction, why not shout it out to the rest of the world? Don't be shy. Turn your great customer service into a tremendous marketing tool. Tell the public how you satisfy your customers and what they can expect from doing business with you. Your customers want to hear this information. In many cases, it can represent a value-added benefit that separates you from the competition. Excellent customer service really does play a vital role in the marketing approach of a company. It's no longer a departmental issue. It's a company issue.

Guarantees and Warranties

Remember watching those commercials on TV that proclaimed "Money Back Guarantee"? You might have thought there was something wrong with the vendor. After all, who would be so foolish as to put themselves at risk and offer a money back guarantee?

Well, companies that offer a money back guarantee tend to be some of the most successful companies out there. And it's not because their products are so superior. Don't get us wrong. Most of them have quality products! But what's important here is not only their quality, but also their willingness to stand behind their quality. These companies have figured out that a very small percentage of people really do ask for their money back (unless the product is truly not working as promised). So their perceived risk in offering this guarantee is far outweighed by the extra business it brings into the house.

Think about when you purchase something. Do you feel a little bit more secure if the product you are purchasing is backed by a money back guarantee? You bet you do!

At Your Service
Guarantees eliminate customer risk, which can be a barrier to customers trying your product. Guarantees also can help distinguish your company's claims of quality from other competitors. Plus, they provide you with an opportunity to identify your weak links: a product that fails to deliver as expected is more likely to come to your attention when the customer seeks warranty service than if the customer simply replaces your product with one from a competitor.

137

Tales from the Real World

A few years ago, Don bought a Compaq personal computer because of its reputation for reliability—backed by a three-year warranty. Two years and nine months into the warranty, the computer's motherboard—the real brains in the box—failed. A call to a toll-free 800 number found a helpful technician who recommended taking the computer to any one of several local authorized service centers for an immediate, free replacement of this very expensive part. The computer went into the service center at Office Depot at 10:30 on a Sunday morning and was back in operation, good as new, Wednesday afternoon. No hassles. No fits. No charge. Cool!

Watch It!

Whatever your policies are on guarantees and warranties, make sure they're clearly spelled out in legible print. Put them in your instruction manuals, on receipts, etc. Don't leave any room for confusion, which can lead to disputes and negative impressions.

Word to the Wise

According to our friends at Oxford University Press, a *guaranty* is a formal promise or assurance that a promise will be fulfilled or that something is of a special quality and durability. A *warranty* often involves accepting responsibility for defects or liability for repairs needed over a specified period of time.

Other traditional guarantees and warranties include:

Limited Time Refunds—Some companies will provide you with a full refund if the product is returned in a specified period of time with a receipt. Some companies, like Nordstrom, will not let a lost receipt interfere with providing satisfaction to a customer.

Exchanges and Credits—Some vendors will offer additional guarantees after the initial period for refunds has expired. These guarantees are in the form of exchanges or credit for an extended period of time. L.L. Bean offers guaranteed satisfaction without regard for how long you owned the product.

Limited Warranties—Some companies provide extended warranties for defects over a period or lifetime of a product. Usually, these warranties aren't valid for damage caused by wear and tear beyond "normal" circumstances (such as using your passenger car as a delivery vehicle). Other limited warranties will provide protection for certain parts and services, but not for day-to-day service. An example is in the car industry. Major repairs like transmission work may be covered in the first three years, whereas oil changes and other routine maintenance are considered normal operating expenses and are the responsibilities of the customer.

But even here, some dealers are expanding warranty coverage to include routine maintenance (Don's Toyota Camry came with a free oil change every 7,000 miles from the dealer). And some car manufacturers are trying to eliminate routine maintenance all together. Some Chevrolet models go 100,000 miles without a tune-up. And virtually all car batteries no longer require frequent checks on the water level. The goal: create customer satisfaction and loyalty.

Unlimited Warranties—Some companies, like Hammacher Schlemmer, a retailer "offering the best, the only, and the unexpected for over 149 years," value relationships with their customers too much to argue with them about whether or not the problem was related to normal wear and tear. They will provide refunds and exchanges with no questions asked at any time. They feel the costs involved in this strategy are far outweighed by the loyalty developed with their customers.

Transform Your Complainers into Referral Champions

You can view your customers who complain as being a nuisance, or you can view them as potential champions of your long-term success. Turning complaints into positive experiences is a sure-fire way of developing loyal customers who are guaranteed to spread the word. Studies show that customers who complain and receive fast, satisfactory resolution to their complaint are actually *more* likely to be repeat buyers than customers who had no problem with the product in the first place!

When you offend a customer, you need to implement a turn-around experience. One way is through giving something beyond a strict one-for-one exchange of products. The give-aways you're willing to part with in order to promote goodwill with your customers in times of conflict might be called Turn-Around Promotions.

In addition to Turn-Around Promotions—which always take place after you've disappointed a customer, you can generate Goodwill Promotions with your customers by using a variety of promotions to show appreciation for your customers' business on an ongoing basis. This helps foster a general sense of appreciation for your customer's business and makes it much easier for her to forgive you when you do occasionally disappoint (as you inevitably will). Let's take a look at some examples of both types of goodwill-generating promotional gestures:

> **Word to the Wise**
>
> *Goodwill Promotions* involve gestures on your part—rewarding customers for their patronage, like offering 6 shirts for the price of 5 shirts. *Turn-Around Promotions* involve giving a peace offering to help make up and compensate for any inconvenience.

➤ **Volume Rebates**—You can offer customers rebates or price discounts in exchange for certain amounts of business. Examples include Preferred Customer discount cards, frequent flyer bonus miles, the cash-back feature of the Discover credit card.

➤ **Goodwill Freebies**—This is all the free stuff you offer customers in return for their patronage. A free after dinner drink at your favorite restaurant is an example.

➤ **Recovery Freebies**—Offering services or products for free in addition to replacing those that were damaged to begin with.

➤ **Recovery Interaction Personally**—Calling someone to handle and solve a complaint.

➤ **Goodwill Interaction**—Writing or calling your customers to tell them how much you appreciate their business—not because they have a problem, but because you really do appreciate their business.

➤ **Goodwill Follow-up**—Regularly scheduled calls to make sure your customer is satisfied with his purchase.

> **Quote, Unquote**
> We don't feel we're particularly good at or are experts in customer service. We'd rather practice it than talk about it. We know that good customer service is a fluid situation and that it can change the moment a customer has a negative experience. We are vigilant in doing what it takes to avoid this from happening.
> —Nordstrom Spokesperson

➤ **Recovery Follow-up**—Calling a customer to see if the solution provided to a previous complaint is satisfactory to the customer.

➤ **Goodwill Inclusions**—Including, at no charge, extra costs such as shipping and handling when the customer places a large order.

➤ **Recovery Inclusions**—Paying the costs of overnight delivery when the product didn't arrive on-time as promised.

As you can see, Goodwill Promotions are good marketing tools. The Turn-Around Promotions transform your complaining customers into champions who will freely promote your business and excellent service to their colleagues, friends, and family. While both of these types of promotions are important, which one do you think carries greater impact?

The True Cost of Service

You have a great product. You've trained your personnel to be warm and cordial. You've given them all the systems and processes to use to help satisfy customers. With all of this support, why is it that some customers are still not satisfied?

Well, some people are never satisfied. But if you're failing to please many of your unhappy customers, it likely has to do with the limitations of your support system. In order to satisfy a disgruntled customer, does your staff have to get approval on every action that would please a customer?

It's very clear that some of the best service companies create a responsive, customer-pleasing system by empowering their line employees to satisfactorily resolve customer issues. From the bellhop at a Marriott hotel to the sales clerk at a Nordstrom store to the salesperson at an industrial equipment company: responsive service comes from responsible service people.

The Cost of Responsibility

There's a legitimate question about how much authority you should give employees in making final decisions on service. After all, you don't want to give away the store, do you?

The idea is to construct a system that doesn't restrain or discourage employees from handling situations immediately. The trick is designing a system that empowers employees to do what they feel is right at the time while being held accountable for their actions.

Some organizations authorize their employees to exercise their judgment up to a certain dollar limit. For example, giving a customer a refund or credit up to, say, $500 or $1,500 without another approval.

Some retail stores pay their sales clerks commissions and/or bonuses. This type of pay motivates the sales clerks to do whatever they can to make a customer happy and want to come back. While at the beginning they may sacrifice some commissions by incurring a charge back for returns, they ultimately will receive far greater commissions from the future business a satisfied customer is likely to bring both directly and indirectly through referrals.

Both of us believe there needs to be some fiscal restraint and responsibility in an organization. You need to place reasonable fiscal limits on your trust. The fine balance is between your cost and the risk of having a customer feel they were improperly treated—never to spend another cent with you.

To determine whether or not your current system of empowering employees to handle complaints is adequate for your business, please take a moment to answer the questions that follow.

> **Quote, Unquote**
> We empower employees to do what it takes to satisfy their customers without management approval. It's important that the customer is happy. Only then will the customer keep coming back and continue to buy more from us. Returns do alter department sales revenues and commissions, but salespeople look at the total picture vs. the short-sighted viewpoint for maximum return. As for training our employees on how to satisfy our customers, we concentrate more on hiring nice people and getting out of their way.
> —Nordstrom's Spokesperson

Are You Worthy?

Ask yourself the following questions to determine the worthiness of your current service process:

1. To handle complaints and make exceptions, do your service personnel need management approval? ___ Yes ___ No

2. If you answered yes to Question 1, does the process for management approval slow down the process for satisfying your customers? ___ Yes ___ No

141

At Your Service
You can tell customers anything you want to. You can tell them how much you appreciate their business. How their time is valuable and how your intention is to do whatever you can to make them happy. Say whatever you want. But it's your actions that count. Your customers will only hear and believe what you have to say through your actions. Make sure your actions support your mission and promise to the customer.

3. If you answered yes to Question 2, then the most important question of all is: Does your service process of gaining management approval negatively affect your overall mission and promise to your customers?
___ Yes ___ No

If you answered yes to Question 3, then you must re-evaluate your current system and make appropriate changes. You'll find some helpful ideas in Chapters 15 and 19.

You can be bold and rely on human nature to make the right calls in resolving customer conflicts. You can also help by educating your employees in how to respond and the various ways they can respond to create a PPMI without giving away the company. Only you can decide how much freedom you want to give your employees to make things right for the customers. Just make sure your process doesn't restrain your employees from carrying out your overall mission and promise to the marketplace.

The Least You Need to Know

➤ Customers who complain are your best source for problem detection and improvement ideas.

➤ Complaining customers can lead to profitable solutions and repeat customers.

➤ Make sure your guaranty and warranty policies support your mission.

➤ If you do it right, you can turn your complaining customers into referrals for life.

➤ The risks and costs you take in satisfying upset customers usually provide far greater payoffs than doing nothing at all.

➤ Employees need support systems and clear authorization to please disappointed customers without jumping through bureaucratic hoops.

Chapter 13

Just the FAQs

In This Chapter

➤ Understanding the law of time

➤ Utilizing frequently asked questions

➤ Uncovering FAQs and FGRs

➤ Answering internal FAQs

➤ Realizing the power of FAQs

"Customer Service, how may I help you?"

"Yes, I bought your ABC switch and I can't figure out where the batteries go in. Can you help me?"

"You know, I heard some other people were having this same problem. Let me find out from my colleagues what the answer is. Do you have about 30 minutes to wait while I get the answer?"

Click!—Dial tone.

It's a fact that you can substantially reduce your customer service response time if you can collect the data on the questions your customers most commonly ask and make the appropriate answers readily available to your customer service representatives. In fact, it is imperative that you do this in order to deliver outstanding customer service today.

It's Your Time—How Do You Want to Spend It?

In Chapter 8 we talked about how you are likely to waste more time with a complaint by not asking the right questions up front in order to solve the problem properly. In this chapter, we will take the argument further by adding that if you don't predict what the most commonly asked questions are going to be, you're likely going to spend a substantially greater amount of time fielding your customers' questions. This additional time is a costly resource that you cannot afford to waste in today's competitive market.

Action Now!

The more time you spend on the phone uncovering customer complaints and providing answers, the more money you're going to spend on labor dealing with these issues. The more time it takes to field a customer service call, the more bodies you will need to field them in an acceptable time frame. By reducing the time it takes to field each call, you can increase the volume of calls each customer service representative (CSR) can handle effectively.

> **Watch It!**
> Today's high tech world carries a double-edged blade for all those who play the technology game. Ever more sophisticated technology allows people to do things faster and faster. People accustomed to saving time through technology expect the time that it takes them to get answers to their problems using that technology to be just as fast.

Not only will you increase your CSR's productivity, but you also will ensure that your customers won't be exposed to long waits for service. There's nothing more aggravating than waiting for a long period of time on hold, especially when you are in an agitated state. Let's face it. If you're having problems with a software application, you're calling the technical hot line because you're aggravated. The problem is annoying because it's frustrating, not to mention a disruption in your schedule. The longer you have to wait to solve the problem and get on your merry way, the more agitated you're likely to be.

Less Stress

Your CSR's stress level can rise with the time your customers are forced to wait. The longer the wait, the more agitated the customer is. As the customer's state of agitation rises, so does his or her level of nastiness in the interaction with the CSR who has the unfortunate luck of dealing with a valued but upset customer at the wrong time.

So the question then becomes where do you want to spend your time? Would you rather spend it on the front-end by trying to predict what the most commonly asked questions are going to be? Or, would you rather spend the time on the back-end by taking longer to field the calls and risk the possible alienation of both your customers and CSRs? Time spent on the front-end is usually time well spent. You wind up spending less time overall and doing a better *job* overall. (In fact, by wisely using information gathered from your customers and employees, you might eliminate customer calls—angry or otherwise—altogether. See Chapter 15 for more ideas.)

What Are Your FAQs?

Ever since the online services like America Online (AOL) and CompuServe became fashionable, the world at-large has been exposed to a whole new language—computerese. All of a sudden, we're inundated with weird acronyms like FAQs.

What's a FAQ? It's an acronym for a phrase that's no stranger to customer service organizations. A FAQ is a Frequently Asked Question. What an invention! A Frequently Asked Question.

Every product and service develops a life of its own. As part of the process of life, symptoms of pain peculiar to a particular product or service often arise. These symptoms of pain are the common questions that arise about how to use your company's specific products and services.

Frequently asked questions arise for a variety of reasons. Let's take a look at some of these reasons:

➤ **Unclear**—It could be that the instructions accompanying your product aren't clear enough and therefore lead to additional questions on the part of the users. (Or maybe your customer missed the version in their language!)

➤ **Too complicated**—The instructions may be clear enough for a certified rocket scientist, but not simple enough for your everyday user.

➤ **Not enough detail**—The instructions may overlook certain steps with the expectation that the customer will know what steps to insert and where to insert them. Or your information may assume that a customer is familiar with a certain procedure or knows how to use a related tool. Customers baffled by the missing information are likely to visit your hot line in a frustrated or angry search for the missing pieces of information.

> **Word to the Wise**
> A *FAQ* (Frequently Asked Question) is a question that's commonly asked of your CSRs (customer support representatives). They are a result of instructions that are incomplete, too complicated, or unclear. FAQs can easily be handled by identifying them and having answers readily available. *FGRs* (Frequently Given Responses) are the answers to the FAQs your customers ask.

➤ **Doesn't cover all the bases**—The instructions may be clear and simple enough, but don't go deep enough in anticipating "what if" scenarios for any number of things that can go wrong with the product or prevent the product from performing at optimal levels.

What Are Your FGRs?

For every FAQ, there is at least one FGR (frequently given response). For some FAQs there may be multiple FGRs.

If a customer calls with a question about why the batteries aren't working, there may be several reasons for and responses to this problem. It could be the batteries are dead, or they weren't inserted properly, or they're the wrong batteries for the product, or the switch wasn't turned on. The best way to solve a FAQ is to think of all the possibilities that could affect the problem in question and provide solutions for all of them. These become your FGRs. If you don't do this, then the FAQ won't be handled swiftly and appropriately by the CSR and more time will be needed to solve it. The value of a FAQ is to predict all potential problems and issues and have the answers at your finger tips.

Tales from the Real World

When America Online (AOL) implemented a flat fee of $19.95 per month for unlimited usage, it was overwhelmed by the increase in usage generated by the new pricing scheme. As the time users spent online swelled, so did the calls to its support hot line. In attempting to handle the flood of calls as effectively as possible, AOL urged all users who dialed into its 800 support line to go online if possible to receive service. It stressed that most callers could get answers to their questions online by visiting the service's FAQ section. It tried to limit the calls handled on the 800 support line to users who could not log on at all.

Using an online forum that handles FAQs can be an important way for companies, especially those experiencing growth like AOL, to adequately support their client base without massive infusions of additional support personnel. If AOL had to depend on human interaction and phone support for all the questions its frustrated customers had, it could not long afford to sustain such a massive operation.

For example, high and low technology companies employ numerous methods to meet impatient customers' lesseningneeds for fast answers. Such methods include:

➤ Menu-driven recorded announcements with answers to common questions

➤ Using automated fax-back systems (covered in more detail in Chapter 25)

➤ Variable staffing for peak demand periods

➤ Outsourcing call overflows to contract call centers

➤ Providing better instruction manuals with products (see Chapter 11)

➤ Eliminating the need for a customer to call in the first place

Obviously, in an ideal world there would be no need for customer service calls. But if your customers do have to call you, at least make the experience a pleasant one and cut out as much time as possible from when they call to when they get their answers.

Uncovering Your FAQs and FGRs

Now that you understand the concept of FAQs and FGRs, the question becomes how do you uncover your FAQs and FGRs? Here are some ideas you can put to use immediately.

Sampling Top CSRs

Over a catered lunch, or during an end-of-shift snack or desert party, invite your top CSRs into a brainstorming session and create a master list of the questions they're most frequently asked. For each question asked, identify all of the possible responses that can be linked to the issue being questioned. Then, list all of the answers for all of the possibilities. Depending on the nature of your business, do this at least three or four times a year (or much more frequently) to stay current.

Tracking Calls

If you have the technical resources, track all customer service calls and identify the frequently asked questions. If you're not using computers (you are using computers, right?), manually log all calls and track the issues being discussed. In addition to tracking the questions, also track the answers being given. They are your FGRs.

> **Watch It!**
> If you're preparing product support FGRs for use in recordings, fax-backs, Web pages, and so on, write the information in simple, easy-to-understand language. We have seen and heard far too many canned support messages that were so technical or so poorly worded that they only caused *more* confusion and frustration. Test them on people other than your engineering staff!

Tracking Surveys and Complaints

The complaint letters you receive and the information obtained from surveys are another source for identifying your FAQs. FGRs also can come from the letters your customers send relating success stories on what works and the results they have obtained by using your products and services.

Using Your FAQs and FGRs

Uncovering your FAQs and FGRs is only half the battle. The other half and most important part of the battle is putting them to good use. All of your CSRs need to be kept updated on the latest information. They need to be apprised of what the FAQs are and what FGRs are available. And both change over time.

Lotus Domino and Notes, for example, will allow you to conduct real-time updates on your FAQs and FGRs based on the customer information being logged in on a real-time basis. If you're not using programs like Lotus Domino or Notes, you can provide the updates with paper or electronic memos. But the more old-fashioned methods likely will lack the coordination, ease of access, and instant availability that more sophisticated systems offer your support staff.

The ideal setting is to have some kind of database that allows the CSR to input a key word for an issue and have the screen uncover a menu of related issues and solutions. By having this information readily available in a couple of key strokes, you are drastically reducing the amount of time it will take to answer the question on the phone.

Quote, Unquote

Effective communication within a company—up and down the chain of the organization—certainly has a great impact on customer relations. If a firm's staff is knowledgeable about its products or services, and about its practices and procedures, the firm's face to its clients will appear to be responsive and knowledgeable. Only when people within a company feel listened to, their questions heard and responded to, and their ideas respected will they believe they have a voice. When this happens, it can only mean a positive attitude all the way around—from top management on to clients and customers.

—Billie Jean Potter, principal, Camp Dresser & McKee Inc.

Internal FAQs

Just as there are frequently asked questions from your customers, there are frequently asked questions on the minds of your employees. The trick is to uncover the questions to begin with. For various reasons, employees either do not have the chance or aren't encouraged to ask questions. Some of these reasons are:

➤ Fear of being considered a trouble maker.

➤ Belief that no one cares about their questions.

➤ Management not having the time to ask their employees if they have any questions.

➤ Fear of looking "stupid" by asking a silly question.

There are probably a few more reasons you can add to this list. The key point is no matter what the reason is, if employees are carrying out their tasks with questions unanswered, there is a high probability that your customers are feeling the effects in the level of service they're receiving. If employees are lacking information, how can they be expected to provide a high level of service?

Camp Dresser & McKee Inc., a global consulting, engineering, construction, and operations services company focusing on the environment and infrastructure, understands the value of answering their employees' questions. They demonstrate that through their Employee Suggestion Program (ESP) that was developed by one of their principals, Billie Jean Potter.

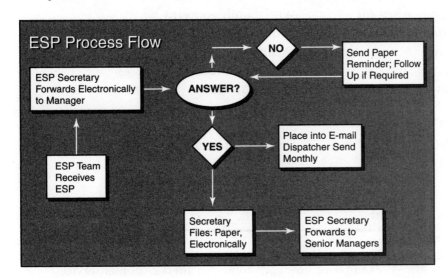

Employee Suggestion Program process flow chart as implemented at Camp Dresser & McKee Inc.

CDM's ESP system, as illustrated, uses the company's e-mail system. You don't need an e-mail system to have an Employee Suggestion Program. But since most companies do use e-mail, why not use it for another value-added service? You can modify your system like CDM has to ensure anonymity of the suggestion providers.

All employee suggestions are received at CDM electronically by a team of four staff people. The suggestions are then routed to the appropriate manager at CDM for answers. The answers are then e-mailed to the employee if the person has included his/her name, while a record is filed electronically. Senior managers are kept apprised of all suggestions and answers. If a manager doesn't respond to the suggestion after a certain period of time, a second request is automatically made.

The beauty of CDM's Employee Suggestion Program is that all employees benefit from each other's suggestions. On a monthly basis, employees receive via e-mail a recap of all suggestions and answers. This is one of the most important tools CDM uses to enhance its ability to communicate efficiently within the organization.

Word to the Wise
An *ESP* (Employee Suggestion Program) provides a vehicle for all employees to ask any question they have regarding any matter relating to their jobs, the company, and current developments. By keeping its employees fully informed and answering all of their questions, employees are further empowered to provide their customers with great service.

Table 13.1 Topics Addressed by CDM Via Its ESP Program

Cost cutting issues, suggestions	Policies, rules, brands
Mentoring	Incentive compensation
Employee recognition/reward	Work/family concerns
Office environmental hints	Sexual harassment
Company reports	Quality
Training issues	Company meetings, programs
Technology issues—World Wide Web, computers, software, training	Social activities
	Manners
Benefits—medical, 401(k), vacation	Smoking
Marketing suggestions/feedback	Corporate functions— Accounting, HR, facilities, communications
Teamwork	
Rumors	Company culture
Communications	Promotions
Venting—gripes, complaints	Silly stuff

From looking at this table, it's easy to find at least one example of how each topic can affect customer service.

Not Touchie-Feelie

Some people might think an ESP is like a big, useless warm fuzzy for employees. Let's take a look at reality. The reality of the matter is companies like CDM don't use such programs if they don't produce benefits that positively affect the bottom line. The following are some of the results that CDM has realized from their Employee Suggestion Program:

➤ Created openings for dialogue on key issues

➤ Changed policies

➤ Implemented suggestions for improvement

➤ Raised awareness for management and staff

➤ Changed culture from fear of speaking out to acceptance of diverse opinions, constructive criticism

➤ Management gaining comfort with feedback

With all of these results being realized from CDM's ESP Program, it is impossible for them not to realize an increase in customer satisfaction—both internally and externally.

Watch It!
Employee Suggestion Programs like the one used at CDM are useless if the suggestions aren't taken seriously and acted upon. In fact, you can do more damage by having an ESP Program and not acting on the suggestions than by not having a program at all. Asking for suggestions and not doing anything with them is a clear message to your employees that they and their ideas do not count. Keep this from happening at all costs. Ignoring well-intentioned input from employees is a sure-fire way to miserably fail at customer service.

The Collective Mind

As with FAQs from your customers, employee suggestion programs tend to provide answers to the same questions on the minds of several employees. As with customers, not every employee is bold enough or willing to take the time to ask the question. Thanks to the few that do, many employees benefit from the responses to the questions. It's management's role to take the initiative and be proactive in seeking out the questions of its employees. If management doesn't take this initiative, then there's a good possibility that questions will go unanswered, information will be missing, and your employees won't be fully equipped to do their jobs well and service your customers appropriately.

Employee feedback systems sometimes work better when they give employees the option to raise questions and issues *anonymously*. While some managers may fret that an anonymous system may invite mostly complaints and whining, experience shows this not to be the case.

Don set up a system in a company that automatically stripped the sender's name from e-mails sent to the "New Ideas" mailbox. For the writer to be identified when sending an e-mail to the small task force monitoring the New Ideas box, he or she had to type their name in the body of the message.

Thousands of business-improving suggestions and questions were sent to the New Ideas mailbox. Well under one-percent were of the bellyaching variety. And most of those were carping about legitimate problems. This, in a company going through major restructuring in response to a rapidly changing market.

Don't be afraid of what employees have to ask or say. Embrace the opportunity.

The Power of FAQs

Just like complaints (see Chapter 12), FAQs are an incredibly valuable indicator of changes you must make to serve your customers better. The concept of FAQs is really to serve your customers more quickly, not build a huge library of questions and answers. The more quickly you eliminate reasons for customers to raise questions, the better.

When customers have the same questions, it indicates problems with the instructions given or understanding of how your product and service works. When you start to see a trend developing with certain questions, you should pass this information on to the people who can make the changes to prevent these questions from coming up in the future.

At Your Service
Great customer service doesn't end with answering your customers' questions expediently. It should continue further by making the necessary changes to eliminate the questions from arising in the future. The ideal customer service environment is when customers don't have to call for assistance at all. Think of those commercials with the Maytag repair people sitting at their desks bored and praying that the phone rings. Your goal is to get as close as possible to this situation.

A good FAQ process should be geared toward achieving the following two results:

1. Identifying the FAQs that need to be addressed and acted upon in the pre-sale and post-sale process in order to eliminate them completely.

2. Predicting the questions your customers are likely to ask—even though you tried to make your system bullet-proof—so you can service them faster by having quick answers ready.

The Least You Need to Know

➤ You are going to spend time with your customers, so you might as well spend the time to figure out their questions and answers before they call you.

➤ Log all of your questions and answers and create a list to help your CSRs serve their customers more quickly and more knowledgeably.

➤ Seek and answer the questions of your employees. If they aren't answered, your customers will ultimately suffer.

➤ Frequently asked questions become action items for future changes in your products and services.

Chapter 14

Survey Says...

In This Chapter

➤ Realizing that surveys can't tell the whole story

➤ Understanding that surveys can tell you a lot

➤ Making decisions based on your results

➤ Doing surveys well is a must

You keep hearing and reading that success in the marketplace comes from giving your customers what they really want. So, how do you know what your customers really want?

Well, for starters, you could ask them!

Excessive Directive: Exceed Customer Expectations

The cliché in customer service is that you need to exceed customer expectations—then everybody will truly love you. That requires you to wrap your arms around what "great service" means to your customers. To help you, there's no shortage of free advice:

"Give the public what it wants."

"The customer is always right."

"If you want to know what customers want, just ask 'em!"

Unfortunately, much of the common wisdom isn't as wise as you need it to be.

Well-Researched Busts, Flops, and Duds

Think about this: If market research could tell a business all it really needed to know about what customers truly value, no major, well-funded, sophisticated marketing company would ever stumble in the market. There'd be no product flops by the Big Boys.

But we know they screw up as much—or maybe more often because of their sheer size—as anybody. (PC jr, anyone? How about a McRib or McDLT sandwich? Or a New Coke? Have you used Federal Express Zap Mail recently? Or an Apple Newton? Flown Pan Am or Eastern Airlines lately? How's your Miata or Fiero?)

Walk through a supermarket today, and about a hundred products won't be there a year from today. That's despite a whole bunch of sophisticated research that can *prove* the world really wants and loves these products. Then next year, in the place of the failed hundred, another new hundred or so products will be introduced with the hope of catching your fancy and repeat purchases.

Likewise, certain opinion surveys can prove to you that no one reads supermarket tabloids, no one watches trash television, and most everyone faithfully patronizes public broadcasting.

No Surveys?

Are we suggesting that you shouldn't use customer surveys in trying to understand customer needs? No. We think they're an important part of your information gathering/ market feedback process.

154

Tales from the Real World

Recently, Ron took his Chrysler Town & Country Minivan in for servicing to his dealer, Ramsey Chrysler/Plymouth in Ramsey, NJ. Already a fan of the dealership because of the customer friendly sales staff, Ron was impressed by the testimonial letters hanging from floor to ceiling on the wall in the service waiting area. Speaking with Keith Reiner, the Service Manager, Ron found out that Ramsey Chrysler consistently averaged a customer satisfaction rating of 3.6 out of a possible 4.0 rating.

Keith claims that the feedback they get from the surveys and letters acts as a barometer of how well they are doing and what areas they need to improve upon. In Keith Reiner's words: "The day we stop reading these letters and surveys is the day you will see our rating dip below 3.6. As long as I am here, no letter and/or survey will go unnoticed." Is it any wonder that Keith Reiner has been happily working at Ramsey Chrysler for 24 years?

In this chapter, we're going to give you some valuable pointers on how to use customer surveys effectively. But we want to start off with this important caution: You can't make critical decisions about what customers want and value based solely on market research—no matter how expensive or apparently sophisticated it is.

Seek and Ye Shall Be Confused

So let's return to that oft-repeated, sage advice: Ask people what they want. Sounds reasonable. But there's a catch. Most people often don't know what they want.

Now, let's be more specific. Some people know what they want at a minimum: their hot food served hot. Friendly service. A clean, inviting place of business. But they often can't tell you the things that they'd absolutely love... because they genuinely don't know what they are!

Look at some examples of the most popular consumer products and services:

➤ Video recorders
➤ Portable personal stereos
➤ Minivans
➤ Home finance software
➤ Camcorders
➤ Cable TV movie services
➤ The Internet
➤ Microwave ovens
➤ Automatic Teller Machines
➤ Cellular phones
➤ Post-It® Notes
➤ Voice mail

These products didn't result from popular demand but rather by risk-taking marketers who offered their customers what they hoped would be pleasing innovations.

155

Why Good Surveys Can Yield Bad Information

People responding to surveys want to help the person or company asking them such important questions. So they give answers that sound good at the time. Even though they may have no basis in reality whatsoever—at least as far as predicting actual customer behavior in the future.

> **Quote, Unquote**
> People are unpredictable by nature, and although you can take a nation's pulse, you can't be sure that the nation hasn't just run up a flight of stairs.
> —E. B. White

"Are you likely to buy this?" asks the researcher. "Sure," comes the reply.

"Are you willing to pay for technical support?" "No. Wait. Yes; er, no. Maybe."

"Which of the following product and service attributes are most important to you?" "They all are."

Oh. Well. That's enlightening, huh?

Woe to the business that tries to set its priorities around these sorts of often conflicting insights.

This is why it's so terribly difficult to determine, through surveys alone, definitively what service constitutes the kind of service or product innovation that your customers would view as important to them.

Getting at True Customer Value

Trying to divine what customers really want is both art and science. Surveys, focus groups, and other market research tools are simply incapable of providing you with the answer to this important question: What do your customers want?

So how do you get at that slippery treasure? A few ways are as follows:

➤ Watch your customers. Their actions will tell you more than their words. Observe what they look at—or don't—when they evaluate your product before a purchase. What goofy things do they do when they use—or try to use—your product. (Wish the guys from the record companies were around to see their customers struggle to open the goofy plastic packaging that some compact discs come in.)

➤ Monitor customer behaviors that tell you how they really feel about your company and its products: repeat purchases; whether the value of customer purchases is getting larger or smaller; the frequency of customer purchases (getting more or less often?); the amount of referred business your customers send your way.

➤ Collect information from your customers at every opportunity. Listen closely to what they tell you when they call or stop by with questions or problems. (See Chapter 13 and the section, "The Magic's in the Database," later in this chapter.)

➤ And yes, talk to your customers. One on one. At the time when they're actually using your product or service. Ask them to be blunt in their evaluation and criticism. Ask them pointed questions about why they bought what they did. Or didn't buy what they didn't.

➤ Ask them what they really like about their favorite businesses to buy from, even if it's totally unrelated to your industry. Get a sense of what kind of treatment your customers value from whatever the source. Then figure out how to capture those attributes in the products and services you offer them.

➤ Get to know your customers as *people*. The more you know about their lives, the more you have a context for how your products and services fit with the whole of their lives. That's where you may draw the inspiration for products and services that customers would never think to ask you for, but you can create for them because you understand them perhaps better than they do themselves. The more you know about your customers, the better equipped you'll be to modify how you do business to increase the performance and acceptance of your products and services.

The bottom line: serve your customers well by understanding them deeply. Use surveys and other formal tools of market research, but don't simply defer to them. They give you some of the information you need, but not all. They're no substitute for what Don calls "breathing customer air"—being where your customers are, really using and evaluating your products and services.

Tales from the Real World

After keynoting a reseller conference for a computer manufacturer, Ron was retained to develop and administer a survey of its resellers to identify ways of improving the company's relationships with them.

The surveys indicated that an expensive incentive trip the manufacturer offered for top performers wasn't really viewed as being valuable by the resellers. They preferred to see that money invested in product and service innovations.

Ron, along with executives from his client, presented the findings to the Reseller Advisory Council (a group comprised of resellers who met regularly with the manufacturer to discuss issues at hand). The council agreed with the findings and it was their recommendation to scrap the trip.

This is a clear example of how a survey can lead to identification of trends to be discussed and validated by appropriate parties. This mix of surveys and validation makes a tremendous tool for getting a good sense of how your customers really feel about certain issues.

Let's Talk Surveys

Survey cards are everywhere! They must be mating and reproducing.

You can't eat at a restaurant, shop in a clothing store, or visit a dry-cleaner, without seeing one of those "Tell Us How We're Doing" survey cards.

Tales from the Real World

While donating blood recently, Don came across a customer satisfaction survey card sandwiched in between the pretzels and donuts. It said:

"The Blood Services staff work very hard to make donating blood a pleasant experience. One of the best ways we can continue to improve is to listen to those in the best position to know how well we do: our donors. Please answer the questions inside. Your opinions will be given careful consideration."

After recommending that blood be drawn without needles, knives, or other invasive instruments, your slightly blood-deprived, possibly light-headed coauthor further recommended ample helpings of lobster thermidor and filet mignon to replenish vital nutrients lost in the bloodletting. As a special bonus, he gave a little free sample of his management consulting expertise, recommending that the Red Cross launch a multimedia advertising campaign repositioning blood donations as a chic, with-it way to "lose weight—one pint at a time!"

And you wonder why you can't rely on customer surveys.

Keep in mind that customers who choose to complete surveys may have very different opinions than those customers who do not. Be very careful in making sweeping changes based on survey forms customers pick-up and choose to complete. Now, if nine out of ten tell you about the same problem, look into it!

What Surveys Can Tell You

Competently designed surveys can usually give you a good indication of when customers love or hate something. But everything in between isn't really very conclusive.

What's the difference between *Somewhat Satisfied* and *Somewhat Dissatisfied*? Partly sunny or partly cloudy? Would you throw out a policy because it leaves many of your customers feeling Somewhat Dissatisfied with it? Would you promote a feature that many of your customers described as leaving them Somewhat Satisfied?

As Ron discussed in Chapter 8, you must clarify the words your customers use. One customer's definition of what satisfied means could be vastly different than the definition applied to the same word by another customer. Therefore, we urge you to not only give choices, but to attach clear definitions describing each choice. For example: Satisfied = you liked the product or service and will order again from [Your Company] the next time the need arises.

To make your surveys more reflective of how customers truly feel about your product, use scales with emotional words. "Love It" is more intense and probably more accurate than "Very Satisfied." Likewise, "Hate It" registers at a gut level more than "Quite Dissatisfied." In the middle range, something like "It Was Just Okay" is probably more real a sentiment to your customers than "Somewhat Satisfied."

Watch It!
Would you be surprised to learn that many customers who say they are *Satisfied* with their purchase from your company don't think twice about doing business with one of your competitors?

What You Can Learn

What you find out in surveys depends on what you ask customers about. The following are many possible areas you could try to assess in satisfaction surveys. These are specific attributes you could assess in a satisfaction/expectations survey.

Sales Representative:

➤ Knowledge of customer's business

➤ Knowledge of [Your Company's] products

➤ Accessibility

➤ Courtesy

➤ Helpfulness

➤ Responsiveness

➤ Promises kept

Product:

➤ Functionality (specific product or service attributes)

➤ Reliability

➤ Performs as promised

➤ Instructions thorough

➤ Instructions clear

➤ Ease of use

➤ Appearance

Delivery:

➤ When promised

➤ Product arrived intact

➤ Order accurate, shipment complete

Service Staff:

➤ Accessibility

➤ Knowledgeable

➤ Courtesy

➤ Helpfulness

➤ Responsiveness

➤ Resolution of inquiry or problem

➤ Promises kept

Billing:

➤ Payment terms

➤ Clarity

➤ Accuracy

➤ Timely

159

Technical Support:

➤ Knowledge of customer's business

➤ Knowledge of [Your Company's] products

➤ Accessibility

➤ Courtesy

➤ Helpfulness

➤ Responsiveness

➤ Resolution of inquiry or problem

➤ Promises kept

➤ Timely response

➤ Clarity and ease of instructions

Promotional Communication:

➤ Information value

➤ Clarity

Competitive Standing:

➤ On all other attributes listed

➤ Price/value

➤ Quality

➤ Guarantees

➤ Distribution channels

➤ Reputation

Just Do Something

Watch It!
Survey research is a numbers game. A few surveys may be worse than no surveys, for they could lead you to false conclusions drawn from a group of customers too small to reflect what the majority of your customers think. Again, get expert assistance to increase the likelihood that your surveys reflect reality and not a distortion of it.

Here are some important questions to ask *yourself* about surveys before subjecting your customers to them:

➤ What do I expect to learn from the survey?

➤ What do I need to find out to be more competitive?

➤ What would surprise me?

➤ What would be signs of progress?

➤ What would be signs of trouble?

➤ What will I do based on the information I receive?

The last question above is vital. Surveys and other research should be undertaken only if you're prepared to act on the information. Gathering a shelf full of "interesting" customer feedback is a waste of your money and your customer's time.

Gather information to act on it. Otherwise, don't bother.

So What's Your Interpretation?

Many people like the "middle of the road." They may feel neither particularly positive nor negative about something. Still, you need to assess whether your product or service struck them as more positive or negative. One way to do this is to offer only an even-numbered set of choices for a rating scale. If you have only four categories instead of five, for example, there's no middle ground. People have to declare themselves as being either on one side of the line or the other.

If you're using one survey form to cover a variety of customer experiences (which we would recommend against), you may need a check-box on the survey that says "Did Not Experience." This is better than Not Applicable (or NA—which many people may not understand at all). Not Applicable may seem like the neutral choice to some people. And you want them to indicate whether they had a positive or negative experience.

There is no one "right way" to do surveys that all the experts would agree is best. People with Ph.D.s in the research field often seriously disagree about methods and conclusions. But there are many mistakes the unknowing could innocently make. If you plan to make business-altering decisions based on your surveys and other customer research—and that is why you should do research in the first place—get some expert assistance.

Survey methods are part of the formula; analyzing the pounds of resulting data is the other. How you cut the data can significantly color the conclusions you might draw from a dizzying stack of numbers.

Bad information—or misinformed interpretations—can yield bad, even disastrous, conclusions. Don't do a good thing badly.

Power Questions

It's one thing to ask customers how *satisfied* they were with their recent experience with your company. It's quite another to really put those feelings to the test.

Here are some tough questions that get to the heart of the matter. *Based on your experience with [Your Company]:*

➤ How strongly would you consider buying from it again? [Scale]

➤ Would you *enthusiastically* recommend to a close friend or associate that they do business with [Your Company]?

➤ To how many people in the past year have you recommended [Your Company]?

➤ If you could make your recent purchase choice over again, would you still buy from [Your Company]?

Watch It!
Just because you have information from a survey about what customers say they want, it doesn't mean you will automatically succeed by meeting those wants. Before putting both feet in the water, come up with a prototype and test your target-customer reactions to it. Use focus groups and test markets before proceeding to a grand scale introduction. See if your customers truly value your solutions.

161

Or how about:

➤ Based on your experience with all companies—across all industries—how would you rate the service you received from [Your Company]?

- ❏ The absolute best
- ❏ As good as any you've had
- ❏ About what you normally receive
- ❏ Less than what you've come to expect
- ❏ Disappointing
- ❏ Truly awful

Revealing Open-Ended Questions

Sometimes customers can provide you with the best insights when they get beyond the confines of your prepared questions and can answer in their own words.

Here are some questions to spur revelations:

➤ What's the one thing about [Your Company] you'd change if you could?

➤ What's the single most important reason you choose to buy from [Your Company] rather than its competitors?

➤ In the past year, do you think [Your Company] has been gaining ground or losing ground?

➤ What's something that [Your Company] could do to improve your experience with it?

Over-Surveyed?

The phone company calls to survey you about service. Credit card companies call to survey you about service. Your auto repair shop calls to survey you. The post office wants you to complete its survey.

Quote, Unquote
A point of view can be a dangerous luxury when substituted for insight and understanding.
—Marshall McLuhan

Everybody, it seems, has jumped on the satisfaction survey bandwagon (where every tenth or hundredth or thousandth customer transaction is automatically selected for a survey). So why does service seem so bad so much of the time? That's another discussion. The point here is that your customers may have had it up to their eyebrows with satisfaction surveys. You might find response rates to mail surveys declining, or experience more resistance to your phone surveys as survey-weary customers begin to lose interest or resent the intrusion on their time.

What to do? Try fewer surveys. More selective surveys. If you deal with customers face-to-face, ask them for four minutes of their time to help your "improvement efforts." And then stay within the four minute time frame unless the customer wants to give you more time. Make sure that whatever you say, you give your customers a good reason for why they should take the time to fill out the survey. How will it benefit them in the future?

If you do phone surveys, hire people with a pleasant, understandable phone presentation. Sorry to labor you with the obvious; too many companies obviously overlook the obvious.

If you have the opportunity, try to use one or more of the following to encourage people to take their valuable time to answer your questions.

➤ Offer to make a donation to a charity of your survey respondent's choice.

➤ Offer to share survey results. (This may be of particular interest to industrial customers where there is—or you'd like to create—a feeling of partnership between vendor and customer.)

➤ Have members of your customer service or sales staff ask their customers to complete the surveys, or have them do the actual interviews (stress with them the vital importance of absolute candor and accurate, uncolored recording of customer responses).

➤ Offer a variety of methods to provide responses such as e-mail, paper, phone interview, and so on.

The Magic's in the Database

A potent way to understand what your customers want, and what they value, is to capture information about what they've been buying from you, and how much they've been spending with you already. That makes it a lot easier to determine what they might want from you in the future.

Even though we don't know the specifics of your business, we're willing to bet that not all your customers buy the same things from you or spend the same amount of money with your company. Do you know the range of spending, the average per customer, and the spending total for every one of your customers? For this year, for last year, and the year before?

You should. And you can do this with a *customer database* that keeps track of all the purchases and other transactions made by each of your customers.

> **Word to the Wise**
> A *customer database* is a system that records the sales and transaction history for each of your customers. In addition, it could include extensive personal information about individual customers. A customer database can be the lifeblood of your business. The information stored in it can give you ideas about what your customers are looking for, how to serve them, and how to market to them. The value of the database deteriorates if it is not kept up to date. For information to be valuable, it must be current and accessible.

Your database, depending on the size and complexity of your business, could take a variety of shapes. A local restaurant might keep an index card for each of its patrons, recording the dates, days of the week, and time of day for each visit, along with what the patron ordered. The card could have the customer's name, address, and telephone number. Imagine eating at a restaurant you occasionally visit and having the food server ask you if you'd once again like to have the raw fish with peanut butter sauce that you so enjoyed on one of your last visits.

At large companies with huge, complex computer systems, a customer database might draw on many different sources of information from the sales department, the credit department, customer service, order processing, shipping, market research, and so on. People from each department that has some interaction with your clients can enter information about them into the central database. Then, anyone interacting with a given customer can see what experiences others have had with the customer, and in turn, record new insights about preferences and desires.

Having access to centralized, up-to-date information helps you to both understand your customers better and to serve them in that special way that is most relevant to them. A good system will help you get information beyond routine transactions (sales, billing, credit, and so on) entered in it. We mean data that might be useful to a design team, to the market research folks, to technical troubleshooters, and so on.

Tales from the Real World

In today's world of wanting things fast, people don't want to have to call several different people to get answers regarding their accounts. Henkel Corporation, a chemical company, realizes this. They're introducing a new system that will enable their customers to truly experience a one call event for all their questions—making one call to place the order, check delivery, clear credit, and handle any other requests. This can only happen if you have an interactive database that links all of this information together from the major operating arms of the corporation.

The key is to capture as much information about your customer as you reasonably can so that you can complete a picture of who's buying from you, and what they want, need, and desire. This enables you to get a sense of what your customers really value so you can anticipate their needs to serve them better than they expected. And, in the process, get ahead of all those competitors who would be happy to take your customers' money.

Sample Customer Satisfaction Survey

The following is a sample customer satisfaction survey. This is not the *ultimate survey*. Read it to stimulate your thinking about the questions you might ask your customers.

*Please check the box to the left of the term that best describes your feelings about purchasing from [*Your Company*].*

All things considered, the experience of doing business with [Your Company] is:

❑ Delightful   ❑ Positive   ❑ Somewhat Positive
❑ Unpleasant   ❑ Terrible   ❑ Less than Positive

Overall, was the product you recently purchased from [Your Company]:

❑ Better than you expected   ❑ About what you expected
❑ Not quite what you expected   ❑ Not at all what you expected

Please comment:

_____

_____

How satisfied were you with the overall *value* of the product you bought from [Your Company]:

❑ It was great!   ❑ Good solid value
❑ Something of a let down   ❑ Very disappointing

Overall, how satisfied are you with the service you received from [Your Company]?

❑ I love it!   ❑ I'm pleased
❑ I'm disappointed   ❑ I thought it was awful

Compared to *all* other companies from which you purchase, [Your Company] is:

❑ Much better to do business with   ❑ Somewhat better to do business with
❑ Somewhat worse to do business with ❑ Much worse to do business with

Please comment:

_____

Would you recommend products from [Your Company] to a friend?

❑ Definitely   ❑ Probably   ❑ Probably Not   ❑ Definitely Not

If you could deliver a message directly to the president of [Your Company], what would you want him to know about your experience with [Your Company]?

_____

How could [Your Company] improve its products or services to provide you with greater value?

_____

continues

165

continued

Concerning your recent purchase from [Your Company], was this:

❑ Your first purchase from [Your Company]
❑ Not your first purchase from [Your Company]

How long have you been purchasing such products/working in this industry:

❑ 3 years or less   ❑ 4 to 9 years   ❑ 10 to 15 years
❑ 16 to 25 years   ❑ More than 25 years

OPTIONAL

Your Name _____

Your Company _____

Address _____

Telephone number _____

If you used this survey directly out of the book, you'd likely get some insights into your customers. For more potent information, we suggest you work with a market research professional to develop a survey customized to your business.

The Least You Need to Know

➤ You need to know what your customers truly value.

➤ Watching your customers and talking with them can yield vital insights.

➤ Surveys can tell you some of that important information.

➤ Information from surveys alone will not result in either a clear or complete picture.

➤ Survey research is complicated, requires special expertise, and is expensive. You should undertake it knowing what decisions you plan to make based on the results.

Chapter 15

Great Expectations

In This Chapter

➤ Identifying problems

➤ Solving true causes of problems

➤ Getting better by operating differently

➤ Trying new ways

"You're only as good as your last ..." Finish the sentence. Everyone—inside your organization, as well as your customers—wants to know, "What have you done for me lately?"

Harvey MacKay, businessman and author, says that gratitude is the least deeply felt emotion. (Think about that one!)

The good things you've done for customers in the past counts for little if you can't help them today—*now*. (Sometimes, don't those customers just seem like selfish ingrates!)

With just about every company trying to distinguish itself by its service, customers are getting spoiled. They're often getting good service, so they know what it is and expect nothing less.

Get Better or Get Out of the Game

To keep pace with what your customers expect—what they've been taught to expect by really good service organizations—you've just got to keep refining how you do things. It's improve or perish.

The call to arms in many companies is this rallying cry:

"Continuous Improvement!"

The fundamental way to improve your service to customers is by bettering your operation. And there are two ways to do that.

1. Solve internal problems that stand in the way of delivering great service.

2. Deliver improved services externally by working better internally.

This chapter helps you do both.

Probable Cause

In earlier chapters, we talked about solving your customers' problems. That's removing the speck in your customer's eye. Here, we're going to talk about getting rid of the roadblocks to progress in your own organization. That's taking the logs out of your company's eye. As Don is fond of saying, you can't create service breakthroughs until you stop service breakdowns.

Let's say you know things aren't going right. Product returns are up. Complaints are up. Sales are not.

Word to the Wise
The true source of a problem is its *root cause*. The problem itself is often only a visible sign—a symptom—of the true cause of what's causing what's wrong.

If your company is like most, the instinct that seizes everyone when problems undeniably surface is to start pointing fingers. Everywhere. Like crazy.

Customers complain to customer service. Customer service blames your sales people for over-promising. Sales points the finger at manufacturing for building inadequate products. Manufacturing points the finger at marketing for inadequate product specifications, and at suppliers for unreliable material. Suppliers point the finger back at the company for forcing costs down to unreasonable levels. Round and round it goes.

Look, blame doesn't solve problems. Neither does attacking problems without identifying their *root cause*.

For example, at home your partner closes the refrigerator door and a picture hanging on the wall comes crashing down. Obvious cause? Your partner slammed the door too hard. But the true root cause is more likely a picture that was hung on a screw that wasn't adequately fastened into the wall. (And the cause of *that* may be at the heart of this particular problem, and probably some others...)

Digging to the Root

How can you avoid the blame game and get to the root cause of problems to really fix what's wrong?

We're going to show you a simple method for problem identification. But first, a couple of important points:

➤ Problems are rarely caused by one single factor. In this complex world, everything is part of an inter-related, interdependent system. A problem is a puzzle with more than one piece.

➤ Identifying and solving problems works best when many people—from many different parts of the company—have input into the problem identification process.

Here's a simple method that can help you identify many possible causes of problems. Create a Cause and Effect Diagram. This tool, developed by Japanese quality expert Kaoru Ishikawa, was created to support Total Quality Management efforts in manufacturing. It's just as applicable to service issues.

Watch It!
Beware the Fire Drill mentality. When things go wrong, what do you concentrate on? Fixing the problems at hand or going beyond that to find out what the cause is to avoid future problems? Too many companies today are stuck in the vicious cycle of putting out fires, and creating more fires by not tending to problem prevention because they're too busy putting out fires. If you find and attack the root of your problems, the number of fires you need to extinguish will be drastically reduced.

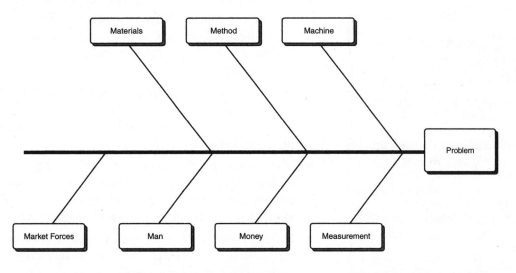

A Cause and Effect Diagram, or fish bone diagram, can identify many different possible causes of a problem.

Watch It!
Money can be at the root of your problems. A cash-starved operation simply can't make the investments necessary to run the business as it should be run. Don't fall into the trap of blaming a lack of funds for all your troubles. That prevents you from seeing other, more likely causes, and blocks innovative thinking for solutions that may have little to do with funding. And, we should note, a company with too *much* cash can have real problems as well. It can get sloppy—drunk with success—spending foolishly and believing it absolutely knows what customers want. (Now *there's* an evil.)

Watch It!
Tempted to blame "pilot error" people problems for your troubles? This should be your last "likely cause." Often, good people perform poorly because the system they work within prevents them from doing better work. Thoroughly scrutinize the system before looking at individuals; you'll likely find your true cause there.

Look at the diagram. Notice how it looks like the skeleton of a fish? That's why many people refer to this tool as a fish bone diagram.

Creating a Cause and Effect Diagram is extremely easy. Look again at the diagram. See the head of the fish? That's where you state the symptom of the problem (or effect). For example, increasing returns, high number of repair calls, decreasing sales, whatever.

Now look at the major branches. See the label at the end? These are the major categories of likely problem-causers. Most every problem has its root cause in one or more of the following areas:

➤ **Machine**. Wrong tools for the job; unreliable tools; out-of-date tools. These factors can be behind the detectable problem.

➤ **Method**. Is it *how* you're doing things that's creating or contributing to the situation?

➤ **Materials**. "Garbage in, garbage out." You can't make products better than their components. Faulty parts make for faulty products which make for service nightmares (repair orders, replacement or refund requests…).

➤ **Measurement**. Do your surveys tell you the vast majority of your customers are absolutely delighted, while they're absolutely abandoning your product? Maybe they really aren't so delighted. Double-check your attitudometer.

➤ **Money**. No mon', no fun. Inadequate cash flow can starve an otherwise healthy operation, delaying necessary hiring, postponing purchasing computers or phone systems, and so on.

➤ **Man**. (Okay, *people*—to be politically correct—but we'll use Man to keep our alliterative MMMMMM scheme going.) Inadequate staffing can cause problems; so can over-staffing and incompetent staffing.

➤ **Market Forces**. We mean the external environment: forces such as competitive actions, social changes, political, and economic trends.

Putting Meat on the Fish Bone

Here's a simple 10-step process for using the fish bone diagram to identify possible sources of your challenges:

1. Identify the problem you want to solve.

2. Put the problem description at the head of the fish.

3. Gather your colleagues and have a free-flowing idea generating session about possible causes.

4. Identify as many possible causes as possible. Encourage creativity; don't debate the merits of any suggestion—you're simply listing *possibilities*.

5. Group related ideas together under the major headings along the big branches.

6. After filling up the diagram, step back and review what you've come up with.

7. Ask the group for their ideas on what, from all the possibilities you see before you, are likely causes.

8. Explore likely causes further. Take a branch of the fish bone, for example, *machinery*, and create another fish bone diagram for it. The major branches of a fish bone for a suspected machinery problem might be labeled Maintenance, Parts, Methods, and so on.

9. Gather and analyze quantifiable data related to the leading suspected root causes. Verify (or invalidate) your gut instincts.

10. Draw conclusions and take action after *knowing* what the root causes are. This particular cause and effect diagram lists many possible causes in several areas for declining sales of a stereo manufacturer.

The sample diagram shows how a completed fish bone diagram looks. This particular cause and effect diagram lists many possible causes in several areas for declining sales of a stereo manufacturer.

Here's a simple process to help clarify your thinking about problem causation. Ask the following questions:

➤ Where are we now in performance?

➤ Where do we want to be?

➤ What do we *think* is keeping us behind?

➤ What do we *know* so definitively we can prove it?

➤ What do we need to find out?

At Your Service

Idea generating sessions (brainstorming, some call it) are most productive when there's a wide variety of perspective. Invite people from around your company, perhaps some vendors and even customers, to help you see beyond your own (and your department's) limited line of sight.

Watch It!

Cause and effect diagrams can tell you which way the wind is blowing, but they cannot tell you the speed of the wind or the air temperature. In other words, you need *data* to complete the picture. Even if a whole room full of well-informed people review a cause and effect diagram and agree that Factor X is the culprit, they might all be wrong. A consensus gut feel is still only a gut feel. Complete the picture with hard data.

➤ Where can we get the additional information?

➤ What will we do with the information once we have it?

➤ What do we need to do to fix the problem?

➤ Who's responsible for implementing changes?

➤ What's the timetable?

➤ How will we monitor progress?

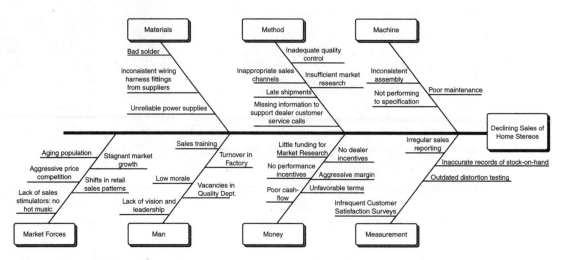

The 5+/20+ Method

Identifying the possible cause of a problem may help you see the surface of the problem more clearly. But to really solve the problem will require you to get beneath the surface.

We've combined a couple of classic problem-solving methods into a process we call the five-plus-twenty-plus method. It's a two-stage process.

1. Take any problem and ask why it occurred. Take the answer to that question and ask why, and so on for at least five levels of detail.

2. When you've gone at least five levels down, and truly believe that you can go no further, begin listing possible solutions to this root cause. List at least 20 possible solutions.

Here is an example problem:

➤ You can't handle all the customer calls coming into the company. Why?

➤ Your company is receiving more calls than expected from customers. Why?

➤ Customers are asking questions about your new Widget 2000 model. Why?

➤ Customers don't understand many of its features. Why?

➤ The features seem to confuse customers. Why?

➤ The ones on the new model work differently than most in the industry. Why?

We thought we knew what customers wanted.

Bingo!

Actually, this line of analysis could go on for a few more levels. Once you get to the root causes—and there probably are a few here, list at least twenty possible solutions.

Notice how much different this list of twenty solutions to the root cause is from what it might have been had you just stopped at the first or second *why*. And notice how much more intriguing your solutions are once you get past the most obvious two or three.

Watch It!
Don't look for the *right* answer to what ails your firm. There's no right answer. There are many, many possible solutions to any challenge your organization faces. And some of the best may be the least obvious. Solving real world business problems isn't like completing a grade school fill-in-the-blank exercise.

If you don't solve for the root cause of the problem, you're not solving the problem.

Progress Through Process

How you do what you do is as important as what you do. In other words, turning the nut on a bolt with your teeth probably isn't as good a method as using a fitted wrench. Both turn the nut. So both do the job. One does it much more efficiently (not to mention painlessly).

Analyzing Work

Could you speed up the service you provide your customers? Could you trim costs by working more efficiently? What if you eliminated unnecessary repetition, delays, approvals, and the bureaucratic steps you have to take to check an order, confirm pricing, review an invoice, answer a technical question, or whatever you do to assist customers?

We have yet to meet anyone working in any company of any size that could honestly say they could not possibly improve their work processes.

Here's how you can begin to analyze your work-flow to seek ways of improving it.

Identify the actual steps in a specific process. Focus on individual work steps—not departments, not jobs, not people.

At Your Service
When examining your work processes, think *macro*, not *micro*. Most work processes include many steps to completing a task or achieving an objective. Rarely do all those steps fall within one work group or department, or report to the same top manager. So think across the organization, and beyond your organization. Picture the whole, not just the part(s) you know best.

Be very specific. It's not, "give service on the telephone." It's:

1. Answer the call.
2. Greet customer.
3. Determine the nature of the inquiry.
4. Query the database for applicable information.
5. Provide appropriate answers.
6. Ask the customer if there is anything else they need.
7. Respond appropriately: Query the database again, or, if necessary, transfer the call, or, ask the customer if she can hold while information is sought; if yes, proceed to obtain information from the sub-system or internal information source; if no, schedule a follow-up call with the customer.
8. Thank the customer for calling.
9. Wait for the customer to disconnect.
10. Disconnect the call.
11. Input the service call and results into the database.
12. Complete any pending information gathering, and so on.

Draw a map of the process, showing each individual step. There's a standard set of symbols for illustrating work-flow (which you can find in many graphics software packages) but don't worry so much about following the "proper" protocol for the map. Devote your energy to identifying the exact steps in the process. If you understand your map and can explain it to other people, it's probably fine for your purposes.

Verify the steps in the process. "Attach" yourself to the work. Walk through it every step of the way, as though you were the question being addressed or the paper or work being handled. Be sure you didn't overlook any steps along the way. If you did, add them to your map.

Ask the following questions:

➤ Why do we do it this way?

➤ What if we didn't do this step at all? Who would notice? What would happen? What's the risk involved?

➤ How could we achieve the same objective (assuming its worth doing), by doing it a different way? How many different ways can we think of to do it?

At Your Service

Evaluating processes has evolved to a fine science, with very sophisticated software—and consultants—available to undertake "business process reengineering," known as BPR. Your own company may have people knowledgeable about BPR available to help you redesign your work. You can usually find them in either the finance or information technology departments. Or, if you work for a small company with limited resources, consider doing the analysis yourself or retaining a consultant to help you.

Discuss with your colleagues across the organization ways to streamline your processes. Create plans for alternative methods. Select a new method. Test the new method—on a small scale—before changing the whole operation. Identify and work-out the kinks before turning your company—and your customers—on their heads.

When you begin examining business processes with a macro view, some colleagues may feel threatened. After all, you're looking over their "turf." Likewise, in the process of improving processes, you may find ways to eliminate unnecessary work—and the jobs that do them. While process improvement is vitally important to the quality of the service you provide to your customers and the fiscal health of your company, some of your colleagues may resist the effort. You're more likely to succeed when your effort has the enthusiastic support of top management.

Growing Pains

Change can be painful, but you can't grow or get better without changing. Asking people to change their ways—even to solve a problem everyone agrees exists and is undesirable, can be uncomfortable to some.

Your best strategy is to acknowledge people's very real, very genuine discomfort. Explain how changing things delivers a benefit to your company and your customers. Ask people to join you in that common goal.

Treat everyone fairly in the process. Keep them informed of your objectives and methods. Try to generate excitement for the better future that you imagine.

Quote, Unquote
Change isn't made without inconvenience, even from worse to better.
—Richard Hooker, sixteenth century English theologian

Nonstop Improvement

Some people are never satisfied. Hope they work at your company. There's always room for improvement; always a better way.

Should you spend your time fine-tuning an existing process or looking for ways to replace it?

Seriously, when you make it a way of life to constantly question the way your firm does things, you'll develop a sense for when you need to fine-tune and when you need to overhaul. The key is to keep fine-tuning until you overhaul.

Failure: Always Better

You can't get better doing what you know already works. You have to experiment. Try some things.

The more new things you try, the more likely you're going to have some clunkers. Not everything works.

Quote, Unquote
Ever tried. Ever failed. No matter. Try Again. Fail again. Fail better.
—Samuel Beckett

And if it does, you're probably not reaching far enough. In baseball, they say, you can't steal second base with a foot on first.

New things you try that don't work aren't *failures*. They're learning experiences.

Quote, Unquote
There's only one corner of the universe you can be certain of improving, and that's your own self.
—Aldous Huxley

The Ultimate Improvement

Take a look in the mirror. You're staring at your best bet for improving your operation and your service to customers.

The degree of improvement you can influence depends on how much better you are—personally—at understanding what customers value, and at imagining how your business can provide that value—and how to do it as efficiently and effectively as possible.

The Least You Need to Know

➤ Your customers expect you to keep getting better.

➤ To get better you first need to eliminate your problems.

➤ Problems can be eliminated only when you get to their root causes, perhaps by using a Cause and Effect diagram and other analytic methods.

➤ Improving your work requires a commitment to continuous improvement and a macro view beyond your micro area of work responsibilities.

➤ Improvement is an ongoing process that requires thorough analysis and innovative experimentation.

Part 4
Build It and They Will Come: Creating a Customer Service Organization

Want to build your business based on Personally Pleasing Memorable Interactions? Hey, who doesn't!

To really deliver on the customer service promise, to distinguish your company with The Service Difference, you have to have systems and processes that make great customer service the way you do business.

The next several chapters guide you through the building process: from hiring and motivating top service performers, to setting up a call center where they can be the most productive, to encouraging great service between colleagues within your company, to giving great service to your far-flung customers around the globe.

Chapter 16

Structuring the Service Function for Success

In This Chapter

➤ Seeking the perfect structure

➤ Doing teamwork

➤ Creating self-managed teams

➤ Making cross-functional teams work

What's the best organization chart for a customer service department? Should the customer service department report to sales, operations, marketing? Should the customer service department include credit, billing, and technical support functions?

These are the piercing questions that inquiring minds want to know the answers to!

And we have the perfect answer—one—to all of these probing issues....

It doesn't matter.

Well, maybe that's a bit flip. We should slightly modify our brief, wise-guy retort....

At Your Service
Relationships between colleagues, information sharing, and a collective commitment to great experiences for customers matter much more than how departmental boxes line up on the organizational chart.

Quote, Unquote
Men are forever creating...organizations for their own convenience and forever finding themselves the victims of their home-made monsters. —Aldous Huxley

Beyond Politics

Political issues like organization charts, department lines, and reporting relationships don't matter when everyone in your company wants to give customers the best service possible.

When your organization has truly committed itself to creating The Service Difference by continually generating Personally Pleasing Memorable Interactions for your customers it will manage to do so. No matter who reports to whom. Remember that our premise for this book is this: in order to thrive in today's competitive market, you must view customer service as being a company-wide cultural issue. Not a departmental issue.

If you turned here desperately looking for the ultimate customer service department design, relax. It doesn't exist. And if it did, it would have very little to do with delivering great service. Organizational charts simply don't impact a customer's Instant of Absolute Judgment. Customers don't know how your department or company is organized, and they don't care.

Structural Integrity

While we won't (can't) give you a magic, or even recommended, formula for structuring the customer service function, we suggest that you think about the following.

How you structure the customer service function—who reports to whom in what department—likely depends on these factors:

➤ The available management time and talent

➤ The size and geographic spread of your organization

➤ The company's history and culture

➤ The way information flows (or *could* flow if everyone made a genuine effort to share information, and the company's technology supported the free-flow of information)

➤ The service needs of your customers

➤ The competitive forces trying to outdo your efforts

Let's look at each factor in a little more detail.

Voice at the Table

We're all for the trend in self-managed work teams. And we're delighted to see fewer layers of paper-pushing, over-the-shoulder-watching, and bureaucratic supervisors breathing down the necks of people doing the "real" work of pleasing customers.

At the same time, Customer Service is such an important link to customers that it should have a strong voice in top management. So where the customer service function reports may be best served by whomever can best serve it.

In other words, a strong advocate and champion for bringing the voice of the customer to the executive table is really more important than the title of the executive in charge of customer service. VP Customer Service? Great! But it also could be VP of marketing, sales, operations, or whatever.

Again, the key is that information should be flowing across department boundaries anyway—all the way to the top.

Here or There and Everywhere

The rallying cry of "close to the customer" may encourage distributing customer service functions geographically. If your customer needs differ greatly from region to region, you may find an advantage in decentralized, locally responsive service centers.

On the other hand, technology allows you to serve customers from the world over in centralized operations. We discuss this in greater detail in Chapters 20–26. The point here is that geography need not drive how or where you set up your customer service function.

Uniquely Your Company

Even in the very same industry, two companies of nearly identical size can operate very, very differently. We've talked at length earlier in this book about how people have distinctive personalities that you need to understand. Well, organizations have unique personalities, too.

> **Quote, Unquote**
> There are no such things as self-directed work teams. A CEO sets the direction for the company and teams are given a charter as to what they have to accomplish. Self-managed teams are something else. Here the teams can figure out how they're going to achieve their goals.
> —Mark Sanborn, professional speaker

> **At Your Service**
> Customer service deserves a prominent place at your company's Table Where Big, Important Decisions Are Made. Tragically, we have seen many cases where people on the front-lines knew darn well about critical problems and customer dissatisfaction, or unmet customer needs, but those messages never got to the people at the top of the organization. The people who could really do something with that information simply didn't have it, or didn't realize its significance. Top management should feverishly seek and heed customer input. People responsible for customer service should passionately provide that to top management.

Your company's corporate culture, its personality, has three main factors:

1. The traditions that are ingrained into "how things work around here." In some companies, they are habits based on traditions or values established by one or more founders decades, or even centuries, before.

2. The personality of current top management. The boss puts his or her thumbprints all over the organization. (Ever notice how in a company where the boss wears a bow tie, lots of folks seem to favor bow ties? A case for Mulder and Scully?)

3. The external environment that affects how your company works. If your customers or competitors create a crisis, or at least the threat of one, your company's culture is going to respond (or perish).

So where does the Customer Service department fit in? What business processes are contained in the Customer Service department? The answers come down to this question: What seems to make sense in your shop? And, of course, that answer will change now and then. So make the question:

What seems to make sense in your shop, at this time?

As your company restructures to respond to a changing world, it will likely reorganize functional divisions, reporting relationships, and so on. Here are three key concepts:

1. Keep the overall focus on serving your customers.

2. Keep the information flowing across departmental boundaries.

3. Don't worry about the internal machinations—things are going to change again anyway.

Dry Bed, Trickle, Fire Hose, or Flood?

How well—if at all—does information travel from one functional area to another in your company?

This is the most important question we've yet posed in this chapter. In a way, it's the only one that matters. People often get hung up on organizational charts and department groupings, but what counts is getting information and work processes from *over there* (whether that's an office down the hall, or halfway around the world) to *over here* in order to serve your customers.

You'll get some important ideas in the rest of this chapter for nurturing colleague-to-colleague relationships and creating a flow of information that gets customers helpful information fast, regardless of the formal organizational structure.

Tales from the Real World

When preparing for a presentation to a national association, Don interviewed several people from the association about the challenges they faced. During the course of an interview, a woman described her company as "many smaller teams serving a big team." We've read lots of management literature and attended many seminars, but that off-hand remark probably best describes the ideal way of operating in a company, no matter what its size.

Go Team!

If we had a dollar for each time the word "teamwork" showed up in an executive speech, a company newsletter, or training seminar, we could own both the islands of Bora Bora and Manhattan.

Teamwork is a wonderful concept. Right up there with Mom, apple pie, and Old Glory. But what does it mean? *Really*?

When thinking about teamwork, you really need to ask:

What *kind* of team did you have in mind?

One of the reasons "teamwork" is an imprecise concept is because it can mean many different things. The following figure shows how teams can operate in ways that seem to be almost polar opposites.

Hut, Hut, Hike!

Consider football. Football certainly is a team sport. Yet it's undeniably coach-driven; players follow a tightly prescribed play book and a highly defined game plan. The players on a football team work together, support each other, pull for one another. And they do that operating within rigidly defined roles (an offensive guard cannot go downfield or catch a pass!).

Football, by design, minimizes spontaneity from most players who operate within a tight physical and operational zone. Progress is measured in increments of three feet. It's highly structured, highly regulated, and driven from the top-down (far more plays come from coaches on the sidelines than players on the field). Large, complex, and geographically spread organizations tend to follow the football model for their major corporate team.

Teamwork can follow many different models. When you say you want to "do teamwork," know what you mean by the idea.

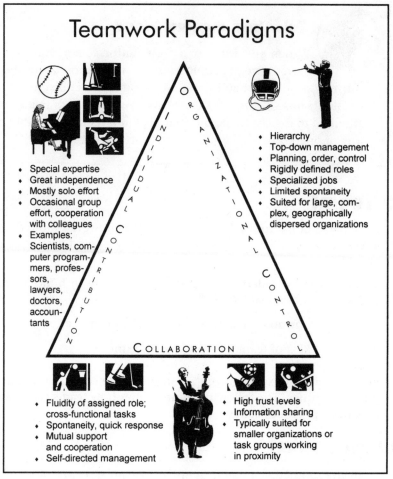

Teamwork Paradigms

INDIVIDUAL CONTRIBUTION

ORGANIZATIONAL CONTROL

COLLABORATION

- Special expertise
- Great independence
- Mostly solo effort
- Occasional group effort, cooperation with colleagues
- Examples: Scientists, computer programmers, professors, lawyers, doctors, accountants

- Hierarchy
- Top-down management
- Planning, order, control
- Rigidly defined roles
- Specialized jobs
- Limited spontaneity
- Suited for large, complex, geographically dispersed organizations

- Fluidity of assigned role; cross-functional tasks
- Spontaneity, quick response
- Mutual support and cooperation
- Self-directed management

- High trust levels
- Information sharing
- Typically suited for smaller organizations or task groups working in proximity

Copyright © 1997 by Don Blohowiak

If sports metaphors don't work for you, an equivalent can be found in the world of music. Football is akin to a symphony, with the conductor providing dominant, controlling leadership, and each member of the team playing a tightly defined—restrictive—role. Ever see a percussionist assume a piccolo player's part on a moment's notice?

Tales from the Real World

One of Ron's clients is TeamCorp NFL, a private licensee of the NFL that produces teambuilding seminars for Corporate America. These seminars revolve around a skilled facilitator, NFL players, and coaches. The sessions facilitated by Ron have been extremely popular because the issues faced by a football team such as varying personalities, coaching styles, selecting good team players, and developing winning game plans are similar to the issues being addressed by teams in the business world. These seminars help companies achieve top results as football teams do—when the entire team is working like a well-oiled machine, where the players want to be on the team and are energized, and where the coaches are doing their jobs as leaders. Championship teams, whether they be in corporations or professional sports, cannot win the big game if the team is disorganized or dysfunctional.

Batter Up!

Contrast the football model with baseball. On the diamond, it is very much an individual's game with bursts of tight coordination between teammates. It's batter versus pitcher working with catcher, then batter versus fielder. An outfielder catches a ball all by himself, but the double or triple play requires the fast, highly skilled interaction of several teammates—each operating within a tightly defined physical and operational zone (like football).

Baseball is characterized by moments of solo performances backed by supportive colleagues, punctuated by lots of downtime between brilliant performances. Certainly, good coaching from the dugout and baseline contributes to both the success of individual players and the coordination of the team effort.

Again, music provides a roughly equivalent analogy. The soloist singer may be accompanied by instrumentalists, each playing their distinct parts, preparing and perhaps performing under the guidance of a musical director.

Many consulting, accounting, law, architectural, medical, advertising, design, engineering, and software firms follow the baseball model. So do academic institutions. These are teams of strong, specialized individuals mostly "doing their thing" with occasional collective, cooperative efforts with colleagues under the guidance of a knowledgeable leader.

Hoop It Up!

Contrast both football and baseball with basketball. Basketball teams operate with greater spontaneous interplay between players. Unlike football's play book and baseball's mostly stationary positions, basketball players are continually on the move. They're constantly reacting to their opponents and interacting with each other.

While basketball players have assigned roles, they enjoy less rigidity and more freedom. The offensive and defensive roles may shift in a split second. While any player can score, a player may literally pass on the opportunity to get the ball to a colleague in a better position to score with less interference.

Just as players on the court constantly communicate with each other to maximize the opportunity of any given instant, so too are they in touch with the coach just inches away from the scene of the action.

Icy Teamwork

Hockey is something of a hybrid, blending elements of the other sports. It has basketball's fast, spontaneous action, *and* an individual goalie with a fixed job and physical zone of operation. All it takes is for one player to not carry out his mission and the goalie has to step up and save the day by blocking a shot from the competing team.

Tales from the Real World

Wayne Gretsky, one of the best hockey players of all time, was once asked what the secret was to his great success in scoring goals. He claimed the secret was knowing where the puck was going to be before it got there. The only way Gretsky could do this was to anticipate future moves and have an instinctive feel for the moves of his fellow teammates.

The secret of a Great Customer Service Organization is anticipating both your customer's potential problems before they arise and the skills your CSRs will need to deal with them. This way, your staff can be trained and ready to assist ably at what could be an Instant of Absolute Judgment.

A musical experience similar to the sports dynamics of basketball and hockey might be jazz. A jazz band plays music in a much freer form than the tightly regimented symphony, and with greater give and take between fellow musicians than typically found between a soloist and her accompanists.

Teaming for You

Which is the best model for teamwork? Better to ask:

What's a team model that's most appropriate to your mission and circumstances?

A football or baseball team is every bit as much a team using teamwork as a basketball team. They just do it differently. A team playing football couldn't do it like a basketball team. The game doesn't allow it. A football or basketball team trying to integrate the individualism of baseball would surely fail. And a baseball team trying to mimic basketball's chatter, frequent movement, and interplay between teammates would likely miss more pop-up flies than it would catch as players ran willy-nilly across the field out of position and into each other. (By the way, this does occasionally happen, even in the big leagues.)

Winning Team Traits

All the sports team models share common characteristics:

➤ Competent players in assigned roles (with some that are clearly outstanding, but effective only as a member of a collective team)

➤ Commitment to success backed by hard work preparing and executing operating plans to meet objectives

➤ Appreciation by all teammates for every player's assigned role

➤ Supportive cooperation between teammates

➤ Acceptance of personal accountability

➤ Acceptance of each team member's strengths and weaknesses

➤ Acceptance and sensitivity to diversity related issues

➤ Quick reaction to unpredictable moves by competitors and opportunities that arise in play

The model that's right for your organization may be none of the above. It's probably a hybrid. On some tasks you play baseball—each CSR on the phone is a baseball player. On other tasks you're playing football—determining refund or discount policies is a coach's job. And yet on others, you're playing basketball—such as collectively generating ideas for enhancing customer value through brainstorming sessions or cross-functional task forces.

Our goal here is to have you realize that teamwork comes in many shapes and sizes. And to get you to be aware of what kind of teamwork you have in mind when you talk about it or try to operate by it.

The value of even your best superstar can't be measured only by individual output. It has to be gauged in the context of contribution to the team. Arguably, Michael Jordan is the greatest basketball player ever. But no matter how many points he scores in any game, he does it with the support of his teammates, *and* his team scores more because of *his* support for his teammates. Playing all by himself, the "Chicago Jordan" would never win a championship, maybe not even a single game. Even the most talented player can't perform the jobs of the others on the team. While Hank Aaron hit all his record home-runs all by himself, he had the coaching and support of his teammates in practice. And he would have had a devil of a time covering the infield, the outfield, and home plate as a baseball team of one.

Tales from the Real World

On the Web page of Bourns, Inc. is this statement: "We know that Customer Service is not just a department in each division that receives orders and answers the phone. Every Bourns employee and Sales Rep provides customer service: whether they put epoxy on a part at a plant, pack units in a box to ship to the customer, review a customer drawing, quote a price or a delivery, answer a corrective action request, visit the customer location, type a letter, analyze a forecast, negotiate a contract, create a new software program, fix a machine, or any of the million and one contributions we haven't mentioned."

Watch It!

Teaming with colleagues from around the organization deeply bothers some people. They feel it infringes on the control they have over their work (or their departments). Some people also have trouble learning how to work with others. They only know how to do it themselves. News flash: With the world as complex as it has become, no person, work group, or department flies solo anymore. Teamwork is not just a business buzzword or fading fashion. Institutionalized collaboration is the way things are and are going to be.

Self-Managed Work Teams

Competent people with adequate information and tools often don't need a boss constantly looking over their shoulder. Self-managed work teams are what the label implies—people who do their work collectively, without constant direction from a boss.

Self-managed teams may:

➤ Propose or even determine their own budgets

➤ Hire and fire workers from the team

➤ Inspect their own work for quality

➤ Buy their own equipment or supplies

➤ Design their own work processes

Would you provide your 17-year-old daughter or son the keys to your car if they'd never been behind the wheel of any car before?

The same principle holds in putting workers in self-managed teams. It's a great idea when:

➤ You have competent, experienced staff who can do the work without constant hand-holding

➤ The people on the team want to try the new method (pilot the concept with eager volunteers; people who resist the idea almost certainly will fail)

➤ The team members are eager to be educated to prepare for their new roles (communication, conflict management, planning, scheduling, or budgeting skills)

➤ Most importantly: you truly trust the people on the team and you really will let them operate independently—even when it's not how you would have thought to do the job! Everyone must be held accountable and accept accountability for their actions.

Cross-Functional Not Dysfunctional

Today's complex market forces companies to operate with tighter cycle times and constant innovation. In responding to these forces, many organizations have found that they need to get more parts of the company working with other parts more often (if not constantly).

You can have both temporary and ongoing cross-functional teams.

A temporary one might be assembled to solve a particular problem (why does this one account experience problems no one else seems to have), or seize an opportunity (what products or services might we offer to the growing segment of people who work out of their homes).

A standing cross-functional team may be one that serves assigned accounts. Members might represent several functional areas within your company, such as sales, product engineering, credit, customer care (the hip name for customer service departments these days), technical support, and so on.

Building a Successful Team

Here are some important factors to build in to the formula for successful cross-functional teams:

➤ Clearly-stated and fully-shared objectives

➤ Well-defined common measures of success

➤ Timely, full sharing of relevant information

At Your Service

Poorly performing teams sometimes fall short of their goals because team members aren't properly educated on the impact their performance has on the entire team effort, both good and bad. Team members need to fully understand how and why their contribution is critical to the success of the team. They must also have a clear understanding of the negative impact they'd make if they do not follow through with their responsibilities. Without question, most human beings don't want to be personally responsible for the defeat of their team. Make sure your team members understand the impact of their actions. Personal accountability goes a long way toward a game-winning team performance.

189

➤ Adequate budgets, tools, and support systems to accomplish the objective

➤ A defined operating structure for the team (who can call meetings, how are decisions reached, how are disputes resolved?)

➤ Calling meetings only when necessary, for a specified amount of time, with an agenda distributed well in advance

➤ Individual performance evaluations tied to team participation and results

➤ Adherence to and acceptance of accountability

Is Your Perspective Correct?

Cross-functional and even intradepartmental work teams add more perspective and insight to any given business situation. The cliché is that two heads are better than one. And they are, when they're both sharing ideas and information and building on the energy and creativity that naturally springs from a genuinely collaborative effort.

When choosing who should be on your team, the idea is to bring together a group of people who do not duplicate the efforts of others. Maximum team performance comes from individuals who each have something of value to bring to the table. It is the accumulation of all these values that results in achieving the overall objective. This is where the well known acronym comes from:

TEAM—Together Everyone Achieves More. If we knew who coined that phrase, we'd give her or him credit, for we could not have said it better ourselves.

Participating on a cross-functional team should not compete with someone's "real job." Team participation must be part of someone's formal job description and performance review. We have talked to far to many people who felt that their boss either intentionally or inadvertently penalized them for their work on one or more teams.

Team assignments represent important work, and supervisors must fully support the people who participate in them—even when it causes a little inconvenience. This especially holds true for cross-functional team members who may be called on to report to another individual on a "dotted line" basis (reporting to someone on a temporary basis, or reporting to more than one boss) for a particular project. Without the support of the regular supervisor, the team member is likely to fall short in performing his team assignment.

The Least You Need to Know

➤ There is no perfect or recommended structure for running a customer service function.

➤ Working through teamwork is most successful when you know what kind of teamwork you mean. Specific tasks and your organization's culture will drive the teamwork model you use.

➤ Self-managed teams can be wonderfully productive and save management overhead expenses when they're adequately supported.

➤ Cross-functional teams help companies meet the challenges of change and competition. To be effective, they need to become part of the normal fabric of day-to-day operation.

CLIFF, YOU'RE FIRED...

Chapter 17

Finding and Hiring Service Winners

In This Chapter

➤ Finding good people

➤ Hiring for personality

➤ Assessing job candidates

➤ Hiring givers

"It's so hard to get good help these days!"

While some people repeat that old saying as a joke, for many companies it's no laughing matter. Especially when employees account for well over 50 percent of the total resource budget. Despite mergers, corporate downsizing, and the flattening of many organizations, there's a real crunch on for qualified human resources at pay rates within your budget.

And as our clients tell us—even those with shrinking staffs—their number one challenge is not competitors, or the economy, or change. They say it's finding and keeping good people. And by that, we're sure they mean the best people.

Good people keep you in the race. The best people win it.

The product you sell will never be unique. But the people who deliver it always will be. You can reach a ceiling for a product's technical performance, but there's no limit to how much people appreciate being treated with respect, kindness, and, yes, gratitude for their business. The competitive advantage in business today comes down to this fundamental: Relationships between people. You bet your business on the people you hire to deal with your customers.

A Tough Job to Love

Let's be brutally honest. Customer service jobs, for better or worse, tend not to be at the top of the economic ladder. And they're usually not most people's dream job. (Don't misunderstand; we think customer service posts can be very rewarding, fulfilling, and lots of fun for people suited to them. But few people in high school or college would list customer service as their ultimate career aspiration. The same can be said for sales and many other jobs.)

Tales from the Real World

Marriott, a service leader in the intensely competitive, service-intense hotel business, has gained considerable notability for its experience in hiring many hundreds of service workers from… the welfare rolls. And it had been doing so for many years *before* it became politically popular to call for programs to move people from welfare rolls to payrolls.

Without shame, the company acknowledges that it employs "the working poor." It's the nature of the business it's in, the company says. But it does so with a caring commitment to its employees and respect for their dignity. Marriott provides extensive training and lifestyle benefits like childcare and education and counseling services to its hardworking service employees. It even maintains what it calls an "employee concierge" to help struggling working people cope with the demands of life that can interfere with regularly coming to work on time.

Not only has Marriott tapped a new source of reliable labor (with turnover rates lower than that for other employees), it's available at the rates the inn-keeper wants to pay, and its efforts have earned the firm prominent coverage in prestigious media such as the *Wall Street Journal*, the *New York Times*, and the *Washington Post*.

Special Generalists

Companies expect many skills from the people they hire to deal with their customers. Hey, you have to. Giving customers personal, pleasing interactions takes many skills and a special inclination for caring. Not everyone is suited to it.

A person good at customer service is part:

➤ Ambassador

➤ Negotiator

➤ Advocate

➤ Accountant

➤ Administrator

➤ Confidant

➤ Detective

➤ Guardian of the corporate coffers

➤ Nursemaid

➤ Troubleshooter

➤ Peacemaker

➤ Teacher

➤ Technocrat

➤ Salesperson

➤ Gracious host

To get people on your payroll capable of delivering the Service Difference for your company, you need to do these three things:

1. Attract qualified (or moldable) people.

2. Identify them *before* you select them to join your organization.

3. Shape, modify, and alter them to embody your cultural values and accomplish the work tasks you set before them.

A Successful Commitment Example

Publix Super Markets, a large ($10 billion in annual sales) and fast-growing grocery chain in the southeastern U.S., has won wide recognition, customer loyalty, and financial success from its commitment to customer service. President Ed Crenshaw tells us that the chain's award-winning service comes from a commitment to service that begins on the first day of employment for a new employee (or *associate* in Publix parlance). He points out that many times a new employee may be only 16 or 17 years old. (How would you like to bet your reputation on a 16-year-old kid holding your valued customer's Instant of Absolute Judgment in his or her hands!)

"We really can't tell in advance if an employee is going to have the commitment to service that we require," Crenshaw admits. But he says that his very young employees tend to be impressionable and eager to please. So they can be shaped into the Publix mold of award- (and loyalty-) winning service. And, according to our analysis, the grocer does seven critically important things to increase their odds of perpetuating a culture "Where shopping is a pleasure."

Here is what Publix does to get employees off on the right foot:

1. They ask their employees to recommend new hires. Nice, friendly, service-minded people tend to associate with others cut from the same cloth. Friends and relatives of good employees often make good employees.

195

2. They indoctrinate new hires into the culture of service on their very first day on the job. They watch videos about the company's service commitment. They hear from store management and their new coworkers about the importance of service, service, service.

3. New Publix associates are paired with a "buddy"—an experienced, service-minded associate—who essentially shares a job with the new associate until, in the buddy's opinion, the newbie is ready to fly solo. "That raises our operating costs," says Crenshaw. "But we feel the investment in assuring good service is worth it." (And, no doubt, the practice motivates the tenured "buddy" whose skill and judgment are affirmed as valuable.)

4. Publix hires new associates on a probationary basis. If store management guessed wrong about the new hire's ability to deliver high quality service, they urge the person to pursue an alternate career (or at least one that takes him or her some-where else).

5. Publix pays wages slightly above market. "We expect a bit more from our associates so we pay a bit more," president Crenshaw says.

6. Publix promotes from within. It grows its own. A 16-year-old bagger may not fantasize about the exciting, fast-paced world of green bananas, canned goods, and frozen carrots, but he or she sees a possible career path to good paying management in a business that's about as stable as they come, with good benefits, and, of course, a friendly, pleasant atmosphere.

7. Publix is employee owned. Doing a good job and treating customers right not only helps with job security, it can build long-term wealth through the company stock plan. At Publix, every employee has a stake in how well customers are served.

After starting new hires off on the right foot, Publix tends to keep its good people for the long-run. And that translates into lower turnover that lowers costs, raises service levels, and pleases more customers. And all that leaves competitors—who sell *identical* products often a bit cheaper—eating Publix left-overs.

Personality Is Competence

Most people who hire other people tend to look at education, technical skill, and work experience. Those might be important sometimes, but more often than not, it's the values and personality of the individual in a service job that will determine success or failure.

Before going further, let's briefly explain what we mean by personality. As we define it, a personality is made of:

➤ **Beliefs**. What we believe, at our core, drives our actions. At the most fundamental level, whether we believe that life and humanity is Good (or not) colors our basic approach to life—and work.

➤ **Values**. We all value different things. Some people value working on mechanical things, others would rather pursue scholarly interests, while others would rather spend their time chit-chatting with other people. Some people value free time. Others value the recognition that comes from their work achievements more than they do free time. What a person values drives their behavior. So your values play a major role in shaping your overall personality. Your values impact the decisions you make regarding the level of education you want to attain, the skills you want to learn, and the experience you wish to accumulate.

➤ **Behavioral preferences**. Some people want to socialize with other people. Some would almost rather die than have to socialize on a constant basis. Some people like to analyze things and compartmentalize most everything into highly structured schemes. Some people much prefer to "wing it." Still others want to command a situation, not analyze or talk about it. And yet others want a prescribed structure and set of rules to guide their behavior.

Caring Is Ingrained

You can instruct people to say "Good morning," and "How may I help you," and "Thank you for choosing [Your Company]." But you can't train people to care. That they need to bring to the job.

If you're going to consistently provide great service, the kind that withstands the Instant of Absolute Judgement, your people need to have *caring* imprinted on their DNA. You just can't fake caring—at least not for very long. People who only pretend to care will reveal themselves sooner or later. The more stressful the environment, the faster the real selfish self comes bubbling up. And stressful times are when you need to be the nicest.

It Takes All Kinds

While we do believe there's a caring personality, we're also sure you can't see it with the unaided eye. Just as it's false to think that talkative people make better sales representatives than quieter, more reflective people, it's a mistake to think that people who appear friendly in a job interview are natural "service types."

> **Quote, Unquote**
> You can have standards, but you can't enforce kindness.
> —Holly Stiel

> **Watch It!**
> Hiring a person who isn't a good fit with his job costs you in many ways. It costs you in lost managerial and administrative time for interviews, processing, orientation, and training. It costs you in lost productivity. And most importantly, it can cost you in lost customers, and bad word of mouth—which can cost you even more. Hire your service people very carefully. You're literally betting your business on them.

At Your Service
People who truly care about pleasing your customers don't all look alike, sound alike, or talk alike. Caring comes from deep inside, and can be found within people of all externally obvious personalities. When hiring customer service people, go beyond the superficial to uncover the real person interviewing for the job. That's the person who, day-in and day-out, will be dealing with your customers.

At Your Service
The better you identify the kind of person you really need to be successful in a given job, the better your chances of finding her, and of her being successful in the job. Only when you know what you're looking for will you be able to figure out the questions you need to ask to assess whether you've found what you're looking for.

In an employment interview, many people can be whomever they think you want for the job. Even if you've hired many, many people, you can be fooled. There will be more on conducting the job interview later in this chapter. For now, let's just make this point:

> A true service personality is not something you can directly observe or quickly detect.

What Personality Do You Need to Hire?

All customer service jobs are not the same. Someone processing returns at a discount store may share some characteristics with a CSR in a special service unit of a firm that constructs nuclear power plants. But people in both jobs will likely have distinct characteristics that make them ideally suited for one or the other position.

How do you know what kind of personality will be suited to a particular job? Well, first you need to understand what the job truly requires. How do you do that? You analyze the job. Determine the fundamental skills it takes to perform it well. Some possibilities include:

➤ Analytic

➤ Creative

➤ Computational

➤ Interpersonal

➤ Adherence to strict rules or protocol

➤ Handling multiple tasks at the same time

➤ Project management

➤ Conflict resolution

➤ Supervisory/managerial

➤ Negotiating

➤ Time management

If you assign yourself the task, you can probably identify many of the true skills—*not* job duties—that lie within a particular job function. There are also instruments that help you create a job skill profile. They are usually available from human resource or management consultants (such as your authors).

Before you set off to fill a job, even one you're sure you understand quite well, it's a good idea to view it with a fresh pair of eyes looking at it through the fundamental skills lens. You may have overlooked or underestimated an important skill set that you haven't previously sought in job candidates for the position.

When you match a job's skill characteristics to a person whose beliefs, values, and behavioral preferences align well, you vastly increase the chances for a successful hire.

How Do You Assess Personality?

Trying to understand what makes someone tick might sound like it either requires a degree in psychology, or, perhaps, a crystal ball. But it really is simpler and less intimidating and more chancy than that.

Reading Personalities

If you spend enough time with an applicant, and ask the right questions, you increase your odds of discovering the true person behind the job application. You can further increase your chances for fully understanding an applicant through the use of personality profiling instruments. There are many brands and varieties of these. All pretty much do the same thing: identify a person's preferences for how they would like to act during their waking hours.

You might want to use these instruments to profile the behavioral characteristics of your most successful people already in the job that you're looking to fill. This can sometimes be surprisingly revealing, and run against your intuition. But it can give you a good benchmark for finding people who will likely behave like Sally and Juan, your star performers, even if the applicants don't seem to be like them at all at first glance.

At Your Service
One of the advantages of personality profiling instruments is that they often rule *in* people who might have been ruled out because they didn't impress an interviewer at first glance. The written instruments can reveal parts of the candidate not visible to even the most open trained eye.

Quote, Unquote
Hire friendly; train technical.
—Bill Marriott, CEO, Marriott Hotels

Ask, Task, and Ye Shall Unveil

When you interview a prospective employee, ask questions that reveal the real person behind the interview mask. Assess the candidate for those characteristic skills you need in the job (which you identified when you profiled the job as recommended above).

For example, if you determined that the job requires a great deal of repetitive work with little variation, you might ask the job candidate about that directly.

Then, later in the interview, try to assess for it indirectly. Ask: *Given a choice between a day filled with many different things to do, or doing one basic job many times over, which would you prefer?* Ask: *Do you get bored easily?* Customer service training firm Kaset International recommends asking this question: *If you have 25 people in a row who have similar questions about a bill, how will you maintain interest in each customer?*

At Your Service
When people interview, they wear a *mask*. It's the face, appearance, and demeanor they feel they need to get the job. Your task is to see through this mask and identify the true person. The secret of how to do this is to ask penetrating questions.

At Your Service
Behavioral scientists suggest that past behavior is an excellent predictor of future behavior. Based on our work with clients, we tend to agree with this. To get a good picture of the candidate, ask him to go back in time and describe instances of when he needed to perform the skills you are looking for—whether that was in a paying job, volunteer role, or other situation. Ask him about any difficulties he may have had. Have him tell you of two instances where applying those skills made for a success. Then ask about two instances that weren't so successful. Many times you learn more from these answers than you do from the answers describing success. Hey, we're all human and we all make mistakes. Did your job candidate learn from his?

Then test the applicant for his or her tolerance for repetitive work. Ask the candidate to fold 200 napkins. If he or she balks or seems irritated at about number 75, you may have a truer answer than any slick interview reply.

Or, if your job requires handling many tasks simultaneously, start the candidate on a test task and interrupt him—several times. Ask him to do several different tasks in addition to the initial one you assigned. Ask him to repeat back to you a list of three things you ask him to remember. How does he handle it?

Can the candidate for a customer contact job come up with five different ways of greeting you? Do you detect an inclination to smile, and is it a genuine, "I like being in your presence" smile?

How does the candidate deal with people not interviewing him for a job? Arrange to leave the room and have some apparent underling pop into your interview space and ask the candidate for information he couldn't possibly have. ("Excuse me, can you tell me how to reach the Information Technology help desk?") Better yet, have a couple of people make apparently unscheduled appearances. Does he greet them? How does he respond to them? Have another "job candidate" show up for an interview? Does he explain that his interviewer stepped out but should return shortly? Is he friendly or combative to his "competition"?

I'm a People Person

Sounds like a great bent for a customer service job doesn't it? Sure. But here's something to explore with your *people person* applicant. Just how much people-ing are they ready and willing to take? Some people like people but only in small doses. Others have an almost physiological need for constant people contact. Both types genuinely like people, in approximately the same way, but not with the same intensity or tolerance. Before you hire somebody to sit in a cubicle, or stand in a store to talk to strangers non-stop for eight hours a day—every day—make sure they're up for it.

Probe in the interview for examples of how much time they tend to spend with people. Real, hardcore, people-people seek people constantly, whether their job calls for it or not.

Seek Giving Servers

"There are only two kinds of people in the world: givers and takers," Don is fond of saying. Well, arguably, that might be a matter of degree, but this much is certain, your service people need to give (and give and give and give). If that giving doesn't come naturally, it's not going to come. Period. When you need givers to serve your customers, hire givers.

Tales from the Real World

A down-on-his-luck taxpayer hitchhiked from out of state to the IRS Ogden, Utah Service Center to pick up his refund check. As it turns out, Ogden doesn't issue checks. But IRS employees there confirmed that he was due a refund. They ordered a check sent to Ogden from a disbursing center. Because the process would take 10 days, and the hitchhiker had no money, IRS employees found him shelter and collected enough food money to see him through until the check arrived.

Perhaps not surprisingly, that same IRS center earned a prestigious Presidential Award for Quality.

Givers give, wherever they're employed. And it shows.

How do you know who's a giver? You can't test with certainty, but you can look for telltale signs:

➤ Have they done volunteer work? (Occasional blood donor counts, so does Brownie troop leader, or PTA, or Get Out the Vote, or Walk-a-thons, and so on.)

➤ Did they work professionally at a charity or do-gooder organization? Takers tend to avoid these.

➤ Did they work in a small company where they needed to wear many hats?

➤ Were they once members of, or did they want a career in, a "helping profession" like teaching, nursing, day care, or social work?

➤ Did they wait on tables? What percentage did they average in tips? What did they think of the way customers treated them? Yours won't be perceived as any better—believe us—no matter how much "better" a clientele you have.

➤ Did they serve in the military? The armed services teach people to treat other people with respect (yes, sir; yes, ma'am) or at least deliver a convincing approximation of it.

➤ Did they ever deal with the public before? What kind of experience was that? What was the worst and best day on the job? What would they have changed? Listen closely here.

You might ask about the sacrifices your job candidate has made in life. People who have never sacrificed probably don't know much about giving. And those who've sacrificed but recall it with bitterness don't know much about giving either.

True givers are people who serve with joy. They find fulfillment, meaning in it. Hire people like that, and you will please your customers.

And Now, This Diversion

Diversify. That's good investment advice for a stock portfolio. And it's a good hiring policy, too. If you've been to any industry conference, picked up a magazine, or read a business book lately, you've probably heard lots about diversity.

In short, it makes good sense to hire a wide variety of people. People of different color. People with different professional backgrounds. People with different accents. (If they speak clearly, communicate well over the phone, and can otherwise do the job, don't hesitate to hire them.) Listen closely to TV anchormen Dan Rather and Peter Jennings. They speak with accents. Rather is from Texas; Jennings from Canada.

With more diversity on your payroll:

➤ You gain a wider perspective in your workforce

➤ Your service group will more accurately reflect the population at large—your customers

➤ You'll enjoy a richer, more satisfying work environment

Variety is the spice of life... in all things.

The Least You Need to Know

➤ The quality of the service you provide your customers depends on the quality of service people you hire.

➤ Good service people are multi-talented and have a "service personality" which is not necessarily readily apparent.

➤ You need to assess the kind of personality that will best fit into your service jobs and then screen applicants for those characteristics.

➤ Good service comes from people who are givers, and they can come in all varieties.

LET'S GET OUT THERE AND WIN! WIN! WIN!!!

Chapter 18

Enable Your Winners to Win

In This Chapter

➤ Motivating through responsibility

➤ Motivating through recognition

➤ Motivating through reward

➤ Enabling great performance

➤ Terminating non-performance

People make the difference in providing high-quality service. And motivated people are more likely to provide great service that positively impresses customers than people who aren't.

Case in point. Airlines. All airlines have an identical fundamental product: delivering you safely to Airport B after taking off safely from Airport A. So, many of them have tried to create a competitive advantage in the service they provide. That theme is reflected in their calling card to the world, their familiar advertising slogans:

➤ The friendly skies.

➤ We love to fly.

➤ Ready when you are.

➤ Something special in the air.

➤ Wish you were here.

> ### Tales from the Real World
>
> Some years back, TWA emerged from some financial difficulties with its employees owning a substantial chunk of the airline's stock. Its advertising boasted about the appreciative treatment you'd receive from the employee-owners (a claim also made by Avis, the rental car giant, and other companies where employees have a real stake in their employer's prosperity).
>
> Don recalls flying that newly invigorated TWA and experiencing a refreshing enthusiasm from the staff who were visibly happy about the renewal of their employer's financial health. The employee's new role as owners of their employer obviously gave their morale—and service levels—a boost from before when they were only "hired hands."
>
> The challenge, of course, is to create that kind of enthusiasm day-in and day-out year after year.

No matter what industry you're in, the quality of your customer service distinguishes your company one way or another. Which way depends on you.

Peak Performance

In the previous chapter, we talked about the importance of selecting people who are oriented to giving great service. Now let's say you've hired well. You have the right people in jobs they're well-suited for. They care about their work, and seem willing to work hard.

Here are some piercing questions for your consideration:

➤ Is each person on your staff performing at or very close to his personal best?

➤ Consistently?

To have your company performing at its peak capacity, you need every individual performing at peak capacity—at their personal best, not just doing enough to keep from getting fired.

Closing the Motivation Gap

Think of the issue this way. Conjure in your mind's eye the ideal customer service employee. We're talking perfection here. Let's create a 10-point job performance scale with that ideal employee performing at the top—a perfect 10.

Next, estimate where each of your employees fall onto the scale—when giving the job their absolute best effort. Do you have a team of eights and nines? Great!

Now, assess where each of your service people's work performance falls on the scale *most of the time*. Are you still looking at eights and nines? Or is it more like fives and sixes?

The difference between your employees' personal potential and their usual performance is what we call the Motivation Gap.

The Three Rs of Motivation

Your under-performing employees are, in a way, holding back. They're not doing their best—most of the time—because… Because why?

There are a couple of basic reasons why employees deliver less than their potential to you. They believe:

➤ You don't really expect their best.

➤ Their extra effort isn't appreciated or rewarded—so they hold back.

Both these reasons stem from a *choice* the employee makes. Most of the time, that choice is made subconsciously. Few people say to themselves, "I think I'll just do only a little bit more than enough to get by—not so much that I really fully invest myself in my work." (Can you imagine anyone talking like *that* to themselves!)

So going "above and beyond" isn't simply a matter of skill or even values, it's a matter of choice.

Watch It!
It's unrealistic to expect people to work at their maximum capacity all day, every day. Yes, you can try to limit your employee's periods of less-than-peak performance by creating conditions and an environment conducive to optimal performance. But even under the best circumstances, there will be times when people aren't performing at their best, for whatever reason. As humans, we're all subject to some degree of mood swings and are influenced by the rhythms of life that can affect our work performance. Some days, and some hours of the day, are going to be less than peak. So, be reasonable in your expectations. Create conditions where people are encouraged to deliver their best work, while neither expecting nor demanding perfection.

Getting your employees to produce outstanding work has been treated by many business people and consultants as some kind of great eternal mystery. If anything is mysterious about it, it's this fact: It's really very simple. You can fully express the "secret" in three words beginning with the letter R.

Responsibility

To give someone responsibility for their work says to them, *I trust you*. It says, treat this work as a source of both pride and joy because you own it, and because you own it, you can freely invest yourself in it.

When people don't own their work, they feel incidental to its progress—they're nothing more than an anonymous cog in an impersonal corporate machine. When people own their work, it's an important part of themselves—something they want to nurture, to make the best it can be.

At Your Service
Motivation is very personal and comes from deep inside. Each of us is motivated by different things—related to personal values, as we discussed in Chapter 17. Because motivation comes from within a person, a boss cannot motivate her employees. They motivate themselves. However, she can create situations and conditions where employees find themselves responding positively—with motivation for producing great work.

At Your Service
Customer service work can be emotionally draining. It's constantly giving care and too often receiving abuse for circumstances over which the employee had no control and likely no involvement. Taking responsibility for continually rescuing the corporate reputation can be emotionally draining and physically exhausting. For your people to have the stamina to do that hour after hour, day after day, they need support and they need rest.

Most people want to take responsibility for their work. As humans, we draw much of our personal identity from our work. A job well done is a source of pride. We say to ourselves, "I did that!" Taking full responsibility for our work heightens our sense of involvement and satisfaction in our work. It encourages us to do better work. Responsibility is a motivator.

Here are some ways to give people responsibility for their work:

➤ Tell them they're responsible. Express your confidence in their competence, and your availability to support them.

➤ Trust them to do the work. Build their skills and competence to take an increasing share of responsibility for the work (work design, scheduling, team inspection, team correction, and so on). Trust is a high compliment and a superb motivator. You'll never get exceptional, inspired work from employees who believe you don't trust them.

➤ Specify quality expectations. Provide the necessary tools and support and tell people they're accountable for meeting the standard. Allow them input into or give them responsibility for designing the system of work necessary to meet the quality standards.

➤ Make clear the negative and positive impact their actions will have on other employees and the company's overall reputation in the eyes of the customer.

➤ Establish boundaries for ownership. How much money can the individual or team spend without an additional managerial approval? Can they set their own priorities? Determine their schedules? Can the team hire their own members? Fire one of their own under certain circumstances? Be clear about the limits of ownership so people can operate fully within the limits but not exceed them. As skills and competence increase, expand the boundaries.

➤ Let them autograph their work. In some hotels, housekeepers leave signed cards in guest rooms. ("This room was prepared for your comfort by Angela. I do hope you find your stay most pleasant. If you need additional towels or would like the room refreshed, please call Housekeeping at extension 456.") In some packing and distribution centers, workers insert little slips of paper into their shipments ("Your order was inspected for completeness and personally packed for you by William T.")

➤ When problems arise or quality slips, give the individual or team the task of correcting the situation. Express your interest and willingness to assist, but respect the boundaries of ownership. If you must assert greater involvement in the process, do so as a partner, not as a thief of the ownership you tried to establish.

When someone owns something, it is theirs. You can't give your employees responsibility for their work while constantly looking over their shoulders, reserving all decision-making, and second-guessing them. That just delivers this double-whammy message: I don't trust you, but I will hold you accountable.

That's a lose-lose proposition that will do nothing to inspire great work.

Recognition

While everyone who works for a living expects a decent paycheck in return, we have yet to meet someone who didn't appreciate a little appreciation as well. When you've done good work, don't you feel proud of yourself? And no matter how self-motivated you are, isn't the good feeling you get from doing good work amplified even more when someone else notices, too? (*Gee, dear, thanks for cleaning the bathroom; it looks great!*)

Watch It!
If you tell employees that they have responsibility by telling them they're *empowered*, explain what you mean by that. Empowerment is a fashionable word not found in some dictionaries. People may not be clear about what you mean when you use the word. Do you know, precisely, what you mean when you say you want to empower your employees? Clarify it for yourself. Clarify it for your employees. And don't think you can fool employees by using the word *empowerment* as a motivational tool with no backbone to it. They will see through the fluff as fast as it takes to say the word empowerment.

Watch It!
You can overdo a good thing. Just as you wouldn't take 20 aspirin when two are sufficient, don't chase after your CSRs shouting "great work, great work!" all the time. Use positive, reinforcing comments when they're deserved. A degree of rarity tends to increase the value of anything—even recognition for a job well done.

Ways to recognize good work:

➤ Post letters from satisfied customers, and from colleagues in other areas of the company who noticed and appreciated the good work done in customer service

➤ Immediately after observing or hearing a particularly strong interaction with a customer, let the customer service rep know you noticed and valued the strong performance. Point out what was done exceptionally well.

➤ Ask a top performer to present some of their winning ways to colleagues.

➤ Provide additional educational opportunities to your top performers. The best usually want to get better. Skill enhancement can be very rewarding.

➤ Discuss effective customer interactions in a newsletter, highlighting particular case studies. It doesn't have to be fancy. We'd advise using paper (it's physically tangible and commands attention, and can be highlighted and stored for future review) but in a pinch, e-mail is better than nothing.

➤ Send handwritten notes to recognize exemplary work. For greater impact, send them to the employee's home.

➤ For truly extraordinary performance, consider public recognition. This could be at a staff meeting, or even a special event, a luncheon, or how about a special snack event in the break room in honor of your achiever. Plaques, certificates, gag gifts; all symbolize the achievement with a lasting, visible reminder to inspire similar behavior in the future.

Watch It!
We love to compete, but strongly caution you about using contests that pit employee against employee as motivators. The idea should not be to have a limited number of winners, but to have an increase in productivity by everyone. Use contests where people receive rewards for certain levels of productivity, not winner take all. It's the cumulative increase in productivity that will give you the greatest increase in overall perceived customer satisfaction. Contests that pit employee against employee can have negative consequences.

While the ideas we mention here are great for recognizing employee successes, remember that what may motivate one person may not be perceived as motivating by somebody else. Try tailoring your recognition gestures to the person receiving the gesture. This will increase the desired effect.

Reward

Sure, your employees receive financial compensation for the work they do. And the company rightfully expects good work from employees for its investment in their salaries. But shouldn't exceptional work be worth a bit more?

Compensation should be related to performance, or else it has no value beyond discouraging people from looking for another employer.

Here are some considerations for using compensation as a motivator:

➤ Tie financial rewards, such as a bonus, closely in time to the behavior that earned it.

➤ Modest rewards in the form of gift certificates, movie or play or concert tickets, can have much greater impact than their equivalent in cash.

➤ Clearly identify the behavior that earned the reward (or, in the case of substandard performance, the behavior that didn't).

➤ When performance is the result of a team effort, reward the team. Celebrations such as pizza party lunches, or catered breakfasts, or mid-afternoon ice cream sundae socials for meeting team goals are a nice way to say thank you to a group, and help foster interactions between colleagues.

➤ When tying compensation to results rather than behaviors, keep the link to results that the individual had control of, or at least influence, over. (An individual CSR exerts negligible influence on a company's stock price.)

Watch It!
Be careful what you reward. Some rewards may yield the opposite results you're looking for. Rewarding a CSR for reducing the amount of time he takes per call—without any accountability for results produced in those calls—can be devastating to your customers. If the employee is self-centered or feels great pressure to slam through the transactions, all he cares about is quickly getting the customer off the phone, with or without a viable solution.

Enabling Through Education

Question: What do you do to help good people turn into great performers?

Answer: Everything you can.

Want better skilled employees? Educate them.

Both of us despise the word "train" when it comes to teaching skills. You can train animals, but you educate people. Animals are trained to carry out specific, limited acts. People apply what they have learned to their jobs, and continue learning, developing, and growing from their experiences. Service isn't an act. It's a response, both pro-active and re-active to the needs and desires of your customers. So we use the word *educate* in place of the word *train*.

Even if you lack internal staff to do extensive employee education, there are a wealth of alternatives.

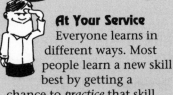

At Your Service
Everyone learns in different ways. Most people learn a new skill best by getting a chance to *practice* that skill. That's why on-the-job training is both very popular and extremely effective. For teaching conceptual material, we favor the method that inspiring teachers have used for millennia: the example. We have seen far too many corporate training programs with students sitting passively listening to an instructor go on and on with so much seemingly abstract blah, blah, blah. As people who give many, many presentations, we know that there's a valid and important role for classroom-style instruction. But it must be engaging, relevant, and directly involve the participants in the learning.

➤ **Community colleges.** Many offer contract instruction right at your company in a wide variety of skill areas. The instructors are often highly capable business people from the community.

➤ **Contract instructors.** Many highly skilled people have jumped on the outsource bandwagon, freelancing their employee development skills, hiring out their instruction or facilitation skills for a half-day, a full-day, or on an on-going contract basis.

➤ **Performance improvement companies.** These consulting and instructional companies provide on-site expertise or certify your employees to become facilitators. Often these companies customize their programs to meet a company's specific needs and offer a variety of instructional methods and media.

➤ **Public seminar companies.** For a modest investment, you can send employees to learn basic business skills such as interpersonal communication, project management, and team-building at a public seminar. Usually held for a day in a hotel meeting room, the public seminars feature competent instruction, take home materials, and the opportunity to purchase additional resource materials.

➤ **Mentor/Mentee programs.** An incredible wealth of knowledge and experience already resides on your payroll... in the minds of your veterans. Have them take part in the training process by mentoring newcomers.

Tales from the Real World

Marriott Hotels assures continual skill development by its employees through a commitment to on-going education. Not only does Marriott offer tuition reimbursement programs, it puts its philosophy of improving service to customers into action at its hotel properties every day. Each shift, every day, begins with 15-minutes of skill enhancement instruction for employees.

Improving customer satisfaction doesn't happen by accident. Continuously improving operations require continuously improving human resources.

Several studies have shown that money spent on the majority of all training interventions was wasted. The reason is that the emphasis was on the training event itself and not on the daily implementation of the information covered in the training. Psychologists tell us that it takes upwards of 28 days of practice to develop a new habit. Education is about developing new habits. If you're going to involve your employees in educational programs, be prepared to have a plan of implementation after the program is over. Otherwise, save your money.

Multi-Function Experience

Some would call this cross-training. We don't for two reasons. First, we dislike the term training. Second, we know that for someone to develop competency in a job, they need to *do* it, not just learn about it, observe it, or try it once. Having a team of players ready to move into a variety of positions means having a group of people with experience in multiple jobs.

That multiple job experience could be as simple as being the driver of the garbage truck one day, and a garbage handler the next, and a truck washer the day after that. Marriott Hotels combined the positions of bell hop, front desk clerk, and doorman into a Guest Services Agent. So now, everyone staffing the front lobby area does what needs to be done, when it needs doing. Guests are served faster, better, and by people who know that serving guests is their job, not performing a small, specialized set of tasks.

Companies who use this multi-functional method swear by it, and here are some reasons why they do:

➤ Greater flexibility in scheduling

➤ More available competent help in critical areas during peak demand periods

➤ Greater employee morale (more job variety, more knowledge and skills)

➤ Greater employee retention

➤ Happier, more satisfied customers

➤ Insurance against the unthinkable—leaving your customers with no one to service their needs

➤ Avoiding being held hostage by a certain employee with special skills or knowledge

> **At Your Service**
> The greatest reward on the job is doing great work. When you've hired right, you've got people who want to do more than the minimum, who aren't happy just getting by. Encourage them by enabling them. Provide the tools, systems, policies, and managerial support to make doing great work as effortless as possible.

The Terminator

Okay, so you have listened to all the great advice we've given you. In fact, you even tried it all. And for whatever reason, nothing seems to work with a certain employee who isn't responding. What do you do?

Have you ever trimmed a tree of dead or out-of-balance branches? Did you notice how that can make a tree healthier and stronger? Well, sometimes you make an organization stronger by weeding the corporate garden. John F. Welch, CEO of General Electric, says you can't be an A+ organization with grade C people. You have to cut your losses.

For evaluating employee performance, here's the essence of a four-quadrant scheme that has been used successfully by many organizations.

Quadrant One: Motivated, Incompetent. When you hire a new employee, the employee is motivated by the new challenge, but is incompetent in terms of the procedures and policies of his new company. He needs to ramp up his knowledge on how the company operates to do his job well.

Quadrant Two: Motivated, Competent. This is the ideal quadrant for all employees to be in. They are motivated, competent, and working at peak performance.

Quadrant Three: Competent, Unmotivated. This is the quadrant where your employees are most dangerous. Here is where the disgruntled employees congregate. You know, the ones hanging out at the water cooler telling everyone else how everything stinks, creating a drag on morale that spreads like a cancer. You have only two choices here. Either correct the situation and help the employee move back into quadrant two—or terminate the employee. If you let the employee sit in this quadrant too long, you will lose a lot of money from their lack of productivity and the negative effect they have on others—including your customers.

> **At Your Service**
>
> If you have employees who routinely don't serve customers with joy, and who refuse to keep up on their technical knowledge, send them on their way. Either to a position that better suits them, or else fire them. Your customers aren't forgiving. You can't be either. Don't carry deadwood. You may bring down an otherwise healthy organization. Prune to prosper.

Quadrant Four: Incompetent, Unmotivated. This is the quadrant of termination. This person is doing you no good. Not only can't they do their job, they're complaining and dragging down morale, too. Sometimes, a previously competent employee's seriously de-motivated state leads to total incompetency. When you find someone in Quadrant Four, you need to act fast. If the employee doesn't quickly turnaround or decide to leave on his own, you will be forced to show him the door. And fast. Any delay only tortures the employee, his co-workers, you, and your customers.

Of course, your job is to keep employees from reaching Quadrant Four. By the time someone lands here, you've wasted the money invested in an employee who didn't work out and will need to spend additional money on finding, hiring, and educating a replacement.

As uncomfortable and painful as it is to fire people, occasionally you might have to terminate an employee for the sake of the rest of the organization.

While we don't recommend termination as the best solution to employee performance deficiencies—they may need better information, skill development, or managerial support—sometimes it's the only real solution. You must be prepared to take this decisive action in order to do your job—to serve your customers—appropriately. The good news is that most of the time termination is avoidable by hiring right and providing the proper environment for people to
excel in.

Remember, hire smart; manage tough.

The Least You Need to Know

➤ Motivation is very personal and comes from within, but management must create a motivating environment.

➤ To motivate employees, remember the 3 Rs: Responsibility, Recognition, and Reward.

➤ Enable great performance—get the best from everyone through education and multiple job experience.

➤ Realize certain individuals may not respond to education and motivation and their employment with your organization may need to be reconsidered.

Chapter 19

Who's Sitting Where?

In This Chapter

➤ Dialing for Dollars

➤ Feeling so good; environmental issues

➤ Outsourcing as a resource

➤ Helping with a Help Desk

➤ Sharing information

Did you ever wonder where that nice customer service person on the other end of the phone was located? Here you are calling the reservations desk at American Airlines using a local number in New York City, and without your knowledge, you might be speaking with a reservations agent in Tucson, AZ. Does this bother you? Not if you are receiving the level of service you expect.

You may have heard that Omaha, NE is the capital of telemarketing centers. Its nearly-smack-dab in the middle of the country location made it attractive from a telephone cost standpoint; and lots of downright friendly folks made it attractive from a labor standpoint.

Today, call centers for the companies with whom you do business can be located anywhere in the world without you knowing about it. Some of these call centers are company owned, and some are independent contractors.

Depending on your needs, there are different methodologies for how you would construct a call center. In this chapter, we are going to discuss the following topics:

➤ How to construct a productive call center

➤ The questions you need to ask to determine if you should build an in-house center versus sub-contracting the service

➤ The pitfalls to avoid with whatever setup you decide to use

The bottom line that needs to be answered by you is does your current setup effectively support the mission and value you wish to provide your customers on a consistent basis?

Dialing for Dollars

We know that most customer service organizations are structured as a reactive (in-bound calls) response to customer calls for service and complaints. Some customer service centers are also proactive (out-bound calls) in that they call the customers to solicit opinions on their level of satisfaction and to possibly sell additional products and services.

Quote, Unquote
We are working to make our Customer Care Center Sun Microsystem's most compelling business advantage.
—Brad Saathoff, Director of Customer Care Center, Sun Microsystems Inc.

Regardless of whether your call center is reactive or proactive, it's important to understand that the level of service provided by your center will have a direct impact on the profit margins of your company. If handled correctly, the call will result in additional dollars. If a customer calls you up and is satisfied with your service, he is likely to continue buying from you. For those of you who sell service plans like software support groups, a satisfied caller is likely to buy one of your plans. If you are a proactive caller and the customer is happy with your style, then she's likely to buy any additional products and services you have to recommend. Both incoming and outgoing calls are all about dialing for dollars.

Feeling Good, Working Well

As with any situation involving the art of influence and public relations, people have to be given the proper environment in which to excel. As we have found out with our clients, establishing several decentralized call centers around the country does not necessarily equate to better service. In the past, many managers believed that decentralization would allow them to react faster to customer inquiries. You know, "close to the customer" and all that jazz.

However, with technology helping to erase the barriers of time and distance, those same companies are now consolidating their call centers to one or two locations. The reason why? They can better afford the systems necessary to properly support a call center in one or two locations than at a dozen locations. It's cheaper and more productive to build a huge center with the right management, equipment, and environmental set-up than to attempt doing the same thing in 12 locations. Usually, companies found out that they wound up offering lower quality in decentralized operations than in centralized locations.

> **Word to the Wise**
> *Decentralized service* involves creating several customer service locations. *Centralized service* involves reducing the number of customer service locations, instead consolidating them into bigger centers.

> **Tales from the Real World**
>
> Kaiser Permanente, one of the largest HMOs in the country, consolidated its 41 member service departments in California to two call centers in Northern and Southern California. The call centers have a combined square footage of 7,500 square feet.
>
> The two centers allow members from anywhere in the state to call with issues such as the physician list, service questions, eligibility, and billing. In a four month study ending 30 days after the opening of the regional call centers, satisfaction with the HMO increased appreciably. The new call centers were built with the right technology to support both the training and mission of the customer service representatives.

How's the Environment?

If you were to talk with any successful customer service manager, she would be the first one to say that her people are only as good as the environment in which they have to work. As you know, you can have the most gifted and talented individuals working for you, but if their environment isn't conducive to maximizing their truest potential, your customers are going to be the first ones to feel the pain. And oh, how painful that can be for everyone.

Let's look at the environmental issues you need to address.

Customer Service Representative (CSR) Workstations

Today, *ergonomics*, the study of the problems people experience in adjusting to their environment (thank you, Webster), plays a big part in how workstations are constructed.

Some companies believe in making sure that all the equipment is at arm's length at all times. This allows the CSR to reach and use any piece of equipment without having to stretch uncomfortably and strain himself. Most organizations provide big computer screens to reduce eye strain. The main focus is on eliminating the common stresses associated with repetitive and tedious motions. The key to eliminating most of these stresses lies in the level of flexibility offered by each individual workstation.

Tales from the Real World

Matthew Gibble, P.T. and Gary Flink, P.T. are physical therapists and co-owners of WorkRight in Fort Lee, NJ, a company that specializes in workplace injury management. Through a comprehensive program involving work site analysis, management/employee education, and ergonomics team education, they have successfully reduced the amount of money their clients spend on workman's compensation and lost productivity.

Factors such as sustained sitting, poor physical condition, ergonomics, posture, and repetitive motion have led to an increase in worker compensation claims of over 76 percent in recent years. With this problem being so widespread and serious, it's no wonder why Matthew and Gary have been so successful. As Matthew says: "Even if your CSRs don't file claims, that doesn't necessarily mean you don't have a problem. If your CSRs are in pain, how can you expect them to do their jobs correctly? Unfortunately, when they suffer, so does everyone else who has to depend on their efforts."

Flexibility today isn't restricted to the height of your chair and desk. It also has to do with the tilt of the computer screen. The right angle of the screen can avoid neck strain and headaches. The proper height and tilting of the keyboard can avoid the disease spurred by technology, carpal tunnel syndrome. In fact, carpal tunnel is becoming a major liability for companies that aren't prepared to prevent this condition from afflicting their employees. Human beings come in all shapes and sizes. The equipment they use must be flexible enough for each individual to make appropriate adjustments and achieve maximum comfort.

Flexibility also involves giving the CSRs the option of how they want to be positioned when they're on the phone. Hertz, for example, builds flexibility into their workstations to allow their CSRs to stand as well as sit on a chair when they're on the phone with customers. Hertz realizes that the comfort of their CSRs impacts the level of service they provide to their customers.

Remember, comfortable CSRs can give warmer, friendlier service than CSRs in pain. And maintaining comfort, hour after hour in a little phone cubicle means paying attention to basic creature comfort. The most comfortable chair you've ever sat in gets tiresome after a while. Our bodies change throughout the day—some muscles relax, others tense up or just get tired of being in one position. To keep your people feeling refreshed, they need equipment that quickly and easily adjusts. Don't skimp on the tools that will keep your people productive and pleasing customers.

Tales from the Real World

Carpal tunnel syndrome can be a crippling disease that limits your ability to perform a job. It is not relegated only to customer service representatives. Anyone who uses a keyboard a lot to perform his job is susceptible to this disease. Ron knows this firsthand as he was forced to have surgery to correct the situation. Having his hand go numb and dropping a cup of coffee was not a fun way for Ron to start his day. Besides the surgery, Ron had to readjust how he positioned himself at the keyboard to avoid a recurrence of the situation. As with any new advances, there are drawbacks if the advances aren't properly used.

Partitioning: Sweet or Sorrow?

Another part of the workstation to give consideration to is the height of partitions. Some companies don't use partitions to foster an open environment conducive to freedom of communications with one another. Other companies that do use partitions sometimes use a 5 foot height versus the standard height of 6 feet. The reason for this is people can usually see further out in the room over a 5 foot high partition than over a 6 foot high partition. Restricting one's distance of sight can have a negative effect on an individual's stress level. (Would you want to spend every work day in a little grave-sized box?)

Another issue to address in partitioned spaces is the ability to reduce external office noise, thereby allowing customer service representatives to concentrate fully on the issues of their customers. Many partitions are manufactured with noise reduction in mind.

Watch It! Providing windows for your CSRs to gaze out may be a morale booster on bright, cheery days. But what about gloomy or snowy days or nights? Some customer service managers believe that a pleasant, consistently controlled environment removes the weather variable. (Ever notice how even the fanciest hotel meeting rooms almost never have windows?)

Call Center Designs

There is a debate among customer service managers about whether or not you should make use of windows in the call center. Some centers reduce the number of windows installed to reduce the glare on computer screens. Other centers, like Kaiser Permanente's call centers in California, use big picture windows to help create a bright, relaxed environment. Manager's offices are located on the interior walls so that CSRs have access to both the light and views from the windows.

As for the set-up of the actual call stations, there's a move by some companies to move from a partitioned format to an open environment format. Some believe that the open environment structure facilitates open communication between CSRs.

Tales from the Real World

An open environment structure doesn't foster open communications if the culture of the organization doesn't allow for it. Detroit Edison promotes employee input through its "Chow and Chatter Program." The program invites employees to have lunch and chat with their managers about anything without fear of repercussions. Some other companies use the circle format to allow for impromptu talks among its CSRs to facilitate the flow of information. Are you walking your talk? Is your company line claiming that it fosters open dialogue? If so, do your actions support this position? As with customers, making promises to your employees and not keeping them is considered to be a capital offense.

Hertz arranged its call center in Oklahoma City in a semicircle format. In each cluster, there are 5 semicircles with a supervisor situated in the middle of the curve (180 degree range). The semicircle format increased the level of communications between the CSRs themselves and with their supervisor. The net effect was an increase in customer service satisfaction.

Breathe Deep

Another issue addressed in call center structures is ventilation. Some setups involve individual air vents for each workstation. Regardless of whether or not you use individual venting, you must make sure that all CSR areas are properly ventilated to maximize individual alertness and productivity. Stale air leads to stale service.

Time-Out Rooms

If you have small children or know people who have small children, you probably have come across a new disciplinary technique known as time-out. When a child acts up, you call a time-out and send the child to a secluded location (room) to get control of himself and calm down.

In customer service, time-outs are given not because the CSR is bad, but because the CSR needs to regroup from a dialogue with an agitated customer, a difficult problem, or just a long string of calls from which the CSR needs to take a break.

To help CSRs rejuvenate themselves during a time-out, companies have literally installed "time-out" rooms. Time-out rooms are usually bright, equipped with music, TVs, and other pieces of equipment that help CSRs relax and remove themselves from the mental stress associated with their jobs.

To Outsource, or Not to Outsource!

When is it best for you to build an in-house call center versus using an outside contractor? The answer depends on your size, budgets, and service situation. Here are a few examples of how *outsourcing* is used and when it should be used.

Here are some special situations to consider:

Overflow—If your call center is structured around a set number of resources (CSRs) and a back-up develops with customers waiting on hold, you can build your system to route the callers on hold to an outside call center. This back-up system prevents your customers from having to wait long periods of time on hold.

After Hours—If you need to respond to callers beyond normal business hours and don't want to staff a call center for after hours, you can switch all calls after hours to an outside call center. This is ideal for 24-hour response times and handling calls from customers who are in different time zones.

Seasonal Service Times—You may have peak periods of customer calls during the year or seasonal periods that coincide with certain promotions. Outside call centers can help handle your calls during peak periods without requiring you to add permanent staff.

> **Word to the Wise**
> *Outsourcing* refers to engaging the services of a third party to operate call centers on your behalf. They provide the equipment, staff, and resources necessary to operate the call centers. They are compensated in a number of ways, including charging a fee per call, for hours of availability, total hours spent on customer contact, dollar volume of sales made to your customers, and so on.

Limited Resources—If you're starting a new customer service call center and have limited resources for providing adequate response, outside call centers might be a cost effective means for handling customer service calls. If you cannot afford the staffing, physical facilities, equipment, and management structure, contract it out. The bottom line is not who provides the service, but whether or not your customers receive the service they expect from you.

Regardless of what your situation is, you have options—including third party call centers—for handling your customer care logistics seven days a week, 24 hours a day.

Help for the Helpers

Where do your CSRs go to when they need help themselves on certain issues in order to properly serve your customers? Why, it's the Help Desk of course! A Help Desk is another version of a call center, except that it's internal. Examples include:

Employee Information

Companies may have internal support services to back up their customer service employees, answering any questions they may have regarding the products or services the company sells. Employees may also call the Help Desk for information on policies, departmental responsibilities, and so on.

Technological Roll Out

A new technological advance may be rolled out by your company, such as a new computer system or enhancements to a phone system or software program. A Help Desk can be set up in advance to help employees with any questions concerning the conversion. This is an extremely important tool to help minimize confusion and ensure that the conversion is transparent to the customer. In other words, you want to make sure that if anyone feels the pain of change, it's not your customers.

This type of Help Desk is crucial in situations involving mergers. When two companies are united, they usually come with their own systems. At some point, the newly found entity needs to make sure everyone is working on the same

Watch It!
Not all call center contractors are alike; not all provide the same value for the dollar. Check 'em out. Look at client lists. Call your counterparts at some of the call center's clients. Are they happy with the service? Are their *customers* happy with the service? Test the centers. Call the numbers for some of their client companies and pretend you need information or assistance. See how well you're treated.

At Your Service
Any change of systems, manual or technical, should include the use of a Help Desk to handle all employee questions and concerns. For example, a company may change the way it reconciles its store receipts for the day's business or any other business processes. For these changes, the company may set up an internal help desk (temporary or permanent depending on the situation) to handle any questions pertaining to this issue.

system and from the same page. Conversions are a necessary evil of mergers, but don't necessarily have to involve a great deal of pain if handled appropriately.

Customized Support

Some companies offer free phone support for any technical questions relating to their products and services. Questions about how to customize the use of their products and services to further meet customer needs may be referred to a third party. Many software companies, for example, have a list of third party consultants to help integrate the software to meet the needs of your company. Who does the third party consultant call when he needs help? Why, the manufacturer's Help Desk, of course.

Tales from the Real World

ACT!, a leading Customer Contact Software Management program sold by Symantec, inserts in all of its packages a Guide to Certified Consultants and Authorized Trainers. These companies and/or individuals are resources who will help you customize ACT! to provide the solutions your company requires. Customizing the program is considered to be beyond what is expected in technical support calls and is therefore referred to qualified individuals who provide support for compensation. Both Symantec and its third party consultants have vested interests in this venture. Symantec provides the quality training and support its consultants need to service the customer. In turn, the third party consultants spend a great deal of money and time training on the product and getting certified. The use of third party consultants allows Symantec to make available a sophisticated level of support for its customers in a feasible and acceptable manner.

The Symantec story shows how the manufacturer can provide a support function (Help Desk) to enable its certified service providers in assisting the end user. Whether you're using strictly internal CSRs or relying on outside consultants for service, you must make sure they're equipped with the latest information necessary to service your customers. Many times it will involve an internal customer service support system.

Sharing the Information

Having the proper environment, the proper seating arrangements, and the right staffing levels and support will mean nothing to your customers if the CSRs aren't provided with the right information they need to answer their customers' questions. This applies to both internal support groups and third party call centers. In Chapter 13, we discussed the concept of how FAQs (Frequently Asked Questions) can arm your CSRs with the information your customers are likely to inquire about.

Quote, Unquote
When the Castle Group is engaged by a client, the client is expecting the highest level of support and experience. The Castle Group is proficient in the ACT! product. But when new versions are released, it requires a new skill set. The Castle Group is quick to embrace the new changes, but it's the collaboration between ACT! internal support personnel and The Castle Group that provides the optimal level of support to the customer.
—Tony Castle, president, The Castle Group Inc.

There are other types of information your customers expect your company's customer service people to have. For instance, when a customer calls, can you pull up his profile instantaneously? A proper profile should include all pertinent personal information like address, phone numbers, products used, and so on. It should also include a history of all previous conversations and requests. There are lots of different software database packages available, PC or mainframe based. The package suitable to your application will depend on the size of your call center and the volume of data you're looking to store and access. There are even customized packages available for certain industries such as plumbing contracting, medical offices, and insurance companies.

The proper environment—the one most conducive to satisfying customers—involves both the physical setup as well as the informational setup. Whatever information you decide to compile on your customers, you must make sure it helps you serve them and provide the perception that you really do care about them. When you have achieved this level of service, you truly are giving your customers *great customer service.*

The Least You Need to Know

➤ How you serve your customers will have a direct effect on how many dollars they spend on you.

➤ If you expect your CSRs to deliver outstanding customer service, provide them with an environment that supports and encourages their best work.

➤ Sometimes, it's wiser, easier, and cheaper to use independent third party call centers.

➤ CSRs may need their own Help Desk in order to serve their customers.

➤ The more you know about your customers, the better equipped you will be to serve them.

It's an Internal Organ

Consider this statement: Your employees are unlikely to treat your customers any better than they feel they're treated by your company.

Would you agree?

What do you think of this statement: The service your customers receive is only as good as the service your employees give to each other.

Service Is an Inside Job

Many of the most successful, best run companies we know operate with a philosophy that their first customers to please are the good people on the company payroll.

Many well-run companies also operate with a philosophy that says each employee should treat other employees as their customers. And that's especially true for the administrative arms of an organization: the Human Resource department, Accounting, Purchasing,

Legal, Facilities, and so on. These are people whose job is to support the other people in the company who are making products or directly interacting with customers (sales, customer service, technical support).

Tales from the Real World

Some companies allow for competition between internal support functions and external vendors. Take a company's internal Information Systems Department. These folks are supposed to identify the computing needs of their internal clients and supply the appropriate hardware and software. Many times in their consulting work, Ron and Don have run into clients who had to go outside the company to purchase the right solutions because their internal support system didn't supply the appropriate technology.

Internal support departments have a monopoly, but need to act as though they were earning their customer's business. While you may have a monopoly inside, it still won't prevent your customers from going to the outside if you don't provide the desired level of service.

Help Your Colleagues Help You

When running a sales support department many years ago, Don was fond of saying, "We give great service, but we can't read minds, and miracles require a week's notice." He was referring to an all too common frustration faced by internal support departments: they're expected to produce the impossible on demand, with no advance notice.

At Your Service

If your service team supports the actions of the sales team, you should communicate all service-related issues to the appropriate salesperson. If the salesperson deals with her customer without full knowledge of everything that's happening with the account, she won't be prepared to appropriately serve her customer. Of course, this is a two-way street. Your customer service support system should support this kind of two-way communication.

The basic key to support departments making their fullest contribution—giving the best service they possibly can to their internal customers—is to be "in the loop." The more information internal support units have about what they may be required to do to support everything the company wants to do to please customers, the better they can do it.

Let's say your customer service group is going to need to upgrade its telecommunication equipment, move to larger quarters, hire more service reps, and upgrade the skills of your current customer care givers. The sooner you bring your computer support people, your facilities people, purchasing, training, and HR people into the discussion, the sooner they can help you get the job done and create the appropriate customer service environment.

Good internal service is usually dependent on good internal communication. And good communication is at the heart of good service. That's true with external customers and it's true with internal ones. Talk to your colleagues in the departments that serve the customer service function, and the ones you serve (sales, marketing, manufacturing, shipping, etc.) The more you interact on a colleague-to-colleague basis, the more likely you are to get the benefit of information exchanged informally.

Companies with good casual information exchange always respond more quickly and smoothly than those dependent upon formal memos and meetings. After all, what is bureaucracy but an excess of formal communication and procedure?

Look in the Mirror

We know that a place of business isn't supposed to be a party. And that working isn't supposed to be a non-stop fun-fest. But we also know that happy people who believe in their employer and feel that their colleagues are supportive of their work give better service than miserable cynics who feel like they're fighting their own co-workers.

Try to answer these two questions:

1. How well treated do your employees feel?
2. How do you know?

If your answer to the second question is: "Because I know," there's a strong possibility that you really don't know the answer to the first question.

Knowing how your employees feel they're treated is paramount to your ability to provide great service to both internal and external customers. Unfortunately, many times executives answer the question from their own point of view instead of seeking the opinions from the people who count. Then they don't have the answers, only dangerous assumptions.

Employee Surveys

We encourage companies to formally survey employees about their satisfaction with the company. The objective is to gauge their support for the corporate mission and to identify their concerns. Employee surveys can reveal roadblocks that stand in the way of your firm providing the greatest value to customers, which prevents negative experiences and can create negative Instants of Absolute Judgment.

If you've not had a tradition of surveying your employees, you might find a healthy dose of skepticism as a reaction to your first survey. Assure employees that the surveys *are completely anonymous*, and that you're interested in the results to build a better company. What should you expect for a response rate? The first time out it could be anything. If you have an employee problem, and the trust level is low, the response level will likely be low. If employees trust you but are eager to tell you of problems, you may see a response rate greater than 90 percent. The average response rate in companies for employee surveys is right around two-thirds. When participation isn't voluntary, employees may feel coerced and that probably will negatively skew the results.

Sample Employee Satisfaction Survey

The following is a sample employee satisfaction survey. It's probably longer than what you would want to use with your own employees, but it gives a broad range of questions that you might consider using with your own colleagues.

As an employee of [Your Company], you are a vital contributor to its success. Your candid opinion is very important to shaping priorities at [Your Company]. Please complete this survey to help top management understand how well [Your Company] is operating, and to get an idea of your concerns. This survey is being sent to all employees and is completely anonymous to encourage honest responses.

Please indicate to what extent you agree or disagree with the following statements.

In your own mind, you have a clear understanding of [Your Company]'s mission, goals, and priorities.

❑ Strongly Agree   ❑ Agree Somewhat   ❑ Disagree Somewhat   ❑ Strongly Disagree

Describe, in your own words, what you think the mission of the company is.

_____

_____

_____

What, in your own words, are the company's top three priorities?

1. _____
2. _____
3. _____

Top management of [Your Company] is genuinely committed to producing quality products [providing quality services].

❑ Strongly Agree   ❑ Agree Somewhat   ❑ Disagree Somewhat   ❑ Strongly Disagree

Overall, [Your Company] is genuinely committed to satisfying its customers.

❑ Strongly Agree   ❑ Agree Somewhat   ❑ Disagree Somewhat   ❑ Strongly Disagree

My immediate co-workers are genuinely committed to satisfying customers.

❑ Strongly Agree   ❑ Agree Somewhat   ❑ Disagree Somewhat   ❑ Strongly Disagree

---

The various departments of [Your Company] generally work well together.

❏ Strongly Agree   ❏ Agree Somewhat   ❏ Disagree Somewhat   ❏ Strongly Disagree

The people in my department usually cooperate and work well together.

❏ Strongly Agree   ❏ Agree Somewhat   ❏ Disagree Somewhat   ❏ Strongly Disagree

My immediate manager encourages cooperation between the people in my department.

❏ Strongly Agree   ❏ Agree Somewhat   ❏ Disagree Somewhat   ❏ Strongly Disagree

Usually, I receive the cooperation and support from other [Your Company] departments that I need to do my job well.

❏ Strongly Agree   ❏ Agree Somewhat   ❏ Disagree Somewhat   ❏ Strongly Disagree

At [Your Company], we generally work to prevent problems rather than react to them.

❏ Strongly Agree   ❏ Agree Somewhat   ❏ Disagree Somewhat   ❏ Strongly Disagree

I have a clear idea of what customers expect from [Your Company].

❏ Strongly Agree   ❏ Agree Somewhat   ❏ Disagree Somewhat   ❏ Strongly Disagree

On a day-to-day basis, I know what is expected of me in order for [Your Company] to provide quality products and services to customers.

❏ Strongly Agree   ❏ Agree Somewhat   ❏ Disagree Somewhat   ❏ Strongly Disagree

On any given day, [Your Company] operates in a manner consistent with its announced policies.

❏ Strongly Agree   ❏ Agree Somewhat   ❏ Disagree Somewhat   ❏ Strongly Disagree

For the most part, I have the freedom to use my judgment in getting the job done.

❏ Strongly Agree   ❏ Agree Somewhat   ❏ Disagree Somewhat   ❏ Strongly Disagree

I have the information I need to do my job well.

❏ Strongly Agree   ❏ Agree Somewhat   ❏ Disagree Somewhat   ❏ Strongly Disagree

I have a clear idea of what top management considers important.

❏ Strongly Agree   ❏ Agree Somewhat   ❏ Disagree Somewhat   ❏ Strongly Disagree

I have the support from management I need to do my job effectively.

❏ Strongly Agree   ❏ Agree Somewhat   ❏ Disagree Somewhat   ❏ Strongly Disagree

continues

continued

I have the authority I need to do my job effectively.

❏ Strongly Agree   ❏ Agree Somewhat   ❏ Disagree Somewhat   ❏ Strongly Disagree

I have the tools I need to do my job effectively.

❏ Strongly Agree   ❏ Agree Somewhat   ❏ Disagree Somewhat   ❏ Strongly Disagree

I feel genuinely encouraged to share my ideas for operating [Your Company] better.

❏ Strongly Agree   ❏ Agree Somewhat   ❏ Disagree Somewhat   ❏ Strongly Disagree

I have received sufficient training to do my job effectively.

❏ Strongly Agree   ❏ Agree Somewhat   ❏ Disagree Somewhat   ❏ Strongly Disagree

I understand how well the business is performing.

❏ Strongly Agree   ❏ Agree Somewhat   ❏ Disagree Somewhat   ❏ Strongly Disagree

I am treated fairly by [Your Company].

❏ Strongly Agree   ❏ Agree Somewhat   ❏ Disagree Somewhat   ❏ Strongly Disagree

[Your Company] management appreciates and recognizes employees for high quality performance.

❏ Strongly Agree   ❏ Agree Somewhat   ❏ Disagree Somewhat   ❏ Strongly Disagree

My manager treats me with respect.

❏ Strongly Agree   ❏ Agree Somewhat   ❏ Disagree Somewhat   ❏ Strongly Disagree

My job involves little unnecessary "make-work."

❏ Strongly Agree   ❏ Agree Somewhat   ❏ Disagree Somewhat   ❏ Strongly Disagree

On the whole, [Your Company] operates without unnecessary bureaucracy.

❏ Strongly Agree   ❏ Agree Somewhat   ❏ Disagree Somewhat   ❏ Strongly Disagree

I would recommend a career at [Your Company] to a friend.

❏ Strongly Agree   ❏ Agree Somewhat   ❏ Disagree Somewhat   ❏ Strongly Disagree

I have been employed by [Your Company] for

❏ 2 years or less   ❏ 3 to 10 years   ❏ 10 to 20 years   ❏ More than 20 years

I am a:

❏ Front-line employee   ❏ Professional employee
❏ Supervisor/Manager   ❏ Senior manager

If I had the chance to tell the president of the company some things I think she should know, I'd tell her:

_____

_____

_____

_____

Here are some other things about the company from my perspective that I'd like you to know:

_____

_____

_____

_____

Scoring

There are many ways to score the results. Some companies will put certain values on each answer such as:

> Strongly Agree = 3
>
> Agree Somewhat = 2
>
> Disagree Somewhat = 1
>
> Strongly Disagree = 0

These values help you tabulate and come up with the statistics you're looking for. Our purpose here is not to teach you how to tabulate surveys, but to suggest that you need to think about it or engage the services of a qualified research professional or firm to help you. Information not properly analyzed is useless to you.

At Your Service
In every survey you use, it's important to include a section soliciting open-ended comments from your respondents. Many times, they'll tell you things you didn't even imagine to ask about. The bits of information you can get in this section are nuggets of gold vital to your success.

Action!

Just as we advised in Chapter 14 concerning customer satisfaction surveys, you need to use research results as an *agenda for action.*

If a significant percentage of your employees tell you they don't believe they have the information necessary to do their jobs well, then you need to find out what they need but don't have. If they tell you they don't believe top management has a clear direction for the company, you'd better find one or get better at communicating the one you have.

Surveys aren't exercises for satisfying idle curiosity. They cost too much to produce, administer, and tabulate, not to mention taking the productive time of all your employees. You need to take an honest look at the survey results, and then take honest action to address what you find.

> ### Tales from the Real World
>
> Finding out how your employees feel should not be limited to internal surveys. You should be soliciting the same information from your customers, such as: were you treated nicely and politely, and did your customer service representative care about your situation? Many times employees telegraph their anger and hostility through their level of service, especially when they feel they have no one else to talk to. Ron knows this first hand through the service he *used* to receive in the pre-Gordon Bethune days of Continental Airlines. It's amazing what one man can do to help change the environment.

Watch It!
If you take more than one survey of employees without taking real action to address the concerns they clearly expressed in the survey, expect a backlash. Employees don't want to have to tell you the same thing year after year. Why bother? Surveys without action feel like make-work: dig the hole; fill the hole; dig the hole; fill....

Service Survey-Itis

It has become popular for internal service departments such as Human Resources or Information Technology to occasionally survey their "internal customers." To many a manager's surprise, such surveys receive either a low response rate, mostly negative reviews, or both. Sometimes this happens even in the face of what seems to be solid improvements in the work they do to support people in other departments.

To ensure a higher rate of response to your surveys, make sure you clearly describe the value the respondent will receive from his effort in filling it out. For instance, you may want to insert this sentence at the top of your surveys... "We value your time and effort. By taking the time to fill this survey out, we will be in a better position to provide you with the tools and information you need to succeed."

What Gives?

The people responsible for performing the work of your company are under pressure. They're being asked to cut costs, increase sales, create more competitive innovations, and do it in less and less time.

Frankly, they're not too interested in getting a memo that says "This survey MUST be returned by Monday at 9 a.m. sharp."

A common phrase we hear from line department managers about their well-intending colleagues in support departments goes like this: "Those guys forget who's working for whom!"

Of course, everyone on the company team should be working to support the company's mission as it relates to working—together—for external customers. Distractions from the core mission, no matter how well intended, take away from the company's focus, and ultimately, from how well it serves customers.

We once worked with a colleague who grew visibly tired of the time spent on internal "nicey-nice." The executive viewed the surveys and meetings from the internal departments that were supposed to help him do his job better as unwanted assignments and obligations. He became quite bold and vocal about it—frequently repeating a remark reflecting his frustration, "As this company goes out of business, we're going to do it with the best HR department in the industry!"

Sarcastic? Sure. But it sends an important warning.

Watch It!
The quest to improve internal service can take on a life of its own. Formal surveys, "feedback" meetings, and the like can suck up a lot of time that "line management" wants to spend trying to serve the customers that make or break the business: those on the outside. The ones that pay money to your company to do its core work. Yes, you need good internal service. But providing it shouldn't get in the way of providing great service to your *real* customers.

The Least You Need to Know

➤ Employees are important customers; how they feel the company treats them will be reflected in how they treat external customers.

➤ To accurately assess how employees feel they're treated, survey them. Ask pointed questions that go to the heart of how well they feel they can accomplish the organization's mission.

➤ Take action based on survey results. Address employee concerns.

➤ Keep perspective on "internal customers." Service between colleagues is valuable and important, but not more important than service to your paying customers.

It's a Worldly Thing

The year was 1962. Back before man walked on the moon. Before fat-free ice cream. Even before we knew we *had* to have a cell phone, and a desktop, laptop, and palmtop computer, *and* a subscription to America Online (or risk social isolation).

Because personal computers hadn't been invented yet.

Well, way back in those dark days, a pretty serious guy up in Canada named Marshall McLuhan was writing essays and books that no one really understood. But everyone was sure they were brilliant. He said a few profound, memorable things—including "the medium is the message." And he said that with TVs and other electronic communication devices spreading like dandelions in May, the world was fast becoming a "global village."

The Amazing Shrinking World

If you've ever taken a trans-oceanic flight for many long, cramped hours, you know the world is still physically a big place. But McLuhan grasped an important truth those many years ago. Technology has shrunk the barriers to communicating—and doing business—across time and space. Now, just as easily as your customers can be in Sylvania (OH), or Sedalia (MO), they can be in Scandinavia, Somalia, or Slovenia!

And your suppliers might be there, too. Walk through a grocery store. You can find orange juice from Brazil, apples from New Zealand, raspberries from Guatemala, coffee from Africa, jams from England, wine from Italy, Chile, or Romania. Look at the labels in your closet. You may well find items made in Mexico, Bangladesh, Honduras, China, India, maybe even the United States of America.

> ### Tales from the Real World
>
> American companies are renowned for their marketing prowess. To them, paraphrasing Shakespeare, all the world's a market. Don recalls, with mixed feelings of pride and disappointment, his first foray outside the United States. He drove through a tunnel connecting Detroit, Michigan with Windsor, Ontario. What mysterious delights awaited him in this foreign land? He got a hint with the first rays of sun that glared onto his windshield once clear of the tunnel. There, glaring down from the Canadian side of the border's customs and immigration station was a huge, red and white billboard for...Kentucky Fried Chicken.
>
> Likewise, much more recently, while crossing into post-war Croatia, once cleared through the customs and immigration checkpoint, he and his local clients entered the country passing a large, red and yellow billboard for...McDonald's.

We're All Connected

The developed world is now blanketed by cell phones, fax machines, and express delivery services. And then there's the Internet, which makes it possible to travel "around the world in 80-nanoseconds." We discuss using this modern marvel much more fully in Chapter 25.

The point is this: Your market can be as big as the Earth, and your customers any one of its people.

Tales from the Real World

The barriers to trade between nations once included distance, language, and currency.

High speed travel and data lines have effectively reduced distance—it's much cheaper to e-mail or fax correspondence abroad than to have it physically delivered.

English has become the common tongue of commerce.

And currency, while not yet universal, is easily bypassed by credit cards. Or easily exchanged—at globally connected automatic teller machines, ATMs.

Just for the heck of it, while traveling on business, Don has made ATM withdrawals in the local currency in various countries. Using his regular ATM card, he has gotten cash-to-go in such places as a gift shop in London, a baggage claim in Paris, and in the shadow of a thousand-year-old castle in a quaint Italian town square—complete with stone fountain and cobbled streets.

Global village indeed!

Serving Citizens of the World

Because the United States is so large, you could easily spend your entire life traveling extensively and never leave its borders. But when you do leave the good old U.S. of A. —or interact with people who've never been anywhere near it—you realize that the whole world is not a mere annex of our familiar Land of the Free and Pizza Hut. Here are some things you should consider when setting up to serve your customers outside North America.

Toll-Free Isn't Barrier-Free

In North America, 800 and 888 numbers are everywhere. But they don't work from everywhere. Make sure your ads, newsletters, invoices, and other printed customer communications provide a way for people outside the toll-free calling area to reach you.

Ron was traveling in the U.S. when he received a message from a colleague regarding an interested prospect in Canada looking to book him for a speech. Ron called the prospect in Canada and was put through to voice mail to leave a message. Inadvertently, Ron left his toll-free number for the prospect to call back on. After waiting for three days and not hearing from the prospect, Ron called to find out what was going on. It turned out the prospect tried calling Ron but was unable to reach him on his toll-free number from Canada.

If you have a toll-free number, call your long distance carrier and see if it can be accessed from outside the U.S.

Fax Over Phones

Many customers abroad prefer to do business by fax or e-mail. While many of your customers outside North America may speak English, they may be hesitant to call for assistance. They may have difficulty understanding English spoken over the phone, or may be self-conscious about speaking a language they don't use very often to a disembodied stranger.

By using written communication, they can compose their thoughts and take all the time they need to construct their questions—and read your answers—in English.

Fax and e-mail communications also involve less hassle—and time—than dealing with international postage delivery.

Be Mindful of Time Zone Differences

Your customer may be many, many hours removed from your local time. When answering calls from abroad you may want to avoid answering the phone with "Good morning," when it's nighttime where your caller is. Keep a time zone chart (found in many atlases and some computer programs) handy. Confirm dates and times for all follow-up phone appointments (is your *tomorrow* their *yesterday*?). Ask when your customer would like to receive fax transmissions from you.

Observe Differences in Holidays

The fourth of July is just another day to most people in the world. But the fifth of May is as important to Mexicans as our Independence Day is to us. Every nation has its own holidays—and holy days—and they very well might not coincide with ours—not even Christmas, which the Eastern Orthodox church celebrates on a day different than Western Christians. In Arab countries, Friday is their weekly holy day.

Obtain a list of the special days for the countries in which you have customers. Keep a master calendar. Don't offend your customers by calling on, or trying to set-up a phone appointment for, those days.

Set Policies for International Customers

Despite the improvements that come with our modern age, there still are at least a few hassles in doing business internationally—for both you and your customer. Reduce for your customer as many of the uncertainties and complexities as you can. The more you fail to disclose at the front-end, the more hassle you have to contend with later.

Here are some questions to consider and clarify for your nondomestic customers:

➤ Do you require a Letter of Credit (LC)? Most companies will ask for a letter of credit from foreign customers. This is a draft the customer draws up with his bank outlining issues such as payment terms, shipping terms, and pricing.

➤ Do you expect payment in advance or will you bill customers abroad?

➤ If you bill foreign customers, when do you expect payment before considering them in arrears? Is this policy more tolerant than the one for your domestic customers?

➤ Do you accept international money orders?

➤ Must funds be in U.S. dollars?

➤ Must payments be drawn on a U.S. bank?

➤ If you accept payments in foreign currency, which currencies do you accept, and at what exchange rate?

➤ If you require money to be wired to your bank, how does the customer obtain the necessary information?

➤ Do you make these and all your other conditions and policies clear in your offer to sell?

➤ Do you build the value added tax, customs fees, or other applicable tariffs into your order forms?

➤ What documentation does your customer need to serve as proof of purchase for their tax records? Will your sales form suffice? Might you need to supply your customer abroad with an invoice or statement your domestic customers don't require?

➤ What are your shipping terms for international shipments? FOB (Freight on Board) means the shipper pays the shipping costs. CIF (Cost of Insurance and Freight) means the buyer pays the shipping costs.

As we pointed out earlier in the book, customers place a value on your product or service that may be different from how you normally view it. A customer abroad may be perfectly willing to wait weeks for a boat to bring your goods to their country. Or they may be willing to pay more for air delivery. Or much more for express delivery.

Don't assume. Identify the related costs and give your customers the option to spend their money in accord with their needs and values.

Communication and Cultural Issues

The biggest hurdle in doing business internationally and serving customers abroad with service they'll find pleasing is not overcoming the barriers of time and space. It is the barrier of culture and communication.

Special Language Units

Earlier in the book we discussed special teams in the customer service function to serve your special customers. You might consider hiring multilingual staff for dealing with customers in their native language. If you have a large enough customer base that justifies the expense, you could establish special phone numbers dedicated to receiving calls from customers in particular countries or customers who speak a common language (for example, Spanish or Chinese).

Tales from the Real World

Besides the words being used, there might be other language differences you need to be aware of. Ron was invited to speak in Brazil a few times over the last couple of years. On his first trip, he was warned that it takes approximately 30 percent more words in the Portuguese dialect spoken in Brazil as it does to communicate the same sentence in English. Ron, being a fast talker from New York, really had to slow down his rate of speech. Fellow speakers suggested that he speak in sound bites. Keeping this in mind, his programs were successful and the translators managed to keep up with him, although they had to be compensated with battle pay.

It's All in the Translation

If you need to conduct an important transaction with a customer who speaks no English, but don't have anyone on your staff who speaks the customer's tongue, you have some options. You can hire a commercial service for interpretation (spoken words) and translation (written words). If none are available locally, try your local university or college language department. Even if no one there can assist directly, they likely can point you in the right direction for help.

When you hire someone to interpret an in-person or video/phone conference, try to meet with the consultant in advance of your important meeting. Give them a chance to become familiar with your industry and company's terms of art, as well as the business issues you intend to discuss. The more they understand before the meeting, the less chance for misunderstandings during it.

If you're conducting the conversation by phone, you can obtain interpretation services from the major phone companies. AT&T, for example, is equipped to translate some 140 languages (Amharic to Yiddish).

Bilingual or Not?

If you deal with customers in their native language, make sure you do it well. Someone who has taken one of those crash courses in a language, or listened to a cassette tape-based language course, or taken two years of high school instruction in a language, or who happens to own a handheld translation computer, is *not* bilingual!

Likewise, be sensitive to the tongue your customers actually speak. Spanish spoken by Spaniards is different than that spoken by Mexicans or Chileans.

Also beware that someone who has had extensive schooling in a language but no exposure to the culture may well miss a customer's cultural cues and nuances. Spoken communication is more than merely decoding the literal meaning of words.

Welcoming Not Casual

Americans tend to be much more casual in business interactions than people elsewhere in the world. We think it's genuinely friendly to call Robert Smythe Bob rather than Mr. Smythe. Many cultures around the world don't see it that way. If it's not Senora Rodriguez, or Mr. Hamaguchi-san, it may be offensive.

When dealing with customers abroad, adopt an attitude of *respectful* gratitude for their business, and one that is more formal than you would likely use when dealing in the U.S.:

➤ **Use Mr. or Ms., not first names.**

➤ **Speak and write with the elevated language of diplomacy.** Rather than, "Thanks for your business!" it's, "We are honored to serve you, and very much appreciate your confidence in our firm."

➤ **Speak slowly.** Your customer may have great command of English, but he or she is still mentally translating, and may be dealing with unfamiliar terms that your company or industry consider familiar. Over the telephone or video conference, your customer must contend with a slight delay from the physical transmission winding its way around the globe, plus being many time zones removed—where they may be getting quite sleepy while you're still perky.

> **At Your Service**
> Some of your customers abroad who are hip to American TV shows see them in their native country long after they've gone off the air here. You may have customers who want to show their familiarity with U.S. culture by mentioning shows such as *Three's Company*, *Dallas*, or *Kojak*. Just say, "Oh, yes. I haven't seen that one in a while."

➤ **Avoid slang and colloquialisms (regional phrases).** So no *yo!*, *whoa*, or *way to go*. Other examples of phrases likely to be lost on—or even offensive to—your customers abroad include: "How y'all doin'?" "Cool!" "Sorry, but that dog won't hunt," "What's up?" "Awesome," and so on.

➤ **Avoid humor.** You don't need to be deadly serious. But given language and cultural differences, and the generally sterile nature of telephone conversations across great distances, you risk great misinterpretation of your attempts at humor. Your customer abroad may think you are frivolous, rude, and disrespectful. If your customer jokes a bit, great, feel free to loosen up a tad. Otherwise, it's buttoned-down and businesslike.

➤ **Competence with a smile is universal.** Respect, helpfulness, and courtesy are valued and appreciated the world over. Please and thank you are welcome in any language. Pleasant, polite civility always translates well.

➤ **Hold back on the chit-chat unless your customer engages in it first.** Even when your customer initiates small talk, remember, your cultural perspective and your customer's may be very different. For example, it is popular in the States to be openly cynical about politicians. That is not universal the world over. In some cultures, political office holders are held in very high esteem; some are viewed as gods on earth.

➤ **Given the above guidelines, be yourself.** Some customers abroad are very eager to practice their English and discuss popular Western culture. If they sense you are a warm, welcoming person, they may well engage you in discussing the latest movies, pop songs, or political issue. Take your cue from your customer and respond in kind. Two humans who want to communicate with each other tend to do just fine.

Tales from the Real World

When Don was preparing for a European speaking assignment, he spoke with some colleagues who shared horror stories of inadvertently offending their audiences by doing something Americans don't even blink an eye at: the speaker removing his suit jacket.

Armed with that warning, Don began presenting in Italy at a public seminar all buttoned up. At the lunch break, the local host told Don the audience was thoroughly enjoying the information, getting all the humor, and finding the high energy presentation quite refreshing. Don asked about the possibility of removing his jacket in the warm meeting room during the afternoon session. "Sure, no problem," his host assured him.

After working up a good sweat during an interim question and answer session, Don asked the audience if anyone would be offended if he removed his jacket. To smiles and approving nods, he shed the wool jacket, and found no adverse reaction from his audience. But, just in case, he kept the shirt sleeves rolled down. No one walked out. The end-of-day reviews were extremely positive. And Don was invited back by the client.

How Can I Offend Thee? Let Me Count the Ways...

Much of the world watches the movies and TV shows made in the U.S., and increasingly all the world's citizens buy the same name-brand consumer products. However, there are still many distinct cultural differences between Buffalo, Tokyo, Morocco, Mexico, and Jericho (Israel, or Long Island, NY).

All symbolic communication—words, gestures, colors—take on different meanings depending on where on our globe you stand. Death is symbolized in black in the U.S., but in Japan it's the exact opposite: white.

There are many ways to inadvertently offend someone with a different cultural orientation than your own. To serve your customers with the kind of service that keeps them coming back to your company, you need to be mindful of cultural issues.

Your customer abroad may speak better English than you do. He or she may be up on the latest U.S. politics and movies. But that doesn't remove him or her from their native culture. And that's the filter your service will run through.

Language

You might think that simply trying to speak your customer's language, even though you aren't very good at it, will score you points. You might be assuming very incorrectly. While some may find your attempt quaint and amusing, others may take great offense at hearing their beloved tongue mangled—even by someone who's doing it in an attempt to "reach out." The French, for example, tend not to appreciate poorly spoken French. And they detest boorish Americans who become indignant when they encounter French people who do not speak English. The nerve!

You may be better off speaking English slowly and carefully than stumbling through a language you really aren't prepared to speak. Your customer will be both embarrassed and confused for your well-intending but inappropriate efforts.

Gaffes can occur even when the translation is flawless, or your customers speak fluent English. A couple of examples.

➤ We know of one company that wanted to tout its "collaborative" style of customer service. What could be wrong with that? Well, to a North American, *collaborative* may equate with teamwork, partnership, and so on. But to some Europeans, the word collaborative produces a dreaded echo. During World War II traitors *collaborated* with the enemy.

Tales from the Real World

Sitting on a plane, the gentlemen next to Ron asked what he did for a living. Ron answered that he helped organizations dominate their markets and get closer to the people they serve. The gentlemen, with his British accent, paused, and then said that was illegal in Europe. Confused, Ron asked what was illegal. The gentleman responded that companies in Europe cannot openly use the word dominate in their literature. It smacks against the spirit of fighting monopolies. This example proves that sometimes the words we use in this country may be perceived as having different meanings and levels of intensity in other cultures. You may want to check with your foreign colleagues to see if any words or gestures you are using will offend anyone.

➤ Casual or slang words that aren't offensive here might be considered rude to fellow English speakers over there. Example: *Fanny*. To folks in the U.S., that's casual speech for one's seat. To someone in the U.K., it means a part of feminine anatomy that's not spoken of in polite company. Likewise a Brit may speak of *fags* and mean cigarettes…

Don't risk offending your valued customers in other lands. Foul-ups in spoken or printed communications risks offending customers permanently (yet another Instant of Absolute Judgment).

Invest in getting qualified assistance. There are consultants who specialize in "intercultural," "multi-cultural," or "cross-cultural" communication. If you need assistance locating such experts, contact the Institute of Management Consultants, listed in Appendix A, "Resources."

Written Communication

Have your material that's written in a foreign language typed up by someone whose native tongue is that foreign language.

There are many classic stories about well-intending professionals who were competently bilingual but missed some subtlety in the translation. To everyone's embarrassment, they unknowingly declared to the locals product benefits in catchy, but slightly off-the-mark phrases along the lines of "Won't give your mother warts," "Cows think it's delicious," or "Best when used naked."

Chevrolet found its Nova model a tough sell in Spanish speaking countries where the words *no va* literally translate to *no go*.

Unintended Slights

The world's customs and habits are full of gestures that mean "You're great!" in one culture, and something quite offensive in another. Just crossing your legs a certain way, waving a certain way, standing too close or too far away... all these hold the potential for insulting your customer when no insult is intended.

One European asked Don during a seminar break why the Americans had such an annoying habit in their restaurants—the one where the food server keeps returning to the table to ask if everything was okay. "The interruptions aren't okay!" he declared.

So you see, even trying to assure customer satisfaction can irritate or offend someone not accustomed to the practice.

We suggest you develop a deep understanding of the cultures in the lands where you do business abroad. Several excellent books are available in your bookstore covering the subject of doing business internationally. Get some. Heed their advice. Be mindful of your customers' customs and taboos.

The Least You Need to Know

➤ The market today is Planet Earth. Your customers and suppliers can be anywhere.

➤ Doing business on a global scale means preparing to serve your customers outside the U.S. differently than your domestic customers. You need to do your homework.

➤ Because of differences in language, customs, and traditions, there are many ways to offend your customers abroad. Your company must prepare to treat people in the manner they expect.

➤ Good service can be universal when the focus is on pleasing customers, foreign as well as domestic, with polite competence.

Part 5
The Gizmos & Gadgets
of Great Service

Great service depends on a satisfying relationship between Customer and Company. And to your customer, your company is both humanity and technology.

Personally Pleasing Memorable Interactions must be supported by solid technology that enables them. That's technology as a tool for your employees.

And, increasingly, those interactions are totally dependent on technology. In fact, with automated support systems, your customers may be interacting with only your company's technology! In that sense, your technology is more than a tool. It is your service to customers.

The remaining chapters in this book discuss technology: as a tool and as a provider of customer interactions.

We look at everything from headsets for your customer care representatives, to automated phone systems, to e-mail, and serving customers over the Internet.

You can't give great service today without technology. So let's look at how you can make the tools best serve you and your customers.

Hello There!

Providing great service to your customers by picking up the phone to competently handle transactions is only half the battle. Choosing which phone system to install is the other half.

Okay, so you know what a phone looks like. And you know what it does. But have you really thought about the features you need on your phone system in order to serve your customers appropriately? It's a good investment of your time and money to get the right phone set-up. After all, it's hard for your CSRs to perform better than the equipment they have to work with. Whether your phone-based customer care representatives work in a state-of-the-art call center or at a couple of small desks in a corner of a small regional sales office, good telephone equipment can make a real difference in their performance and productivity.

Choosing the appropriate system involves:

➤ Determining how many lines you need

➤ Staying within the budget

➤ The ancillary equipment your CSRs need to make using the phones both easy and capable of delivering full service to your customers

Wear Your Phone on Your Head

Quote, Unquote
According to statistics we have accumulated with our clients, CSRs wearing headsets handle 22 percent more calls than their counterparts who don't. Part of the reason for this is that people using headsets either need less time for breaks or can spend more time on the phones between breaks because they are less stressed and more energized…
—David Yoho, call center expert

Let's begin with the simplest part of the whole telecomm system—headsets.

Headsets deliver great convenience and boost productivity to anyone who spends any significant part of the day on the phone. Yet we're both amazed how many people still don't use them, especially people functioning as CSRs. Let's look at the many ways you can change your life by using a headset.

Mobility

Do you think best when you're standing, sitting, walking, or a combination of all three? Headsets allow you to do all of these things as well as get up and look at files or reach for any information you need to adequately serve your customers. This sure beats being chained to a short cord. If nothing else, having a bit of mobility increases the choices for working comfortably.

Tales from the Real World

Ron always felt like a prisoner tied to a receiver when he was on the phone, until his headset liberated him. Ron was an expressive and demonstrative kind of guy who had trouble sitting in one spot. His headset allowed him to stand when he spoke to his clients and deliver his message with the same energy as he would a speech in front of hundreds of people. He was known to go on walks through his office while speaking to clients. Where he wound up after the call was over was secondary. His primary concern was whether or not he was able to effectively communicate his message in a manner that was pleasing to his clients. Headsets gave Ron the freedom to be himself on the phone.

Lose the Umbilical Cord

If you don't want to be tethered even by long phone cords, you can use a wireless headset that works similarly to cordless phones. If you saw the movie Jerry McGuire (you know, "Show me the *money,*") you saw sports agents using wireless headsets as they roamed the halls and building while they were negotiating on the phones. The point is the more comfortable you are, the better you will handle your customers' problems. For some people, that means cordless headsets.

Hands Free

It's amazing the difference between having one hand free and two hands free. Headsets free both of your hands to operate equipment essential to your work, such as keyboards, calculators, and paper files.

Tension Release

Ever get tired of sitting in one position all day long? Or did you ever have the urge to jump up and down or do some kind of aerobic exercise to release nervous energy or vent anger when dealing with difficult customers? Whatever your needs, headsets allow you to talk in any position your little heart desires to release that tension. Studies have proven that headsets reduce the amount of instances in which CSRs are likely to emotionally respond to customers.

Fewer Headaches

Headsets are a stronger form of medicine than aspirin when it comes to getting rid of headaches and body aches associated with telephone work. Studies show that people who use headsets feel less pain. One of the big reasons for that is that you don't need to crank your neck over to cradle the receiver. Doing that literally makes talking to your customers a pain in the neck!

Watch It!
If you're using headsets or are going to start using headsets, make sure the model you use has a mute feature. With the mouthpiece in close proximity to your mouth, it's very disturbing to the person on the other end of the line to hear you cough, sneeze, or slurp a drink. It's almost like a gale wind blowing in their ears. Also, a mute button allows you to carry on off-line conversations without your customers hearing you, though we advise extreme caution just in case that mute button isn't actually pressed like you thought it was.

Sharper Listening Skills

CSRs using headsets tend to listen better to their customers. Why? Because the sound and quality of sound is focused squarely in the ear. There are no outside noises to cause momentary loss of hearing, and they aren't fumbling with the phone, trying to type with one hand, and so on. Many headsets come with a volume control that lets you turn customers up or down as the phone connection dictates.

Improved Speech Quality

Yes, you can improve the way you sound to the customer by using headsets. The reason is simple. The mouth piece is situated in close proximity to your mouth, closer than a normal receiver would be. And it's adjustable, so you can position it so that if you project your voice or speak with intense breathy-ness, that air doesn't slam into the mouthpiece, causing annoying sounds for your listener. Any unnecessary sounds can be interpreted by your customers to mean anything they imagine (rudeness, aggressiveness, sloppiness...), even if those sounds were innocent and had no meaning at all.

Higher Quality of Work

As if you aren't sold on the power of headsets already, let us provide you with one more compelling reason. Are you ready? People using headsets tend to perform better quality work. Just look at all of the issues addressed in this section and it's no wonder that headsets are the preferred piece of equipment for most CSRs. In fact, headsets probably rank right up there with computers on the top ten list of equipment critical to a CSR's success.

At Your Service

After reading all about headsets, you probably have a different image regarding their importance. Like any other type of equipment that's critical to your success, don't jeopardize your performance by buying equipment of lesser quality. Invest in quality models. After all, if the headset is your communications gateway to the world, don't you want it to be the best gateway available? You wouldn't expect a surgeon operating on you to use anything but the best equipment. Your customers deserve the same from you. You will find sources who sell quality headsets listed in Appendix A in the back of this book.

Oh Dear, Which Phone Do I Need?

If you were to set up your call center ten years ago, it would have cost you tens of thousands or more dollars to fund the necessary mainframe computer, custom software, and application development. Today, for a fraction of the cost, you can create the same functionality of a topflight call center that's able to synchronize the use of your phone and computer systems.

Even for a small business with one to ten employees, you can create a topflight call center. All you need are three components: caller ID from the phone company, products that connect and synchronize your phone system and computerized customer database, and of course, your database. What would have cost you over $100,000 ten years ago will cost you now as little as $500 (maybe even less depending on how well you can negotiate).

Imagine being a CSR working in a bank and when your phone rings, you answer it by saying: "Good morning Mary, how are you today? You must be happy that Jennifer (Mary's daughter) is going to graduate from college in only two weeks! What are you going to do with all the money you're going to save on education?" (hint, hint) We guarantee Mary feels quite welcomed and appreciative with your approach, wouldn't you? This is truly a classic PPMI (Personally Pleasing Memorable Interaction).

Now, we're going to talk about some of the telecommunication systems and equipment that will enable you to build a well-equipped call center.

ACD Anyone?

An ACD is an Automatic Call Distribution system. It is a large scale telephone switch that has a high degree of intelligence geared toward routing calls. In plain English, ACDs allow you to determine how you want the calls routed within your support unit. Examples include:

➤ Route calls to evenly spread the workload among your CSRs.

➤ Route calls to the first available CSR.

➤ Route calls to an appropriate recording when no CSR is available to handle the call.

➤ Route calls on hold to outside call centers when CSRs are not available.

➤ Route calls by skills capability of CSRs (veterans may take more calls because of their capability). For example, a computer company routing software-related issues to software specialists.

➤ Route calls by geographic territory of CSRs.

ACDs are a tremendous resource tool for management. They can generate reports regarding call traffic patterns, how fast the calls are answered, how long the calls take to resolve problems, and so on. ACDs are a vital tool for any customer service executive who wants to obtain a view of how her operation is running at any given time.

Caller ID

If you're using a sophisticated system and your telephone company supports this feature, you can program the system to identify the customer on the line as the call is received. Some high-end systems automatically call up the customer record on the CSR's computer screen before he even answers the call. That way the CSR can say, "Good afternoon, is this Ms. Montas calling?"

Watch It!
Did you ever call someone by mistake and hang up without saying anything so they wouldn't know it was you who made the goof! Don't be so sure you're getting away with it anymore! Caller ID identifies you as the person making the mistake. You might be better off staying on the line and owning up to it or otherwise someone might think you're a prankster. It's amazing how technology forces you to change the way you handle certain situations.

If you're running a small business with a small phone system, you can also identify your customers before you pick up the phone by using Caller ID. Caller ID involves hooking a small LCD unit to your phone station that provides you with the number and name of the person calling. With Caller ID, your CSR can begin a computer record search to obtain the customer transaction information when initiating the interaction.

In addition to identifying your customers before you pick up the phone, Caller ID allows you to know who to call back in case your customers get disconnected. Now that's proactive and great customer service.

Voice Response Unit

Computers have advanced to the point where some can accurately recognize words spoken by a human. This has given rise to hardware and software specialized for automating some customer service transaction work through voice response. For example, you call up your HMO with a question. The system asks you to input your name, account number, and so on. When the CSR comes on the line, they can now address you by name..."Good morning, Mr. Smith. How may I help you today?"

PBX

PBX is an abbreviation for Private Branch Exchange. It evolved from the days when phone connections were physically made using a switchboard. Today, a PBX is a computer-controlled system serving anywhere from fifteen to thousands of phone stations.

Key Systems

These are smaller systems than a full-blown PBX. They allow you to serve anywhere from five to fifteen lines. They usually come with features such as call forwarding, call transfer, and speaker phone.

Networking—for Computers

When you hear the term networking, your initial thought might involve going to a cocktail party to meet people to further your business, or even to get a job. The term networking also plays a big role in today's world of high technology. It involves connecting all of your CSR workstations to access and share customer information.

Two networking terms you might recognize are:

LAN—This stands for Local Area Network. It's a way to share and send information between individual computers in an office. This is what you would use to connect your CSR workstations to each other or a central information bank. A LAN usually has a central server (a dedicated computer) that stores and supplies all data to each workstation. Besides the hardware, you need appropriate networking software to manage the data storage and transfer. LANs usually connect the computers in a single department or building together.

WAN—This is a Wide Area Network. It involves connecting multiple sites. It would connect the LANs at various sites together. So you could hook up your office in Bangor, Maine with the one in Bangor, Washington, or even Moscow, Idaho with your field office in Moscow, Russia (theoretically).

Word to the Wise
LANs and *WANs* simply deal with connectivity, helping to connect all CSR workstations—wherever they may be—to access and share company and customer information.

Look Who's Talking...Video Conferencing

Video conferencing allows you to supply customers with a more personalized service without having to staff experts at each location.

An example is banks. Banks today have hundreds of small locations that make it difficult to staff experts in all product areas. Some banks have systems where you can walk into your branch, call a mortgage specialist (that's if you want a mortgage) located in the bank's headquarters, and discuss your needs. Being able to see the specialist on a screen gives the impression that you're actually meeting the individual in person. In addition, the specialist can show charts and illustrations on the computer screen to help paint a picture of what you're buying. Video conferencing also can be used to serve engineering applications as well as high-end business solutions.

You might consider video conferencing, which uses fairly inexpensive equipment and regular telephone lines, as a way of connecting with important but distant customers. Some companies also use it for connecting far-flung colleagues for meetings and training sessions.

Now What?

You probably came up with many ideas about what you can do with your phone capabilities from reading this chapter. But you also might be wondering what to do first. Any firstclass customer service program takes time to build. The trick is to analyze your immediate needs and pick the one or two technological solutions in this chapter you feel will best help you meet these challenges. Appendix A contains the names of companies that can supply you with the hardware, software, and know-how to equip for performance.

The Least You Need to Know

➤ Use headsets to break the monotony of using the phones and to gain your independence.

➤ Phone systems come with a host of add-on equipment and features that can take your service to the next level.

➤ Networking allows you to connect all of your CSR workstations to access and share information.

➤ If talking isn't good enough, video conferencing lets you look at the person you're talking to.

Help Is on the Line

Remember those good old days when every call you made was greeted by a cheery voice on the other end of the line? The cheery individual was hired to screen your calls and direct you to the proper person. Oh, those were the days.

Okay, so maybe sometimes that person wasn't too cheery or helpful. Like the times you were bounced around to different departments until you stumbled (probably by accident) upon the right party who could help you.

Remember the times you were greeted with the awkward option of: "XYZ Company, could you please hold?" Of course, when the receptionist asked this question, she never gave you the opportunity to say yes or no. It was simply rhetorical in nature because she was going to put you on hold no matter what your answer was, especially when she didn't give you a chance to answer.

Oh, those were the days. At least if you were going to be unduly dealt with, it was by a human being who you could lash out at. Oh, those were the days.

Introducing...Voice Mail!

Remember the old *Superman* TV show theme song? Play it in your mind as you read this. Faster than a speeding mouth. Friendlier than an upset person. More efficient than the best receptionist out there. Voice Mail, everyone's solution for quick and easy access to a customer service representative or a fast answer to a question.

Now, if voice mail works the way it's cracked up to, you won't be longing much for those good old days. It's when voice mail becomes a barrier too difficult to navigate that you yearn for the return of the good old days.

In this chapter, we'll show you how to use voice mail so that you can recapture the fond memories of what it was like to feel welcomed when you called for service. If we do our jobs right, then 20 years from now after voice mail has been replaced by newer technology, your children will be yearning for the good old days of voice mail.

Hello Customer

Regardless of whether you're still using the human answering machine or the electronic answering machine, you must make sure the process supports your overall customer service mission. By process, we not only include how the phone is answered, but also the different phone menu options customers hear when they reach out to contact you.

While voice mail technology does allow you to efficiently handle your customer service-related tasks, it can also serve as a barrier to customer satisfaction if it isn't set up properly. Here are some of the barriers you want to avoid.

Too Many Menu Entries

The idea of voice mail is to make things easier for both the customer and you. Making the customer listen and respond to several layers of messages tends to irritate people and build a perception that the system isn't user friendly. Most of us simply can't remember more than three options. By the time the fifth option is presented we aren't sure if the one that might be right for us was #2 or #3.

And even if you're only given a few choices at a time, if you have to climb through several menu trees to get to the information you really want, it can be awfully tedious.

Watch It!

For all the potential great benefits voice mail technology offers a company, you can overdo a good thing. More than one company we encountered used long-winded recordings to pass along information that was supposed to save both the customer and the company time. But the insufferable messages droned on and on and on with no escape hatch. *Now, before actually helping you, we'd like to take advantage of the fact that you're held hostage on this line. So let us tell you—in great detail—about some special offers we have on a warehouse-full of some really mediocre products that no one else wanted to buy...*

Wasting a customer's time in an attempt to save the customer time makes no sense. Voice mail strikes most people as impersonal enough without adding insult or imprisonment to the mix. If your customers are frustrated when they call for assistance, they won't hang around to hear your messages or follow your instructions. And then they'll start calling around for alternatives to your company.

An example:

Thank you for calling XYZ Corporation.

If you need help with laptops, press 1.

If you need help with desktops, press 2.

If you need help with servers, press 3.

Now suppose you press one for laptops. The next prompt says:

If you are using models a, b, c, d, press 1.

If you are using models h, j, k, press 2.

Now suppose you press one for model a. The next prompt says:

If you can't run applications, press 1.

If you can't run the hardware, press 2.

Now, suppose you press two for hardware. The next prompt says:

If you've owned your unit more than 3 months, press 1.

If you've owned your unit less than 3 months, press 2.

Can you see how this can be irritating, even though there are only a few choices at each level? Some people will be annoyed after the first round of entries. When you're struggling through a series of menus, you probably think to yourself; "Hey, all I want to do is talk to someone. Get me out of here!"

Realize that 30 seconds in reality can feel like several minutes in the mind. You don't want people getting irritated by a cumbersome process merely to access a customer service representative. They're probably irritated enough just from having to make the call.

Granted, the multi-level menu listed in the above example will go a long way toward routing your call to the appropriate support person or recorded information. However, there must be a better way to handle this. Here are a couple of suggestions.

➤ On printed information accompanying your product, put a table listing the various call options next to where the support phone number is printed. For instance, to call for support on a new (less than 3 months) model a laptop concerning hardware problems, simply key in 1,1,2,2, when the voice mail system comes on. Make sure your system allows people to press the numbers without having to hear the entire menu. This will save a great deal of time and not force the customer to listen to the entire message.

➤ Assign a dedicated toll-free number for each product type or department. That's relatively easy since you can now buy several toll-free numbers in a bundle. So you could, in the manuals where you print the support numbers, list the dedicated toll-free numbers for the various product/support functions. Going along with our example above: if you need service on a laptop model a that's under three months old, call 1-888-LAPTOP3.

Avoid Unnecessary Steps

If you're going to ask people to go through a series of menu options or input data, make sure that their effort will result in faster and more efficient service.

Ron once called his mortgage company regarding an issue. When the voice mail system greeted him, it asked for his account number. Ron was irritated because he didn't have it handy and had to go hunting for it. He was hoping that all he had to do was give his name and address to the CSR and have him look up the account number.

Giving into the voice mail demands, he found the number and punched it in. After waiting another few minutes, a CSR answered, "How may I help you?" Ron asked her if she had his information up on her screen. She said no and asked for his account number. Flabbergasted, Ron asked why was he forced to enter in his account number if it didn't do anything. The CSR responded by saying that the system requesting the account numbers didn't work and she didn't know why it was still asking for the numbers.

This is a classic case of having customers put forth effort that's unnecessary. If you ask for account numbers or other information, it better be used to advance the service process.

Confirm Actions

When the automated system receives input from a customer, especially one with a long string of digits, confirm for the customer that the transaction was received.

Don once called a credit card company's toll-free number three times to activate a replacement card mailed to him. The process was supposed to be automated and quick but after completing the procedure as instructed, the automated voice system never closed the loop by saying: "Thank you. Your credit card is now activated." Instead, the system accepted all the input from Don—with many, many key presses on the phone—and... and nothing! Finally, on the third call, Don listened to the menu of choices and opted for a live operator (see the following section). The human representative confirmed that Don activated his new credit card twice already. When Don suggested that she mention his experience to her firm's technology or marketing departments, she was polite in her brief response. Don is sure he heard her giggling madly as they disconnected the call.

Operator Assistance

Never develop what we call a closed loop system. We have heard and personally experienced instances where you would be trapped in a vicious voice mail circle with no way out. The only escape sometimes is to just hang the phone up. How many people do you think gave the company a second chance by redialing the customer service number? Maybe customers were forced to call back if they really needed the information. But the annoying process certainly did nothing to encourage customer loyalty. Remember, the Instant of Absolute Judgment can come at any time in sales or support transactions. So always allow the customer to access a live operator at any time. There are several reasons for this:

> ➤ The customer may not be clear about what option to choose to address his specific issue.

> ➤ The customer may not want to deal with voice mail. Some people hate it even when it works elegantly.

> ➤ The customer doesn't have time to go through the menus.

> ➤ The customer wants to speak with a manager after a bad service interaction.

> ➤ The customer may not have a support question but isn't sure how to contact the appropriate company resource.

At Your Service
On a regular basis, pretend you're a customer and make a customer service call to your company. Find out personally how easy it is to access the voice mail system, how long it takes to get through to a CSR, and if the system is providing the right perception you want your customers exposed to. Many times, problems arising in a customer response system aren't intentional. They just appear because the company isn't aware of them. There's no excuse for this. Constantly monitor your systems and make the appropriate adjustments. Customers rarely give you a second chance once they have had a bad experience.

Playbacks

Sometimes a customer will forget where he wanted to go and will want to hear that menu of options again or revisit a previous menu. Make it easy for your customers to playback previous messages.

Time of Delay

Voice mail systems might route a customer to the right person, but that doesn't mean anyone is immediately available. Some computer technology can actually calculate and tell a customer how long the expected wait may be (and suggest a more optimum time to call back with a much shorter expected delay). If a customer hears that the wait is expected to be 45 minutes, she may decide on her own to call back later or possibly solve her problem through the company's fax support system or Web page. Either way, she has

Watch It!

If your customers have to wait 45 (or 15) minutes on your help line before someone assists them, then your help line is in need of help itself. Think about how much the average person could accomplish in 45 minutes of her lifetime. And how much more they'd rather be doing anything other than sitting on *ignore*. Vigilantly check your systems to make sure they spare your customers from experiencing the injustice of *terminal wait*.

the opportunity to decide and that's what customers value the most, the freedom to make their own choices. Well actually, they value instant and competent service most of all. But short of that, they'd like some choice in the matter.

Interactive Voice Response

Part of your voice mail can be set up to use an interactive menu to offer information on store locations and directions, hours of operations, and special promotions. Again, if you're using voice mail to provide store hours and directions, please make sure the customer can replay the message or access an operator at anytime. There's nothing more irritating than having to listen to a message that's irrelevant to what you're looking for, or to listen to a long message, finally get to the part you wanted to hear, and only catch part of that vital piece of the message. You then have to call and be tortured a second time. Ugh!

Ron was trying to find out which store locations of a certain office product chain carried a certain product. He called the first store location and had to listen to a message that seemed to last several minutes on how to get to the store. At the end of the message, there was nothing else. No operator access, nothing. To find his answer, he would have had to drive to the store. Ron bought the product from a competitor who was more than happy to tell him on the phone; "We've got what you're looking for, so come on down!"

The store that lost the sale was guilty of two sins: A) Making Ron listen to directions he didn't need, and B) Having no operator available to answer his simple question.

Phone Etiquette—Say What?

Regardless of whether you're using voice mail or a human being to answer your calls, there are certain rules of etiquette that should be followed.

Voice Mail Etiquette

Here are a few things to keep in mind:

➤ Thank people for calling—Having your voice mail system answer by thanking you will go a long way towards building a comfort level with the customer. Example:

"Thank you for calling XYZ Company."

➤ Tape Disclaimer—Companies will usually tape the phone calls for educational purposes and analysis. If you tape phone calls with customers, you have an obligation to make them aware of this through a message at the beginning of the service call. Ron heard a great one as he was writing this chapter:

"Your call may be taped to help educate and develop our customer service associates." (to which we'd add, "… to provide you with the best service humanly possible.") Some systems will also offer you the option of rejecting the taping of your phone call if you desire—again, giving the customers the option of how they want to be treated.

➤ Operator Assistance—At the front end of the call, you should have a message that says:

"If at anytime you wish to speak with an operator, simply press the # key."

Of course, your system has to allow for such a feature and we highly recommend it.

➤ Beginning Instructions—Explaining to the customer how best to use the system to get the answers they want is crucial for a positive interaction. For example:

"Please listen to the following options and select the one that you are looking for."

➤ Clearly Understandable Voice—The voice must be clear and the rate of speech must be slow so everyone can hear and understand the recording. Imagine the customer saying at the end of the message:

"What did she say?"

If the customer cannot understand what you're saying, then he will likely be routed to the wrong person. If you are servicing a multi-lingual market, this is especially important when customers aren't that familiar with the English language. In fact, you might want to consider having the very first menu give the customer a choice of hearing their other choices in another language—whatever is appropriate to your market.

> **Watch It!**
> No matter how good your message is, if your customer cannot understand it, then it means nothing. Everything starts with your customer understanding your message. A basic principle of communication states that all meaning exists in the mind of the listener. No matter how much effort you put into your service attempts, nothing gets resolved if your customers can't understand what you're trying to tell them.

Human Etiquette

When the customer finally gets in touch with the human who can actually provide some help, another set of issues present themselves: effective communication between people over the phone. What follows are some recommendations for making those interactions as successful as possible.

➤ Thank you for calling—Have a bright energetic voice answer the phone by saying:

"Thank you for calling XYZ Company."

➤ Ask how you can help—This is handled by having the operator ask:

"How may I direct your call?"

➤ When getting the party requested, do not transfer the call without telling the customer you're doing so. When this happens, the customer thinks you're being rude and inferring that the customer's call was an intrusion on your day. You should respond with:

"It would be my pleasure to transfer you to my colleagues in the service center."

➤ Saying good bye—When ending a call, you must make sure there is no unfinished business and that the customer goes away feeling fully satisfied. You this by asking:

"Is there anything else we can do for you, Mr. Jones?"

If the answer is no, end the call by saying:

"Thank you for calling XYZ and have a pleasant day." or

"Thank you for allowing us to serve you and have a pleasant day."

Whatever you use, the most important word is thank you! And then, wait for the customer to hang up before disconnecting. That way, if there was any last second issue on the customer's mind, you're still available to her.

Tales from the Real World

In Chapter 12, when discussing refunds, we described how Hammacher Schlemmer, the retailer "offering the best, the only, and the unexpected for over 149 years" was willing to give Ron a full refund on a suitcase. What we didn't tell you was when Ron called customer service to inquire about the refund, the CSR stated up front:

"Mr. Karr, we would be only too happy to give you a refund and pay for the shipping."

Hammacher Schlemmer is not in business to give refunds. However, its promise to its customers is that it will guarantee the customer's satisfaction no matter what. The CSR who took Ron's call backed up this claim with his actions. Ron will never forget how good he felt in this transaction and will probably buy from Hammacher Schlemmer in the future. If the CSR handled Ron differently by giving him the impression of being a pain in the neck, then Ron not only would walk away mad, but he would probably hold it against the company for selling him a product he didn't want.

➤ Handling returns—When your customer requests a return and your policy allows for it, always say up front that you will be delighted to accept returns for credit or refund. It automatically puts the customer in a good mood for the rest of the call.

➤ Having to say no—Rather than restate what's already been said, we recommend that you review Chapter 6. However, the bottom line is do not say you can't or won't do anything. Turn it around by saying what you can do to positively move the call forward.

Effectively providing service to customers via the telephone still depends on the most basic principle of all. Great service comes from someone in your company reaching out—with care, understanding, and compassion—to touch someone who needs help.

Whose Dime Is Being Used?

It used to cost you only ten cents to make a local call. Those were the good old days. When companies review their service operations, this question always comes up: who should pay the phone bill? You have several options that you can mix and match to create the appropriate system for your company.

800/888 Numbers

For initial calls of service, you always want to supply a toll-free number. At least in the first three months of the use of a product or service. Toll-free numbers start with either an 800 or 888 area code. Just about all the 800 numbers have been assigned, so most new toll-free numbers will start with an 888 area code.

Toll-free numbers have their own information line. People not having access to your phone number will likely call 1-800-555-1212 or 1-888-555-1212. In addition, you must make a request that your listing be included in the toll-free directory assistance. Unlike a regular phone number, your toll-free number isn't automatically entered into the database. Some companies don't want their toll-free number listed and available to just anyone. It's their dime, after all.

As mentioned earlier, toll-free numbers can be bought in bundles (several lines). You can also obtain vanity toll-free numbers. Ron's toll-free number is 1-800-423-KARR. If you're looking for a new toll free number, put your name or company slogan in the number if possible. If you do, remember to always list the digits after the word spelling. Ron lists his as 1-800-423-KARR (5277).

It can be downright annoying for someone to have to take extra time to learn the numbers that coincide with the letters being used. If your customer uses reading glasses and doesn't have them handy, you're really in trouble. Imagine forcing someone to find their reading glasses in order to call you for service!

Customer Support Phone Packages

For companies that don't want to offer unlimited toll-free service at their expense, there's another alternative. Some companies, especially software companies, sell service packages based on number of calls or time of service provided. For example, a customer may pay a flat fee for a package of, say, six calls during a year. As part of this package, the company may supply a toll-free number.

If you use add-on service packages, you must make sure the customer gets through immediately to a CSR. Someone paying extra isn't in the mood to wait for service. Premium prices imply premium response. Getting immediate attention is probably the number one reason why your customers bought the plan. Again, it's giving your customers the option of how they want to be treated—no wait service for a premium versus free service that might entail a waiting period.

900 Numbers

We bet that when phone companies started offering 900 phone numbers, no one figured they'd become so popular, especially in the areas of adult entertainment. But hold on, 900 numbers are proving to be valuable for mainstream businesses.

A 900 number offers people a "pay for service" system. Your cost for the call is dependent on how much time you spend on the phone with the CSR. These calls are usually expensive, with charges usually being in excess of $1.00 per minute. A lot of technical support centers use this feature. Companies also use it as a means of reducing the number of calls they must handle on a personal basis. Customers not opting for this type of expensive service can choose alternative methods, such as fax-on-demand (detailed later in this chapter) and service on the Internet.

900 numbers are a source of revenue for whoever uses them. Your company, if you decide to use 900 phone numbers, will receive a nice sum of revenue. In fact, you will gain a new partner in life, the phone company. You can obtain 900 numbers through independent brokers who lease them.

Remote Phone Lines

Technology now allows you to list local phone numbers in various areas and have the calls routed to your support center location. For instance, if you wanted to call XYZ Company for service, they may have a local phone number for you to call in Topeka, KS, even though their CSR is actually located in Miami, FL. This is a great tool for companies that are looking to establish themselves in certain geographic locations without having to take on the expense of opening another location. Today, you can never tell where the person you are talking to is actually located. Unless you ask, of course.

Whatever mix of toll-free, 900, and local phone numbers you use, be sure that your system supports the overall objective of your company and expectations of your customers.

Nothing but the Fax

Fax machines today offer you an array of opportunities to better serve your customers. There are several ways you can use the fax machine as a customer service tool.

Fax-on-Demand

Whenever a customer needs something he can get it 24 hours a day, 7 days week, 365 days a year without having anyone actually staff the phone lines. All the customer has to do is call your fax-on-demand phone number and press the appropriate number from the menu of options available. The caller will then be asked to enter his fax number. Within a little while, your customer is looking at the information he needs to continue using your products or to place a new order. While customers prefer a toll-free number, many are willing to pay the phone freight as a small and worthwhile cost of getting instant and complete information.

The equipment that's required is a PC on your end that's always on and capable of receiving incoming calls and making outgoing calls. It acts as a fax server for the information being distributed. Types of information a customer can access from this system include:

➤ Product lists

➤ Updated pricing lists

➤ Technical briefs

➤ Product specifications

➤ Answers to frequently asked questions (FAQs)

➤ Service locations

The list goes on and on. A fax-on-demand system provides your customers with information in a timely basis without tying up phone lines and using expensive personnel. It also provides a written record the customer can use for the future, again lowering your overhead expense for support personnel.

At Your Service
If you aren't a manager, don't be alarmed. When we talk about lowering overhead, we're not necessarily referring to job reduction. Yes, job reduction may be a by-product of technological advances. But to us, lowering overhead also involves identifying ways of utilizing existing resources to provide a better return on investment while maintaining or improving service to customers.

Broadcast Fax

Broadcast fax means what its says, the ability to broadcast a message to many people at once. Imagine being able to send out 1,000 faxes after loading the document just once.

To use broadcast fax, you need the right equipment. Besides the appropriate software and computer, you need a modem pool. Your PC must be able to hold several digital boards (16–32) with modem connections. You also must have the fax numbers for all of the recipients programmed into your computer. Companies such as Sprint and others will do fax broadcasting for you on a contract basis.

Broadcast fax is ideal for companies that need to distribute information to hundreds, if not thousands, of fax machines at once. It can be used to send out timed updates or special alerts on promotions to distributors or franchises, or for press releases, earnings announcements, and so on.

Watch It!
When setting up a fax broadcast system of any size, be sure to monitor it carefully for wrong numbers and be vigilant about removing such errors. We have an elderly friend who received repeated attempts by a fax machine to connect to his residential phone at all hours of the day and night for three days. Great customer service companies review their fax logs and have a person dial the unsuccessful numbers to verify that a fax machine lives at the other end of the line, not someone's great-uncle.

Sequential Fax

For smaller communication jobs, you can use sequential faxing. All you need to do is log in the fax numbers you want the information sent to. Your computer will send the faxes one after another. If one number is busy, it will store the fax and try later with automatic retries. Reports that detail notification of deliveries are available. For fax jobs involving fewer than 50 faxes, this method is best.

You can carry out this task on a regular PC with one modem and the right software, such as WinFax Pro or FaxSTF. You can even time the faxes to go out at certain times of the day, like off-peak calling periods when the phone rates are low or during the night when you don't mind if the computer and a phone line is tied up for a little while.

Like broadcast faxing, sequential faxes are good for product updates, promotions, change announcements (like change of address), and so on.

The Least You Need to Know

➤ Voice mail should help your customers, not harm them.

➤ Whoever or whatever answers your phone will dictate how well the customer service call is handled.

➤ When possible, offer your customers a toll-free number.

➤ If used properly, fax machines can provide tremendous customer service benefits to your customers.

Chapter 24

ZAP! E-Mail Coming at You

In This Chapter

➤ Discovering e-mail and its benefits

➤ Writing effective e-mail messages

➤ Responding to e-mail

➤ Using e-mail for great customer service

➤ Understanding the ten commandments for using e-mail

Here's a switch for you. How would you like to replace all of your incoming phone calls with a tour through your e-mail box? If you live for the phone, this may not sound so enticing. But for those who want to get away from the phone, freedom is here. Except that now you will be tied down to the keyboard of your computer! Oh well, nothing's perfect.

Welcome to the world of e-mail. The system that allows written messages to be delivered instantaneously. The system where rain, snow, sleet, and hail will not stop delivery of your mail—although electrical problems, phone trouble, software, and computer hardware problems can prevent delivery of your electrified mail!

As with all of the other technological advances we're discussing in this part of the book (such as the Internet, which we tackle in the next chapter), e-mail can provide you and your customers who are equipped to use it with tremendous value if it is used appropriately. It will definitely revolutionize the way you structure your customer service operations. In fact, it will help you streamline your operations and at the same time increase the level of service you provide your customers.

Hello, You Have Mail!

Everyday when Ron and Don sign on to America Online (AOL), if they have mail, they're greeted with the message, "Welcome, You Have Mail." (When was the last time you heard your letter carrier say this to you?) Their messages come from colleagues, clients, friends, and family.

Tales from the Real World

While writing this book, Ron and Don only met once in person. The majority of their communications was done through e-mail. Once a chapter was written, one would e-mail it to the other one for corrections, additions, and comments. E-mail was quite valuable in this collaboration. It saved Ron and Don a great deal of time in traveling long distances to meet and it allowed them to submit their chapters anytime of the day—without worrying if there was enough paper in the fax machine. E-mail allows communication without regard for either time or space. We sent and retrieved chapters whenever and wherever we wanted (or had) to—hotel rooms, airport lounges, the wee hours of the morning on a weekend at home. This flexibility helped create what Ron and Don agree was an enlightening and wonderful collaboration.

E-mail provides customer service organizations with tremendous value, such as the following:

➤ Allows customers to contact you at any time.

➤ Allows you to respond immediately to customer inquiries— thereby meeting their expectations for expedient and gratifying service.

➤ Requires less overhead than having to staff phone lines; you can prepare well-written replies to standard inquiries in advance and then send them instantly to your e-mail correspondents.

➤ Less costly than responding by mail. Save on postage, printing, and paper/envelope costs.

➤ Less costly than responding by phone. No long distance charges. All of your e-mails can be sent at one time to a local phone number for distribution.

➤ Prevents you from interrupting people at the wrong time. Your customers can get your messages whenever it's convenient for them.

➤ Assures both completeness and consistency of your messages.

Composing the E-mail

E-mail, like letters, should be sent with a clear purpose in mind. And they should be sent in response to interest expressed by your customer. In the world of electronic communication, there's less patience for junk e-mail than there is for junk mail sent through the postal system. To send someone commercially oriented e-mail messages that they didn't request is otherwise known as spam (you know, the meat no one claims to have eaten even though tons of it is sold).

If a customer perceives you as sending them junk e-mail, even if you meant well, they will resent you. A big reason for this is they have to read the message in order to determine it's junk. And many of them are paying for the time it takes to read or delete electric junk mail. Whereas with normal mail, most of us wouldn't even open the letter if we thought it contained junk. A customer's e-mail address is sacred and should not be abused.

> **Word to the Wise**
> *Spam* is the word used to describe junk e-mail. You don't want to be accused of spamming someone. Otherwise, you might be sent e-mail by hundreds of people with searing feedback on your unwelcome junk e-mail. This is known as "flaming" a spam-mer. Internet culture has its own mechanisms for self-regulation.

Addressing the E-Mail

As with writing a normal letter, you should use the appropriate rules of greeting customers. If you don't know the customers that well, address them by their last name—Mr. Sanchez or Ms. Sanchez. Use their first name only if you know them well enough to do so.

E-mail Etiquette

The same etiquette used in printed letters should be used with e-mail. All too often we receive messages from friends, colleagues and customers where words are misspelled, letters that should be capitalized are not and so forth. Remember that when a customer reads your e-mail, it is her first and possibly only impression of you. If your grammar and protocol are sloppy, her perception of you will suffer. To excel in e-mail, become an expert on using the keyboard.

> ### Tales from the Real World
>
> One of us once worked for a boss who sent long, rambling, terribly misspelled e-mail messages. This otherwise obviously capable and intelligent executive seriously undermined the respect he commanded from his staff because he didn't take his electronic communication seriously enough. No matter the medium, you always leave an impression on your audience. Don't risk offending a customer with casual or sloppy e-mail.

Be Concise

The person reading your e-mail is probably reading one of several at any given time. Do your customers a favor and be concise and to the point. People don't have patience to read a lot of verbiage that's irrelevant. The purpose of e-mail is not to show off your creative writing skills, but rather to assist your customers. If words are irrelevant to the cause, erase them. Your customers will love you for this.

Signature File

When sending an e-mail to a customer, it's a good idea to use a signature file, which is several lines of text automatically added at the end of every e-mail message. Some e-mail programs such as Eudora allow you to set up a signature file once and with a click of the mouse button, you can automatically append your message with your signature file. If your e-mail system doesn't allow you to use a signature file, you can accomplish the same result by writing out the signature and saving it in a word processor file. When it comes time to use the signature file, all you have to do is copy and paste it to your e-mail message.

Word to the Wise

A *Signature File* is like adding a calling card to the end of your e-mail message. It allows you to include your name, phone number, and a memorable slogan. The signature file is a way of adding both vital contact information and a human touch to the electronic mail system.

The components of a good signature file are:

➤ Your name

➤ Easy way to get a hold of you

➤ Succinct company information or promotional line

For example, your signature file may read as follows:

Ron Karr
1-800-423-KARR (5277)
e-mail: karrqman@aol.com
Helping organizations dominate their markets and get closer to the people they serve.

Or:

> Pete Smith, Hardware Specialist
> 1-800-GO-LAPTOPS ext. 148
> GO LAPTOPS—Your source for excellent computing on the go.

In customer service, signature files are important because they tell the customer how to get a hold of you by phone or e-mail should they have any questions on what you had to say. Ideally, they should always be used when:

➤ You want the recipient to know all the avenues on how to get back to you

➤ It is your first contact with the customer

The times you shouldn't use a signature file are:

➤ When you send e-mail to people who know you well enough and know how to get a hold of you

➤ When it would be overkill and overwhelms the message of your text. If your e-mail is only 2 lines long and your signature file is 3 lines long, that's overkill.

E-Mail Responses

There are several ways you can set up your e-mail responses, depending on your needs.

Small Mailing List

If you wish to send an electronic letter to a small group of people, all you have to do is address it to a recipient, and carbon copy the others. That way, you send the message only once and it goes in bulk to all the addresses listed. You can create group lists in your e-mail program to help you. For example, you may have a list of customers who are in the public relations business. You might call that your PR Group, and keep their names and e-mail addresses in a file on your hard drive.

If you have a large number of people to send a message to, then you're probably better off with an Internet mailing list. This is a mechanism that's run by your Internet Service Provider, and it allows people to subscribe or unsubscribe to the list simply by sending e-mail to a special address with a request. Later in this chapter, you will read examples of how small business people send electronic newsletters to large numbers of people using Internet mailing lists.

Semi-Auto Responders

A semi-auto responder is when you have prepared text all ready to send electronically at the command of a service person. Say you get an e-mail asking you one of the seven most commonly asked customer service questions your company regularly receives. All you

Word to the Wise

Attaching a file is simply adding a file or document to your e-mail message. Most e-mail programs have this capability. Usually all it involves is a click of the mouse on the icon "Attach File," at which point your software will allow you to scroll through your files until you find the one you want. Then you simply highlight it and press the mouse button and the file will be attached to your e-mail.

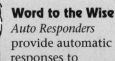

Word to the Wise

Auto Responders provide automatic responses to e-mails. Sometimes they're referred to as mailbots and infobots. Don't get confused. They all are the same thing: automatic responses triggered by a customers request.

have to do is go to the prepared answer for that question in your word processor, copy and paste it to your response, or attach the file to your e-mail message and send it off. This system allows you to cut down on the time it takes to respond to the message, and your customer gets his well-prepared answer fast.

Whenever you automate prepared answers to customer questions, you need to schedule a periodic review of that information. Make sure the information you send to customers—in any form—is current and accurate.

Auto Responders

As the name suggests, auto responders allow you to automatically respond to e-mails. Auto responders are an excellent tool for:

➤ Handling large numbers of requests for information

➤ Providing immediate responses so your customers will know that their message was heard and acknowledged.

The way auto responders work is this: You create a text file that resides on the host computer that has its own specific e-mail address. When someone sends an e-mail to that address, it generates a command that says "send this file." An example is a customer sending you an e-mail to receive the latest customer service bulletin on a particular product line. They simply address their message to the e-mail address for this function and the service bulletin is sent to the customer in a matter of seconds.

Ron received an e-mail from a colleague that was sent to several entrepreneurs. The message encouraged all recipients to immediately write to U.S. Senators concerning the Home Based Business Fairness Act of 1997. The act was written to change several IRS regulations concerning tax deductions for home-based entrepreneurs. To make the process easy, the writer of the e-mail message supplied all the e-mail addresses of U.S. Senators involved with the act.

Ron highlighted this list, copied it, and pasted it into the address section of his e-mail message. Within hours, he received several messages back from the Senators, all of which were sent by auto responders. Below is a copy of one such response. The Senator's name, e-mail address, and state have been deleted from the original message.

Dear Friend:

Thank you for your recent e-mail message to my office.

Please accept this response as acknowledgment that we have received your message and will note your comments. Constituents who have included a postal address in their message will receive a reply via U.S. Mail as soon as possible. If you resend your mail address please include the text of your previous message. Because of the large volume of mail, we are unable to write to citizens from other states and countries so if you are not a resident of XYZ State you may want to contact your senator. (This e-mail also gave instructions on how to access your own Senator through their Web Page.)

I look forward to hearing from you on other issues of importance to you.

Sincerely,

XXXXXXXXX

United States Senator

When was the last time you got a reply to a letter sent by mail to your politician? Without a reply, you didn't even know if he or she received it. And because you didn't get a response, you probably felt like they didn't care for your message or were too busy to respond. Either way, no doubt you were miffed by the fact that you weren't acknowledged. Mailbots, "automated responses," may lack a politician's charm, but they do let you know your message at least got to its destination. Whether your sentiments are being given serious consideration or not, well, that's another story.

The Senators who responded to Ron made him feel important by acknowledging his message, even though it was a form response. At least Ron knows it was received and counted. Ron was also educated on what else he could do to ensure his receipt of a written reply. All of this action transpired while the Senator was probably far away from his office. As a matter of fact, no one had to be in the Senator's office for this process to take place.

This is what your customers want from you: to be heard, counted, and responded to immediately. Auto responders are a tremendous tool that will allow you to do this in a timely and cost-effective manner.

> **Quote, Unquote**
> These days, technology plays an important role in the power and reach of any business. The challenge is to maintain the personal qualities of customer interaction while leveraging the abilities of instant communication on a global scale. Customers still want to know there's a person behind those e-mail messages.
> —Terri Lonier, small business expert

275

Valuable Service with E-Mail

Besides enabling you to respond immediately to customer inquiries, e-mail allows you to pro-actively serve your customers. On a regular basis, or when it's appropriate, you can keep your customers informed with the latest information on issues including:

➤ Price lists

➤ Product updates

➤ Calendar events

➤ Service bulletins

➤ Alerts and warnings

➤ Promotions

➤ Changes in procedures, addresses, and phone numbers

➤ Industry trends

Tales from the Real World

Wally Bock, an expert on using technology to support business strategies, sends out an e-mail every Monday called "Wally Bock's Monday Memo." It is a one-page document with tips and highlights regarding technology and its impact on business. At the bottom of the form is information on how clients can subscribe to receive his other services. Ron gets this memo every Monday and there has never been a week where he didn't receive a valuable tip. Now that's Great Customer Service! Look in the resource section at the end of this book to see how you can receive Wally's Monday Memo.

Tales from the Real World

For several years Terri Lonier, author of a best-selling guide to self-employment, "Working Solo," published a traditional quarterly print newsletter distributed to her customers and the media. Realizing the power of electronic communication, she launched "Working Solo eNews," a monthly e-mail newsletter that offers ideas, insights, and news for entrepreneurs. The electronic format allows Lonier to be in touch with a worldwide customer base on a more frequent basis, and for a fraction of the cost. It also allows her customers to receive current and valuable information essential to their success. Technology has certainly helped Terri Lonier service her customers at a higher level.

If you're going to send e-mail newsletters, or even regular print newsletters, here are some of the elements you may wish to include:

➤ Customer testimonials—success stories about what's working. Of course, get permission from the customer to use her story.

➤ Product information—Highlight certain products and services you have to offer. Be concise and make sure you include the benefits to your readers. Include ways the customer can and should use your products and services.

➤ Industry news—things happening in the industry that could affect your customers.

➤ Company news and updates—changes in policies, key personnel, pricing, and so on.

➤ Response instructions—how to get a hold of you by e-mail, mail, or phone.

As with anything else, frequency is the key. For some firms, it may make sense to stay in front of your customers every week. Or you may decide to send a newsletter by e-mail on a monthly, quarterly, semi-annual, or annual basis. We suggest that you send customers a communiqué on a quarterly basis at a minimum. Otherwise, your messages may be lost over too long a time period between them. When too much time elapses between your messages, they can't have a significant effect on your customers, unless of course you're sending out a special alert or update.

To decide the frequency that's right for your situation, review what your customers' expectations are. Heck, go ahead and ask customers how often they'd like to hear from you. This will help you come up with the right answer. While you're at it, find out if there's information you could provide your customers that they would find really valuable.

E-mails, whether they're newsletters, updates, or responses to customer inquiries, are fantastic tools to help strengthen the bond between your customer and you, which, of course, helps keep out the competition.

The Ten Commandments of E-Mail

If you're going to use E-mail, here are a few things to remember:

1. E-mails aren't private. You never know who can access your messages, especially in internal company e-mail systems. If you're going to write anything that you wouldn't want anyone else to read, protect yourself and don't send it via e-mail. As with cordless telephones, people with a little bit of know-how can eavesdrop on your conversations.

2. If your message isn't fit to print in a public medium, don't print it in e-mail. The last thing you want to do is tick-off a customer with a phrase that they find to be humiliating, offensive, or biased. In these days of being politically correct, you want to be a savvy e-mail user. For some companies, the only exposure you're likely to

have with your customers is through e-mail or on the phone. These companies don't know what you're really like and they aren't going to take the time to analyze what you meant by certain words or phrases. Avoid misperceptions and print what's universally understandable and acceptable.

3. Follow the same rules of etiquette in writing letters we discussed in Chapters 6 and 10. You are writing customer letters when you send e-mails. The only difference is that you're sending your letters over the phone line. And you don't have to lick your monitor.

4. Make sure your customers want to receive your e-mails. Give them a way to communicate that they want to continue receiving them—and provide an easy way for them to withdraw their names from your circulation list. (A common method is to have them reply with this one word as their message: Remove.)

5. Don't send more e-mails than are necessary. The success of e-mail doesn't depend on quantity. It depends on immediacy, quality, and purpose.

6. E-mails aren't a replacement for the human touch. They're an extension for enhancing human interaction.

7. Make sure you respond to all e-mail inquiries sent to you on a timely basis, generally within two business days, if not sooner. Customers have less patience with people who don't respond to e-mail. They sent their message through a medium that communicates instantly, and they expect a response in kind.

Tales from the Real World

If you plan on doing business using electronic mail, you not only need to reply to your customer e-mail promptly, you need a mechanism and process that assures it. In his *Doing Business on the Internet* seminars, consultant Bill Ringle shows examples of companies that respond to e-mail inquiries—the good, the bad, and the in-between, and explains the efforts and investments involved in creating the related customer response systems. Fast response through an auto responder is being used as an effective customer service tool today.

If your internal resources aren't ready to manage such services yet, you can contract with Internet Service Providers (ISPs) to maintain these services for your organization.

8. Keep it brief, concise and to the point.

9. Carbon copy (now there's an antiquated phrase—when was the last time you used carbon paper?!) only those people who are effected by the e-mail message. You don't always have to cc: the whole world on every message.

10. Blind carbon copy—send the e-mail to people who you want to keep up to date without the recipient knowing it is being read by other parties. There are a couple of good reasons for this. First, when you put everyone's name in the "To" box, everyone on the list will see the entire address list—taking up lots of time both to download the message and to scroll through all those names. Second, having all the recipients' names appear on the e-mail gives away your entire subscriber list—valuable proprietary information. Check your e-mail systems to learn how you can use the blind carbon copy function.

The Least You Need to Know

➤ The benefits of e-mail are too significant to not make it a part of your customer service structure.

➤ Like everything else in life, the effectiveness of your e-mail depends on how you use it.

➤ There are different types of responses to meet every e-mail need.

➤ E-mail provides you with valuable ways to enhance communications with your customers.

➤ Using e-mail the wrong way can do your business more harm than good.

Chapter 25

Next Stop: Information Superhighway

In This Chapter

➤ Riding the Information Superhighway

➤ Giving service on the Web

➤ Understanding the components of a Web site

➤ Utilizing the Web as The Great Service Value

Let's take a ride onto the wide-open road of the Information Superhighway.

Is this your first trip? You might be wondering what kind of ride you're in for. We're pleased to tell you that your journey on the Information Superhighway will be delightful, enlightening, and crucial to your ability to service your customers now and in the future.

This chapter will provide you with ideas and case studies guaranteed to help take your customer service to higher levels—electronically. But first, let's take a little time to sort through all the new names, gizmos, and gadgets that are born out of this brave new world. We promise you it will be painless. Hey, if dentists can now work on your teeth with high-speed drills that don't hurt, we can surely provide you with a pain-free primer on the definitions you'll need to get your bearings and safely navigate the Information Superhighway.

The Information Superhighway

If you've been following high-tech developments with one eye and ear (or less), there are probably lots of new words and phrases you have been exposed to but aren't really sure what they mean. Here's our painless version of what you need to know to get your Learner's Permit for the Infobahn, and get you prepared to drive your customer service to the next level.

The Information Superhighway is a metaphor for electronic data flowing between computers, usually over phone lines. Computers use devices called modems to send and receive information in electronic form, including text, pictures, spreadsheets, even software programs, audio (like news broadcasts and music), and video (such as product demonstrations).

Here, explained in simple, easy-to-understand terms, are some common terms associated with barreling down the infobahn.

➤ **Internet**: Our colleague Wally Bock, who helps companies develop strategies and products for the digital age, describes the Internet simply as: a worldwide collection of computers, the links between them, and standards about how information will be shared over those links.

> **Quote, Unquote**
> Think of the gymnasium floor in your local college or high school. On it are different colored lines—red for basketball, green for floor hockey, and gray for indoor volleyball. Each game you play uses different lines, different equipment, and different rules. The Internet is like the gym floor. It is the wires, hubs, routers, and switches that the different services run on. E-mail, Web transactions, file transfer, chat, and other services are the "games" that are played on the Internet.
> —Bill Ringle, Director of Internet Services, Star Communications Group

The Internet involves everything associated with the Information Superhighway. The word Internet means interconnected networks. The Internet is simply many computers connected to each other through phone lines, cables, and satellites. The Internet is a system that lets computers send information in many forms to other computers—all over the world!

With a few basic tools, the Internet lets you become an electronic publisher. That means anyone with a properly equipped computer can access your information from wherever they are. And that, as you soon will see, is a great way to connect with customers—at their convenience.

➤ **The World Wide Web** (WWW or simply Web): An information storage and retrieval system that uses the Internet to present text, graphics, photos, sound, and animation for access by any properly equipped computer connected to the Internet. Such information is made available at distinct locations known as *Web sites*.

➤ **Web site**: This is a place on the World Wide Web where a particular company, organization, or individual makes their unique information available to visitors from the world at large. On your company's Web site, you can post product descriptions, price lists, annual reports, list your locations or contact information for your sales offices...and any other information you would like to make accessible to the world. In addition, your Web site can be interactive—allowing customers to ask questions about billing or technical support issues, check the delivery status of orders, or even place new orders right online. This electronic information is easily transferred between the Web site and the visitor's computer through a *Web browser*.

➤ **Web Browser**: Software that allows you to search for and access any type of information on the World Wide Web. There are several kinds available, including Netscape Navigator and Microsoft Internet Explorer.

➤ **Intranet**: Private Web sites within companies for access by their employees only. Companies use these to post policies, current company information, announcements, and job postings, as well as store—in a searchable form—employee manuals, product information, and so on.

➤ **Keyword**: If you need to find information that you think might be available on the Internet, you can search for it using special software—available right on the Web at no additional cost. All you have to do is go to the section of the search software where you enter the term(s) you want to find (usually titled Keyword or Search Term) and type in a word or name that describes what you're looking for. The browser will then bring to your attention all sites that contain that name. For example, suppose you're looking for IBM's Web site and don't know their address. Simply type in IBM in the keyword section and you will most likely find their Web site address. Click on it, and, wham! there you are, getting the scoop directly from Big Blue.

➤ **Internet Address**: This is the address, like a street address or telephone number, of the information source you are looking for. Techies call it an *URL (pronounced "Earl")*, or universal resource locator.

➤ **URL**: Stands for Universal Resource Locator. It is a path that takes you directly to the desired site on the World Wide Web. For instance, http://www.LeadWell.com/ is Don's URL.

➤ **Hyperlink**: A hyperlink is like an electronic doorway that takes you directly to certain information, such as an e-mail address, or another page on a Web site, or another Web site altogether. You can

At Your Service
Most Web site addresses start with http://www. "Http" sounds like a sputter—if you're used to speaking in English. But it's like an ignition key to your computer's drive-train. Http:// www is the first part of most, but not all, Internet addresses. When your Web browser sees it, it revs up for the open data road. The WWW stands for the World Wide Web. Most big companies have reserved domain names in their company name to make for a simple Web address, as in www.ups.com.

Word to the Wise
You might be wondering what the various suffixes in a Web address—such as *com, org*, and so on—mean. Well wonder no more. Here are some secret codes unmasked.

.com = commercial (assigned to profit seeking organizations)

.org = organization (assigned to not-for-profit organizations such as trade associations)

.edu = education (assigned to schools, universities, and so on)

.gov = government (assigned to civilian governmental agencies)

.mil = military (assigned to military agencies)

Watch It!
If you have a name you want to protect as your own domain, conduct an immediate search to see if it has been used already. If not, reserve it immediately. There are companies that specialize in searching and reserving domains. Most companies that offer Internet services can search for the availability of the Internet domain name your company would like to use for its Internet site, and can reserve it for you for a modest cost.

immediately access that information, which might be stored on a computer clear on the other side of the world, simply by clicking on hyperlink phrase words (usually shown in a different color of text and underlined) or graphics (icon). For example, Don's Web site lists the many books he's written, with links to several online booksellers that let you instantly purchase the books right from your computer.

➤ **Domain**: This is the part of an Internet address that is unique to the organization that sponsors the information location along the highway. The domain name for Your Company might be "YourCompany.com." Domain names are unique. There can't be two companies or organizations with the same Internet domain name, just as there can't be two companies with the exact same telephone number.

As with any word or symbol that identifies your company, it's imperative that you immediately do a search and reserve your company's name or slogan as your protected domain—a name that no one else can use in their URL address. Don's protected domain is LeadWell. Therefore, no one else can use the URL address of http://www.LeadWell.com.

That's it. No more definitions. Now wasn't this painless? You now have the background and understanding of the Internet elements to begin comprehending the value the World Wide Web has to offer you.

The Web for Service

Your Web site is the place where customers come to do their business with you. There are several things you can accomplish with your Web site, such as:

➤ **Retrieve product information**. Most every Web site offers product information hyperlinks (including our own).

➤ **Place orders**. Example: Dell Computer sells about $1 million a day of products ranging from low cost PCs to complex systems costing in excess of $30,000.00.

Revenues are growing by 20 percent per month. Web site orders average 10 percent more than phone orders. Example: 1-800-Flowers. Don uses the Web site of this popular phone-based direct merchant for business and personal floral needs. The site has pictures of the flowers or plants you are ordering—arranged by occasion, type of gift, and price range. And it lets you enter the message for the card exactly as you'd like it to appear.

➤ **Download product/service bulletins in electronic form**. Dell Computer reports that every week 20,000 customers download support information. We go online and visit Web sites for vendors we deal with and associations we belong to. The virtually unlimited capacity of the Internet means you can offer customers detailed and timely information like no other medium in the history of man has ever done. (That may sound puffed up, but it's really true.)

➤ **Track shipments**. Example: UPS ships over 12 million packages a day. Its Web site handles 65,000 tracking requests a day, with that number doubling every 4-6 months.

> **Word to the Wise**
> The word *download* refers to transferring the information from the Web site to your computer's hard drive. *Upload* involves sending information from your computer to the Web site or Internet Address you are communicating with.

Tales from the Real World

Ron wanted to check to see if his materials arrived in time at a hotel in Florida for an upcoming presentation. Instead of calling UPS's toll-free customer support number, he had his computer dial into the UPS Web site using America On- line for access to the Internet. Once he was on AOL, it took only a few seconds to get into the UPS Web site. Once in the Web site, after Ron entered his tracking number, he instantaneously found out the exact time of delivery and who signed for it. Now that's Great Customer Service. Other shipping services, such as Federal Express, also offer the same kind of service options.

➤ **Accounts payable and receivable**. Typically, these functions are protected by passwords and secure technology. Using this technology, you can offer your customers a direct route to seeing if you received their latest payment, and how you applied it.

➤ **Access answers to frequently asked questions** (FAQs, which we discussed in Chapter 13). Research indicates that some 80 percent of the calls taken by call centers are in the "frequently asked" category. So if you could get people to visit your Web site instead of calling your call center, you could help more people faster at less cost. And you could combine your FAQ section with auto-responder technology we discussed in Chapter 24 to send information to your customers in their own mailboxes.

Watch It!
If you go through the expense of creating a Web site and don't immediately respond to any and all e-mails addressed to you at the site, you're committing commercial suicide. You'd be better off saving your money and not having a Web site at all.

➤ **Send e-mail to company executives**. Example: If you go to IBM's Web site http://www.ibm.com, you can click on the hyperlink "About IBM." When that page comes up, you will be able to access IBM CEO Lou Gerstner, read his latest articles, his bio, and even send him an e-mail.

➤ **Find out the latest company information.** Most publicly held companies will have their latest earnings statement on their Web site. You don't have to look for the statements in the newspapers, bug a broker for them, or wait to read them in their annual report. General Electric even puts their entire annual report on the GE Web site.

A well-crafted Web site can allow your customers to handle all business functions electronically if they so desire—and if your system can support these functions.

Creating an Effective Web Site

There are great Web sites and there are Web sites that are nothing to write home about. A Web site is your new Internet calling card. And to some of your customers, it might be the only contact they have with your company. It is a piece of advertising; it is an extension of your relationship with your customers. It may be the first or only piece of advertising for your company that your customers are exposed to. It better be one of your better pieces of advertising if you are going to entice your customers to visit and stay awhile.

When televisions started coming equipped with remote controls, a whole new society of channel surfers was created. Come on, admit it, you're one of us. You will click that remote or mouse button the instant you lose interest in what you're looking at. Just as TV producers work hard to hold viewers' increasingly short attention spans, your Web site has to hold a visitor's interest. It better be informative, pleasant—even entertaining, and easy to use.

To successfully influence your customers, you need two things from them; their time and attention. When someone clicks on your Web site, you have their time. But if you don't grab their attention, your time with that customer will be limited to a few short seconds.

Granted, if the customer is contacting your Web site in search of service, you will have their attention, unless your site is too difficult to navigate and the customer can't find his answer fast. Technology has reduced the amount of time customers are willing to wait for their answers. The faster something gets, the faster we want it to go. Customers, we've been saying, are never satisfied.

One of the changes coming out of the Internet revolution is the disappearance of the line defining service and sales. Today, customers usually refer to both issues in the same breath. If your Web site creates an easy environment in which your customer can do business with you, then you're considered to have great customer service. If it's too difficult to place an order, your service is considered to be poor. Service today no longer refers only to technical and support issues. It's a bigger envelope encompassing the entire relationship between all of your company's resources and the customer.

Your Web site must create an environment where the customer finds it easy to do business with your company. And that, of course, encourages the customer to do more business with you.

Let's take a look at the components of a great Web site:

➤ **Easy to find.** List your site with the major Web directories and search sites. If you have an outside firm maintaining your Web site, they can do this for you.

➤ **Easy to Use.** Your customers want to easily navigate your Web site and find what they're looking for with as few mouse clicks as possible. If you have a section on technical support, it should only take one mouse click to get there once the customer is at your Web site. The more clicks they have to use, the more likely they are to get confused and give up their search. As with voice mail, you don't want your customers going through layers of menu options. Once customers are sure they're in the right place for help, they're usually willing to complete forms, and send your company information that can help you help them.

> **Quote, Unquote**
> We are trying to integrate United Parcel Service (UPS) into our customer's business processes and take our customers out of the customer service business. Now, instead of having to field delivery tracking calls, our customers can have their customers track it themselves on our Web site, or their own Web site. Imagine having the ability of having your buyers track their purchases at your Web site. Whichever way our customers want to handle it, we can provide it to them.
> —Rakesh Sapra, Manager of Interactive Marketing, UPS

Tales from the Real World

When Ron wants to know how much it will cost to ship product and media kits to his clients via UPS, all he has to do is input three things: origin and destination zip codes, weight of the package, and the type of service (for example, next day air). Instantly, he gets the cost information he is looking for. This is UPS's Quick Cost feature on its Web site.

Put the most commonly used areas up-front so people can get to them fast. Many companies put hyperlinks on the first page to areas including Product Information, Technical Support, Ordering, Shipment Tracking, Company News, articles, and so on.

Tales from the Real World

Paul Goldner, professional speaker and author of *Red Hot Cold Call Selling*, was working in Europe for the Dow Chemical Company. He was having a discussion with his contact on how to justify the cost of their sales training programs. Paul promised to send his client an article he wrote on this very topic upon his return to the United States. Before the meeting ended, it dawned on Paul that the article was also posted on his Web page. Paul and his contact immediately dialed into Paul's Web site and printed the article. He was able to solve the customer's problem on the spot. This is what you call Just in Time Customer Service. Another way of saying Great Customer Service.

➤ **Fast Download Time**. Your Web site shouldn't have more graphics than you really need to serve your customers. Remember, you're dealing with impatient channel surfers. If it takes too long for someone to get into your site (anything more than 10 seconds) because they're waiting for the big color photo of your company president—and the dancing logo—to download, poof, they're gone. Once customers are into the site and requesting information or files, let them know the download time. Estimate actual download time, or at least give a little warning ("this could take a few moments, please be patient").

➤ **Fast Response**. Your Web site must be backed up by a computer system that can handle the load of traffic it receives. Again, time is everything here and customers won't wait around too long for answers to their inquiries.

➤ **User-Friendly Design**. The design of the Web site should be pleasing to the eye and able to capture one's attention. This is business with a touch of show business. If the print is too difficult to read or the graphics are sloppy and not appealing, forget it; you've lost the customer's attention.

➤ **Relevant, Well-Organized Information**. The information on your site should be relevant to the needs of your customers. "People will come to your Web site looking for one of two things," technology expert Wally Bock says. "They either want an answer to a question or a solution to a problem." People don't have time to wade through a lot of material they don't have any interest in.

➤ **Reinforce Your Company's Mission and Brand Name Recognition**. Your Web site should serve as a stellar reminder of what your company is known for and how it wants to be remembered. Your Web site must be memorable if you're going to succeed in word of mouth advertising. You want customers telling their friends to check out your Web site—not because it's the most gimmicky, but because it's the most helpful.

Having a Web site isn't to show the world that you're hip to cutting edge technology. Who cares! Your Web site's purpose is to provide a fast, convenient mechanism for communicating with—for serving—your customers. People don't come to your Web site to be impressed with flying logos and multimedia amusements. They come for help. Keep this simple truth central to the design and execution of your Web site.

The Web's Value

Hopefully by now you will have realized the benefits the Web can offer your customers and you. Now let's look at some of the value you can receive from using the Web.

Bottom Line Value

Earlier in the chapter we mentioned that UPS handles 65,000 tracking requests a day on its Web site. Imagine how much money it's saving from not having to handle these requests by phone!

Watch It!
Having an attractive Web site doesn't mean deploying every bit of the latest high-tech bells and whistles. Do you really need your company logo doing the hula in 3-D animation? Those kinds of gimmicks usually increase the time it takes your site to load in your customer's computer, and shortens the time they'll wait before they go somewhere else.

At Your Service
More and better software is becoming available to make transacting business directly on the Web easier and more affordable even for small businesses. Products such as Domino from Lotus allow smaller businesses without huge computer departments to maintain attractive, functional Web sites and take orders directly from customers online.

By using the Web for service, companies can realize the following cost savings:

➤ Phone bills are reduced because the companies receive fewer calls to toll-free support numbers.

➤ Labor costs are reduced because the companies don't have to staff so many phone lines.

➤ Levels of service are increased without having to spend additional resources on additional labor and facilities.

➤ Printing costs may be reduced as brochures, bulletins, pricing lists, and annual reports can all be accessed off of the Internet.

➤ Postage costs (sorry, Mr. Postman) will also dramatically decline as more mail is sent via e-mail and information is accessed on Web sites.

➤ Time it takes to support your customers is reduced. When time is reduced, so are all the associated labor costs.

Watch It!
Building and maintaining a Web site is a big, ongoing job. It requires planning and resources. A Web site must be figured into your total operational plan. It can't be a whim or be loosely assigned to your in-house "computer guru." If running the Web site isn't his "real" job, your site will be in trouble fast. Yes, properly designed and maintained, a Web site can help to lower other service costs and please more customers. But only if it's providing useful and timely information week after week, month after month. Long before unveiling your site to the world, answer this question: Who's going to operate this thing on a day-to-day basis?

In short, the Internet and all of its components hold the potential to drastically reduce the cost of doing business these days—even when you factor in the costs of developing and supporting the necessary technology. The key is to use the technology appropriately.

➤ Make your customers aware of your Internet site and what information and services you offer there.

➤ Build your site to offer maximum value to your customers, not maximum promotion for your company.

➤ Keep your site current. If it's out of date or not functioning properly, you've probably done more harm than good.

Let's face it. The service wars of today and tomorrow are going to be fought on the Internet as well as by phone and in person. As society becomes more and more computerized, more normal daily functions are going to be computerized. It won't be too long before all of us are doing our banking electronically, shopping electronically, and paying our bills electronically (some of us already do all those things now).

Eventually, most every commercial market is going to be "electronically driven." How long it takes to get to that point is a matter of speculation and debate. But eventually we will all wind up there. So you have a choice. You can either wait until everyone is there and you have to play catch-up. Or you can jump on the bandwagon now and strive to be continuously ahead of the curve by leading your industry into the electronic future. That future is now and it's here to stay.

> ### Tales from the Real World
>
> With 10,000 customers checking order status and 20,000 customers downloading support information every week, Dell Computer estimates that its Web site is producing a direct cost savings of $500,000 per month from these two features alone.

Differentiated Value

With very little perceived difference in the types of products and services being offered in many industries, companies are being forced to concentrate on differentiating themselves by how they offer their products and services. Today, the Internet is no longer a luxury or high-tech plaything. It is a serious business tool, and a "must" for any company that desires to excel in the game of customer service with customers who use personal computers.

It used to be that a company that was first to market with a new product was guaranteed the leadership role. Hertz was #1 in Rental Cars, Federal Express in overnight delivery of letters, and so forth. Companies are finding out that today being first represents a limited window of opportunity. It won't be too long before someone provides a similar level of service. Being first is useless unless there's a commitment to stay #1 and do what it takes to stay ahead of the pack.

So here's a rule for you to follow. The moment you come out with a new type or level of service, consider it obsolete. Why? Because it will only be a matter of time before your competition catches up to you with similar offerings. If you aren't developing the next innovative service offering while enjoying the results of your latest offering, you will be crying in a short period of time.

Quote, Unquote

Just a few years ago, having an address at a fancy office building downtown was a status symbol. Today, it's an Internet address, because in the global economy you may never come face to face with many of your business customers. These customers may live in different time zones and different countries, but they want to purchase goods and services from you if they can find you on the Internet and you show that you're responsive to their inquiries.

—Bill Ringle, Director of Internet Services, Star Communications Group

> ### Tales from the Real World
>
> Federal Express was the first to offer package tracking on a Web site. Over time, UPS saw Federal Express's advantage dissipate as UPS began concentrating on providing superior customer service. It started managing all points of customer contact by: drivers, salespersons, phone support, and via the World Wide Web. UPS sees the Web as not only a means for providing customer service, but as a means for doing business—making it easier for their customers to conduct new business. They have taken what FedEx started and are striving to take it to higher levels to achieve differentiation.

Quote, Unquote

At UPS we want to delight our customers. Our Web site is a critical component for providing superior customer service and raising the bar of the value we offer our customers.
—Rakesh Sapra, Manager of Interactive Marketing, UPS

Like time, innovation does not stand still. The clock is always ticking; customers are always more demanding. Dynamic market forces require companies to continuously raise the bar on the level of service they offer their customers. If you don't, then your competition will pass you by and leave you with nothing but their dust.

As you define how you're going to use the Internet to create your differentiated service, remember that it must support the overall mission of your company and the promise you make to your customers. Like any other tool, this technology shouldn't become the emphasis of your strategy. It should support the implementation of your strategy.

See y'all on the Web.

The Least You Need to Know

➤ The elements of the Information Superhighway will help you raise your level of service to your customers.

➤ The Web offers your computer-equipped customers a fast, accessible mechanism for information, assistance, and even transactions.

➤ The Web will save your company money in customer service and help create the differential value.

➤ If your Web site isn't constructed properly, it will hurt you more than it will help you.

Resources

Here are some places you can turn to for additional expertise, support, and resources. This list is not exhaustive; it's a place to start. We don't have direct experience with all of these sources so we imply no endorsement by their listing here. Contact them, hear them out, seek alternatives, and use your judgment.

Associations

American Telemarketing Association (ATA)

4605 Lankershim Blvd., Suite 824

North Hollywood, CA 91602-1891

Phone: (800) 441-3335 or (818) 766-5324

The largest professional, non-profit, trade association that represents and serves the telemarketing industry. It is committed to serving the needs of its members, as well as protecting the rights of consumers and businesses who have telephone contact with its members. Its mission is to provide leadership and education in the professional and ethical use of the telephone to do the following:

1. Increase marketing, sales, and service effectiveness

2. Enhance customer satisfaction

3. Improve decision-making

Help Desk Institute (HDI)

1755 Telstar Drive, Suite 101

Colorado Springs, CO 80920

Phone: (800) 248-5667 (United States and Canada); (719) 528-4202

Provides targeted information about the technologies, tools, and trends in the help desk and customer support industry. Recognized worldwide as a customer support training organization. HDI also provides a networking forum for industry professionals. More than 50 Help Desk Institute chapters, locally formed and operated, thrive in the United States, Canada, Australia, and Europe.

Institute of Management Consultants (IMC)

521 Fifth Avenue, 35th floor

New York, NY 10175-3598

Phone: (212) 697-8262

Fax: (212) 949-6571

Email: Office@imcusa.org

http://www.imcusa.org/

The leading association representing management consultants with members in the U.S. and overseas.

International Association of Business Communicators

Phone: (800) 776-4222 or (415) 433-3400

E-mail: service_centre@iabc.com

http://www.iabc.com

Products, services, activities, and networking opportunities to help people and organizations achieve excellence in public relations, employee communication, marketing communication, public affairs, and other forms of communication.

International Customer Service Association (ICSA)

401 N. Michigan Avenue

Chicago, IL 60611

Phone: (800) 360-4272 or (312) 644-6610

E-mail: ICSA@sba.com

http://www.icsa.com/

Globally, membership tops 3,400; offers a full range of programs, publication of surveys, and member research studies. ICSA members are managers, directors, vice-presidents, owners, and CEOs of companies of all types and sizes in virtually every industry—manufacturing and nonmanufacturing—from the Fortune 500 to the emerging blue chip giants of the twenty-first century.

National Speakers Association (NSA)

1500 South Priest Drive

Tempe, AZ 85281

Phone: (602) 968-2552

E-mail: NSAMain@aol.com

http://www.nsaspeaker.org

The professional association for leading thinkers and presenters at conferences and meetings. Call or visit the Web site (searchable) for the *Directory of Who's Who in Professional Speaking.*

Society of Consumer Affairs Professionals (SOCAP)

801 North Fairfax Street, Suite 404

Alexandria, VA 22314

Phone: (703) 519-3700

Membership is open to all professionals who are in some way responsible for creating and maintaining customer loyalty: vice presidents, directors, managers, and supervisors with responsibilities for consumer affairs, customer service, inbound call centers, market research, information systems integration, sales and marketing, database management, new business development, and operations. SOCAP membership is composed of close to 3,000 corporate consumer affairs/customer support professionals, representing 1,500 companies. Most of these companies are listed in the Fortune/Forbes 1000.

Contract Call Centers

AT&T Solutions Customer Care

Jacksonville, FL

Phone: (904) 636-2340

E-mail: futurize@attmail.com

http://www.att.com/solutions/custcare.html

Provides outsourced customer- and employee-care services including customer inquiry, sales-lead generation, Internet support, order and account management, dealer-locator programs, help desk and crisis care, and administrative support for human resource programs and employee benefits plans. More than 8,000 employees in the U.S., Canada, Europe, and Asia.

Microdyne Support Services

Alexandria, VA

Phone: (703) 329-3700

http://www.microdyne.com

Provides outsourced technical staff and management for telephone technical support (TTS) centers, and warranty and after-warranty service depots with a staff of more than 150 TTS professionals.

TeleTech Customer Care Management, Inc.

1700 Lincoln St., Ste. 1400

Denver, CO 80203

Phone: (303) 894-4000

Operates several customer service centers in the U.S., the United Kingdom, Australia, and New Zealand. Provides services such as customer enrollment, account inquiries, product information, and technical help-desk support.

Customer Service Consultants

The Bentley Company

22 Kane Industrial Drive

Hudson, MA 01749

Phone: (508) 562-4200

Fax: (508) 568-9468

E-mail: info@bentleygroup.com

http://www.bentleygroup.com

Knowledge, expertise, and action for building world class service environments. Assessment and sales of sales force automation; service technology consulting; systems integration and implementation; customer satisfaction surveys; and change management consulting. Other offices in Bellevue, WA; Sunnyvale, CA; Oakbrook Terrace, IL; and Lillburn, GA.

The Castle Group

Tony Castle

1204 Third Avenue

New York, NY 10021

Phone: (212) 333-9373

E-mail: acastle1@aol.com

Other offices in Miami, FL and Ridgefield, CT.

The Castle Group offers a full range of services that include: assessment, implementation, and support of client customer service centers.

Customer Care Institute

P.O. Box 19627

Atlanta, GA 30325

Phone: (404) 352-9291

Fax: (404) 355-5059

Email: info@customercare.com

Bulletin board: http://www.customercare.com/wwwboard/wwwboard.htm

CCI's staff is frequently called upon to assist companies with evaluating and reengineering the customer care function.

Technical Assistance Research Programs (TARP)

1600 Wilson Boulevard, Suite 1400

Arlington, VA 22209

Phone: (703) 524-1456

Fax: (703) 524-6374

Also offices in London and Melbourne.

E-mail: rhett@tarp.com

http://www.tarp.com

TARP is a customer service research and consulting firm offering a wide range of services to help businesses maximize customer satisfaction, customer loyalty, and positive word of mouth. Offers CRIS (Customer Response Information System), a software solution that offers customer call centers complaint and inquiry management. Also offers assessment of standards and policies, benchmarking services, satisfaction surveys, training programs, and communication skills workshops.

Customer Service Training, Conference Keynotes, and Suppliers of Behavioral Assessment Tools

Don Blohowiak

(Co-Author of *The Complete Idiot's Guide to Great Customer Service*)

Strategic Advisory Services

P.O. Box 791

Princeton Junction, NJ 08550-0791

Phone: (609) 716-9490 or (888) LEADWELL (532-3935)

Fax: (609) 799-8271

E-mail: DonB@LeadWell.com

http://www.LeadWell.com

Helps service organizations boost employee productivity and market effectiveness. Award-winning marketer. Author of four other popular books on leadership, marketing, and change. Delivers fast-paced, thought-provoking keynote presentations at leadership conferences around the globe. Plans and facilitates strategic planning retreats. Uses validated behavioral and values-based assessment instruments to improve hiring and team productivity.

Lisa Ford

Ford Group, Inc.

140 Seville Chase

Atlanta, GA 30328

Phone: (770) 394-4860

Lisa Ford delivers high-energy speeches and seminars in customer service, leadership, team skills, communications, and personal power. Her customer service video learning system is one of the all-time best-selling videos in customer service.

T. Scott Gross

HCR #1-561

Center Point, TX 78010-9700

Phone: (210) 634-2122 or (800) 635-7524

Fax: (210) 634-2338

E-mail: tscott@hctc.net

http://www.posgross.com/

T. Scott Gross is the author of some of the most popular books ever written about excellence in customer care, including *Outrageous: Guilt-free Selling & Unforgettable Service* and *Positively Outrageous Service*. Known for his high-energy platform skills, he shows audiences how to turn customer service into an invincible marketing strategy.

Sue Hershkowitz CSP

High Impact Presentations

14826 N. 54th Pl.

Scottsdale, AZ 85254

Phone: (602) 996-8864

E-mail: Hershk@aol.com.

Sue Hershkowitz is an international expert in written communications. She has spoken before more than one million people during the past 17 years. Author of *Power Sales Writing: What Every Sales Person Must Know to Turn Prospects into Buyers!*

Shep Hyken CSP

Shepard Presentations

711 Old Ballas Rd., #103

St. Louis, MO 63141

Phone: (314) 692-2200

E-mail: ShepardH@aol.com.

Shep Hyken delivers presentations combining information, humor, and magic on internal service, customer service, and motivation.

Terri Kabachnick, CSP

Terri Kabachnick & Company, Inc.

160 West St.

Cromwell, CT 06416

Phone: (800) 275-8374

Fax: (203) 635-0477

An expert on retail organizations, Terri Kabachnick brings real world relevance and an engaging interactive style, which distinguishes her presentations, workshops, and retreats. She also offers behavioral and values-based assessment tools.

Ron Karr

(Co-Author of *The Complete Idiot's Guide to Great Customer Service*)

Karr Associates, Inc.

1355 15th St.

Fort Lee, NJ 07024

Phone: (800) 423-KARR (5277)

Fax: (201) 461-5621

E-mail: karrqman@aol.com

Ron Karr is a professional speaker and consultant who works with organizations that want to dominate their markets and get closer to the customers they serve. His clients include Marriott, Hertz, and the International Customer Service Association. He also offers behavioral and values-based assessment tools.

Kaset International

8875 Hidden River Parkway

Tampa, FL 33637-1017

Phone: (813) 977-8875 or (800) 735-2738

E-mail: intouch@kaset.com

http://www.kaset.com

Kaset International is a partner in the Times Mirror Training Group, the world's largest provider of professional training and information services. Helping organizations achieve extraordinary customer relations has been the company's sole mission for nearly 25 years. A fully integrated series of training programs—service quality solutions for the front-line, senior management, and everyone in between—geared to both private and public organizations. Consulting support as needed throughout the training implementation.

Bill Ringle

Internet Expert/Professional Speaker

Phone: (610) 284-0846

Fax: (610) 284-9185

E-mail: ringle@starcomm.com

http://www.starcomm.com/Ringle/

Provides a real-world business perspective and hands-on expertise for putting technology to work.

Mark Sanborn, CSP, CPAE

Sanborn & Associates

695 S. Colorado Blvd. #415

Denver, CO 80222

Phone: (303) 698-9656

E-mail: MarkSpeaks@aol.com

Delivers high-content motivational speeches and seminars on customer service, leadership, teambuilding, and mastering change.

Holly Stiel

Holly Speaks

728 Bay Rd.

Mill Valley, CA 94941

Phone: (415) 383-4220

E-mail: HollySpeak@aol.com

An internationally renowned concierge and author of *Ultimate Service* and *Thank You Very Much*. She delivers seminars and keynotes on hospitality.

Judy Suiter

President

Competitive Edge, Inc.

P.O. Box 2418

Peachtree City, GA 30269

Phone: (770) 487-6460

Fax: (770) 487-2919

Competitive Edge's motto is "be daring, be first and be different" in all training areas including customer service. Also offers behavioral and values based assessment tools.

David Yoho

Professional Educators, Inc.

138 Evergreen Rd., Suite 106

Louisville, KY 40243-1410

Phone: (800) 220-0440

E-mail: davidyoho@compuserve.com

David Yoho, a dynamic speaker and educator, specializes in call centers and tele-service training.

Internet and World Wide Web Services

Avit Corporation

Contact: Dan Doyle

1355 15th St.

Fort Lee, NJ 07024

Phone: (201) 886-1100

E-mail: avit@intac.com or avit@aol.com

Provides consultative and creative/production follow-through for Web site development, video, and interactive CD-ROM programs.

Bock Information Group

190 El Cerrito Plaza, Suite 404

El Cerrito, CA 94530

Phone: (800) 648-2677

Fax: (510) 531-3598

Email: Bocktalk@Aol.Com

http://www.bockinfo.com

Wally Bock helps companies develop Internet strategies and products and services for the digital age. He is the publisher of electronic newsletters such as *Executive Briefing* about using the Net to improve business and is the author of *Net Income: How to Cut Costs, Boost Profits and Enhance Operations Online*. A free trial subscription to *Wally Bock's Monday Memo*, sent by e-mail, is available by sending an e-mail to wbock@bockinfo.com.

Silknet Software, Inc.

The Gateway Building

50 Phillippe Cote Street

Manchester, NH 03101

Phone: (603) 625-0070

FAX: (603) 625-0428

http://www.silknet.com

World Wide Web-based customer service software; Internet-based service solutions that can serve as a replacement for, or complement to, conventional call centers. The "virtual service rep" allows customers to serve themselves through the World Wide Web, thus eliminating hold times while also relieving "live" service reps from performing many mundane duties, so they can focus on truly complex customer issues.

StarComm Development, Inc.

P.O. Box 1013

Drexel Hill, PA 19026

Phone: (610) 284-0846

Fax: (610) 284-9185

E-mail: Info@StarComm.com

http://www.StarComm.com

Internet training and Web site development.

Publications

Call Center Magazine

1265 Industrial Highway

Southampton, PA 18966

Phone: (800) 677-3435

Publication for people who manage call centers.

Customer Service Review (CSR)

E-mail: csr@csr.co.za

http://www.csr.co.za

This Web-based electronic newsletter is published monthly in South Africa. With a global focus and numerous examples from North America, this periodical covers service technology, customer loyalty, case studies, service trends, and checklists for service organizations. Subscriptions are sold in U.S. dollars via major credit cards right over the Internet. A single issue subscription is available for $9; a 12 month subscription goes for $79. A free sample issue is available on the Web site.

TeleProfessional

209 W. 5th Street, Suite N

Waterloo, IA 50701

Phone: (319) 235-4473

Publication for professionals who make their living over the phone.

First-Rate Customer Service

The Economics Press

E-mail: jaymack@ix.netcom.com

Newsletter published every two weeks. Readership of 40,000 people around the world. For a sample copy of *First-Rate Customer Service*, send e-mail to jaymack@ix.netcom.com (don't forget to include your mailing address!).

Working Solo Online

E-mail: info@workingsolo.com

http://www.workingsolo.com

This Web site is designed for independent entrepreneurs, and features an electronic version of Terri Lonier's "Working Solo Sourcebook," a collection of more than 1,200 valuable business resources that's been transformed into a full searchable online database. Other areas take you to details on Working Solo books and products, small business articles and news, and past issues of *Working Solo eNews*, a free monthly e-mail newsletter that's filled with information and ideas for busy entrepreneurs.

Telecommunications Equipment and Customer Service Software Systems Vendors

Applied Voice Technology

Kirkland, WA

Phone: (206) 820-6000

Fax: (206) 820-4040

E-mail: info@appliedvoice.com

http://www.appliedvoice.com

Specializes in solutions for call centers with fewer than 75 agents. Develops, manufactures, markets, and supports a broad line of open systems-based, advanced CTI (computer telephony integration) software products, and basic call answering and voice messaging systems.

Aurum Software, Inc.

Santa Clara, CA, with offices worldwide

Phone: (800) 683-8855 or (408) 654-3463

http://www.aurum.com

Leading provider of customer relationship management software. Offers the Aurum Customer Enterprise, a suite of client/server applications that increases the productivity of an organization's sales, marketing, and customer service functions. Consulting integration firms, including Cambridge Technology Partners, Deloitte & Touche, Ernst & Young, GE Information Systems, IBM, KPMG, and Price Waterhouse, have selected Aurum for delivering enterprise customer relationship management solutions.

Clarify, Inc.

San Jose, CA

Phone: (408) 573-3000

E-mail: info@clarify.com

http://www.clarify.com

Front office solutions for customer service, field service, internal help desk, quality assurance, and sales and marketing. Customers include Amoco Corp., Cisco Systems, GE Medical Systems, Georgia-Pacific, Hewlett-Packard Co., MCI, Microsoft Corp., Motorola, Sprint PCS, and Transamerica Corp.

CTI Interactive

1343 Canton Road, Suite B

Marietta, GA 30066

Phone: (770) 919-9075 or (800) 776-5773

Fax: (770) 218-1494

E-mail: sales@cticid.com

http://www.cticid.com

Computer telephony integration software products and interactive voice response systems including Call Commando, a suite of computer telephony solutions for call centers in small offices and the middle marketplace.

PowerCerv Technologies Corporation

400 North Ashley, Suite 2700

Tampa, FL 33602

Phone: (813) 222-0886

http://www.powercerv.com

Integrated software applications for customer asset management providing sales, marketing, and support management across an enterprise. Applications include sales force automation, and customer support/help desk. Integrates with other supply chain applications for manufacturing, distribution, and financials.

Scopus Technology

U.S. Headquarters:

1900 Powell Street

Emeryville, CA 94608

Phone: (510) 597-5800

Fax: (510) 597-8600

E-mail: info@scopus.com

http://www.scopus.com/

Customer information management systems. The company's integrated product line automates customer support, sales and marketing, and quality assurance functions to enable companies to enhance the quality of their products and services, improve customer satisfaction, and reduce time to market.

Teknekron-Infoswitch

Fort Worth, TX

Phone: (800) TEKNEKRON or (817) 267-3025

E-mail: info@Teknekron.com

http://www.Teknekron.com

Existing global base of more than 500 call center customers (such as AT&T, Wireless Services, American Express, and British Airways), representing over 1,200 installations and 250,000 agents. Developed call center tools and technologies, such as service observation and evaluation software, and computer telephony systems, all devoted to increasing productivity and enhancing customer service. Systems Integration solutions include full multimedia integration of voice, data, images, and screen-based telephony on a single, window-based desktop.

Headsets and Small Office Equipment

Hello Direct

5893 Rue Ferrari

San Jose, CA 95138-1858

Phone: (800) 444-3556

http://www.hello-direct.com

Catalog seller of telephone productivity tools.

KGP Telecommunications

Rosemary Russo

East Wing, Suite 300

4250 Veterans Memorial Highway

Holbrook, NY 11741

Phone: (888) 547-8353

Offers a free 10-day trial, two headsets at a time, and special pricing if you use David Yoho's name. Just tell them Dave sent you.

Ziehl Electronics

Joan Ziehl

115 Meacham Ave.

Elmont, NY 11003-2631

Phone: (800) 654-1066

Offers a free 10-day trial, two headsets at a time, and special pricing if you use David Yoho's name. Just tell them Dave sent you.

Workplace Injury Prevention Consultants

WorkRight

Matthew Gibble, P.T.

Gary Flink, P.T., A.T.C.

1355 15th St.

Fort Lee, NJ 07024

Phone: (201) 224-8717

Fax: (201) 224-6381

Provides assessments of injury risks in your service establishment and any related training issues. Referrals given for specialists in your local area.

Glossary

ACD (Automatic Call Distribution system)   A large-scale telephone switch that has a high degree of intelligence for routing incoming calls.

Auto responder   An automated out-going response to incoming e-mail messages. You create a text file that resides on the host computer that has its own specific e-mail address. When a party sends an e-mail to that address, it generates a command that says "send this file."

Broadcast Fax   The ability to fax a message to many people at once.

CSR   Customer Service Representative, an employee who assists customers after the sale has been made. Some organizations refer to such employees as *customer care providers*.

Call Center   The location where service phone calls are answered.

Call to action   Simply a request for the customer to do something.

Caller ID   The ability to identify the customer on the line as the call is received.

Carpal Tunnel Syndrome   A potentially crippling disease that limits one's ability to perform a job. The disease often occurs when one frequently makes a repetitive movement such as typing.

Clarification Question   This requests customers to clarify their perceptions and meaning of words; useful because words can mean different things to different people.

Closed-Ended Question   This requires yes/no type answers.

Compliant Customer (C Style)   One of the four behavioral styles in the DISC Model. The C Style Customer is your everyday perfectionist. She wants it precise, orderly, and accurately. She is meticulous by nature and diplomatic in behavior.

Conflict Resolution   The fine art of moving from heated disagreement (or icy-cold standoffs) to warm agreement.

Consequence Question   This requests customers to describe the impact your proposed method or solution will have.

Constituencies   All the people served by your organization, including the owners, stockholders, employees, customers, joint venture partners, members of the community, government officials, and even suppliers.

Corporate culture   The distinct personality of your organization that comes from your company's unique history, the customers you serve, the people on the payroll, and your firm's values and traditions.

Credit   Returning goods and services with monetary value to be offset against future purchases.

Cross Functional Teams   Teams comprised of people representing various departments in an organization such as sales, product engineering, credit, customer care (the hip name for customer service departments these days), technical support and so on.

Cushion   An opening statement in a letter that lays a soft landing for when you have to deliver bad news.

Customer base   All the customers you serve. Within that wide collection you might have many different types of customers that can be divided into groups known as *segments*.

Customer database   A system that records the sales and transaction history, and other pertinent information for each of your customers. It can be as simple as keeping an index card for each customer, or as complex as intertwining numerous mainframe computer systems.

Customer Service Representative (CSR)   An individual charged with the responsibility of providing service to customers (sometimes referred to as a Customer Care representative).

Customer Support Phone Packages   Telephone-based product support plans that include either unlimited or a specified number of calls by the customer seeking service after warranty.

Defectionitis   A terrible, possibly terminal condition for your business where your customers take their business elsewhere, causing your business to whither, shrivel up, and die. The antidote is creating an outstanding reputation for providing your customers with Personally Pleasing Memorable Interactions.

Demanding Customer (D Style)   Typically driven people who push for results and expect the same from others. In the DISC behavioral styles model, this style is known as the D Style. They are bottom-line oriented. They do not like a lot of detail and get bored very easily.

Desires Question   Seeks out any other issues your customer may have with which you can be of assistance.

Differentiated Value   A unique feature that offers value to the customer and separates your business from the competition.

DISC Behavioral styles model   A psychologically valid system for grouping people's behavior into four major styles based on the way they do things, such as respond to problems, influence others, respond to their environment, and react to rules.

Domain   The part of an Internet address that is unique to the organization that sponsors a specific location along the information highway.

Download   This refers to transferring information from a Web site to your computer's hard drive.

E-mail (electronic mail)   Messages that are sent from computer to computer over the Internet or company network.

Employee Satisfaction Survey   A study of how employees feel about their jobs and work environment.

Ergonomics   The study of the problems people experience in physically adjusting to their environment.

ESP (Employee Suggestion Program)   Provides a way for employees to make suggestions (perhaps anonymously) on how to improve the company's performance.

Exchange   Replacing goods and services purchased by a customer with other goods and services.

FAQ   Frequently asked questions.

Fax on Demand   System that automatically, without anyone actually staffing the phone lines, provides information by fax to callers who request certain documents (usually by entering a code on a touch tone phone).

FGR   Frequently given responses.

Goodwill Follow-up   Regularly scheduled calls to make sure your customer is satisfied with his purchase.

Goodwill Freebies   Free stuff you offer customers in return for their patronage.

Goodwill Inclusions   Including, at no charge, extra costs such as shipping and handling when a customer places a large order.

Goodwill Interaction   Writing or calling your customers to tell them how much you appreciate their business—not because they have a problem, but because you really do appreciate their business.

Guarantee   Assurance, for a specified period of time, of the quality of products or services offered for sale.

Headsets   Devices that connect to the phone and allow someone to conduct phone calls without having to use a hand to hold the cradle. Headsets have both the ear and mouth pieces attached to them.

309

Hearing   The physical act of taking in through your ears what is being said.

Help Desk   Similar to a call center, except that it is a resource for employees to get answers to their questions.

Hyperlink   Like an electronic doorway that takes you directly to certain information such as a Web site or a particular sentence in a long document.

Illustrative Question   This requests a customer to paint a clear picture of what is wrong.

Influential Customer (I Style)   One of the four behavioral styles in the DISC Model. The I Style Customer is the person who needs and wants to talk and has a need for interaction with people and social recognition.

Infobots   *See Auto Responder.*

Information Superhighway   This is a metaphor for electronic data zooming between computers, usually over phone lines.

Instant of Absolute Judgment   The moment when a customer forms a lasting, decisive opinion about your business. This can come at any time.

Interactive Voice Response   The ability of a phone mail system to offer prerecorded information on various issues (such as store locations and directions, hours of operations, special promotions...).

Internet   Many computers connected to each other through phone lines, cables, and satellites.

Internet Service Providers (ISPs)   Companies that provide access to Internet services.

Keyword   Term(s) in a document you want to be found by search software.

Key System   Telephone systems with features such as call forwarding, call transfer, and speaker phone that are smaller than a full-blown PBX. They usually serve anywhere from 5–15 lines.

KISS Principle   Keep It Sweet and Simple.

LAN (Local Area Network)   Software and hardware that allow you to share and send information between individual computers in an office.

Limited Time Refund   A full refund of the purchase price for a product that is returned with a receipt in a specified period of time.

Limited Warranties   These provide protection for certain parts and services over specified periods of time (a guarantee with limitations).

Listening   The emotional act of understanding what your customer is really saying.

Mailbots   See *Auto Responder.*

Open-Ended Question   This requires detail and free dialogue.

Outsourcing   Engaging the services of a third party rather than having work performed by an employee.

Pay for Service System   A for-charge system (such as a 900 number) where customers call and pay for service.

PBX (Private Branch Exchange)   A computer-controlled telephone system serving anywhere from 15 to thousands of phone stations.

Playback   The ability to replay menu options in a voice mail system.

PPMI   Personally Pleasing Memorable Interactions, the goal of customer service.

Recovery Follow-up   Calling a customer to see if the solution provided to a previous complaint is satisfactory to the customer.

Recovery Freebies   Offering services or products for free in addition to replacing those that were damaged or unacceptable to begin with.

Recovery Inclusions   Paying the costs of overnight delivery when the product did not arrive on-time as promised.

Recovery Interaction   Personally calling or visiting someone to resolve a complaint.

Remote Phone Lines   Technology that allows you to list local phone numbers in various areas and have the calls routed to your support center location.

Root cause   The true source of a problem.

Segments   Groups of customers that have certain characteristics in common.

Self-managed teams   Work groups that determine how they are going to achieve their goals.

Semi-Auto Responder (prepared)   Text ready to send electronically at the command of a service person.

Sequential Fax   Fax equipment and software that has the ability to automatically send faxes one after another.

The Service Difference   The operating principles and specific processes that combine to give your customers a warm feeling of great satisfaction, maybe even *joy*, from interacting with your organization.

Service standards   Guidelines and operations procedures that specify measurable activities that help your company please customers by delivering services in a consistent fashion. For example, specifying the longest time allowable that a customer should sit on hold before being assisted.

Signature file   Several lines of text automatically added at the end of every e-mail message you send.

Status Questions   Seek information such as name, serial #, and so on.

Steady Customer (S Style)   One of the four behavioral styles in the DISC Model. The S Style Customer is an accommodating individual who, when inconvenienced by your product not working, will make sure he doesn't upset you with his complaint. The S Style Customer is patient, relaxed, logical, and systematic.

Tape Disclaimer   A message at the beginning of the voice mail menu indicating that the phone call may be taped for quality/training purposes.

Time of Delay   The ability of a phone system to tell customers how long it will be before a customer service representative comes on the line.

Time-out rooms   Places that are usually bright, equipped with music, TV's and other equipment to help CSRs relax and remove themselves from the mental stress associated with their jobs.

Toll Free Numbers   Phone numbers for which the receiving party pays the charges. They usually start with either an 800 or 888 area code.

WAN (Wide Area Network)   Computers connected at multiple sites.

Warranty   A written guarantee by the producer of product or service regarding the integrity of the product and responsibility for repair or replacement of defective parts.

Web Browser   Software that allows you to search for and access information on the World Wide Web.

World Wide Web (WWW or simply Web)   Information storage and retrieval system that uses the Internet to present text, graphics, photos, sound, and animation for access by any properly equipped computer connected to the Internet.

Upload   Sending information from your computer to another computer such as one connected to the Internet.

URL   This stands for Universal Resource Locator, the path descriptor that directly takes you to a desired site on the World Wide Web.

User-Friendly Design   Design of a product or service that can be easily used by the customer.

Vision and Mission Statements   Declarations that express why the organization exists and give employees and customers alike a clear sense of what the organization stands for and what it is trying to achieve.

Voice Mail   A system that enables callers to leave messages by phone.

Voice Response Unit   Hardware and software specialized for automating some customer service transaction work through recognizing a caller's voice commands.

Volume Rebates   Rebates or price discounts in exchange for certain (usually large) amounts of business from a customer.

Do You Get a Second Chance to Be Your Customer's First Choice?

We've been driving home the theme that one rarely gets second chances. It's what you do with the first chance that counts. And because customers always stand ready to judge, every interaction is yet again your first chance—from which there may or may not be a second. So every interaction counts.

And count they do. Case in point: While on a consulting assignment, Don flew to Central Florida to meet with executives of Publix Super Markets. While renting his car, he asked for directions to the nearest Publix. The rental agent perked right up.

"Do you work for Publix? " she wanted to know.

"No. I have a meeting at their offices."

"Well, you tell them how much I like their stores," she exclaimed.

Hearing this exchange, another agent came to the counter. She began singing the praises of Publix.

"I love their stores! When I can't find something, the people who work there actually know where things are and they'll take you right to them."

As if these unsolicited testimonials weren't enough already, a third rental car agent joined the spontaneous rally.

"I'll tell you what I like about Publix—their people are friendly. They say, 'good morning,' and 'thank you.' They seem so happy. I go out of my way to shop at Publix. There's a different grocery store right near my house, but all the employees do there is grunt—if you can get them to even look at you. I drive right past it whenever I can and go straight to Publix."

With this praise-a-thon in full swing, a *fourth* rental agent interrupted a transaction with another customer at the far end of the counter. She came over and joined the chorus.

"I heard y'all talking about Publix. I love their bakery! And, you know, when I shop there I see the same employees year after year. In the other stores you often don't see the same person twice. And their prices aren't bad either, and I like…"

If this sounds a little fairytale-ish, we understand your skepticism. But it really happened—just the way we've described it. It was spontaneous, heartfelt, and totally unexpected. All someone did was ask for directions to the nearest supermarket, and the floodgates of happy testimonials came rushing out.

So what are your customers saying about you?

And what are you going to do to give them something to talk about?

Wrapping Up

Throughout this book, we've tried to leave you with a few points worth recapping here:

1. Your company will prosper or decline based on how customers perceive your customer service.

2. Great service stems from *Personally Pleasing Memorable Interactions*. Each customer interaction—often measured in just seconds—must stand the test of the *Instant of Absolute Judgment*. Each instant may have a lasting effect that is eternal.

3. Great service results from your entire organization being deeply committed to outstanding customer service—to satisfying customer needs and wants they didn't even know they had. That kind of service isn't a department, a program, or a slogan. It's a way of life.

4. The many principles and methods we've talked about in this book—service standards, communication techniques, state-of-the-art technology, hiring, and so on—mean nothing if they aren't part of an *integrated whole*: an organization where *everyone* truly believes they have a job that is only to happily serve and delight customers.

5. And most importantly, great customer service is a fluid state of perception. You're only as good as your last customer interaction. Great customer service isn't the result of a few excellent customer interactions. Great customer service is the result of consistently creating great customer interactions—time after time. Every failed moment of truth threatens to permanently negate several Personally Pleasing Memorable Interactions—and all of the hard work that went into them.

While the companies discussed in this book serve as examples of great customer service, they, too, have had their moments of inconsistencies. Still, they are proficient in customer service overall because they consistently remain vigilant. They make sure they understand their customers. They treat them with care and deal with them competently to provide interactions that ensure a positive outcome.

When such vigilance disappears, the level of service decreases. Customer satisfaction declines. Customers disappear. Ultimately, the business disappears.

The Way of the Happy Servant

When you consistently follow the path we've laid out between these covers, something wonderful happens. Your customers notice The Service Difference. And they respond. They return to buy again and again. And they become the most motivated, most credible, and most effective sales force for your company that you could ever hire.

Index